The Remarkable Life of Albert Haskell Jr.

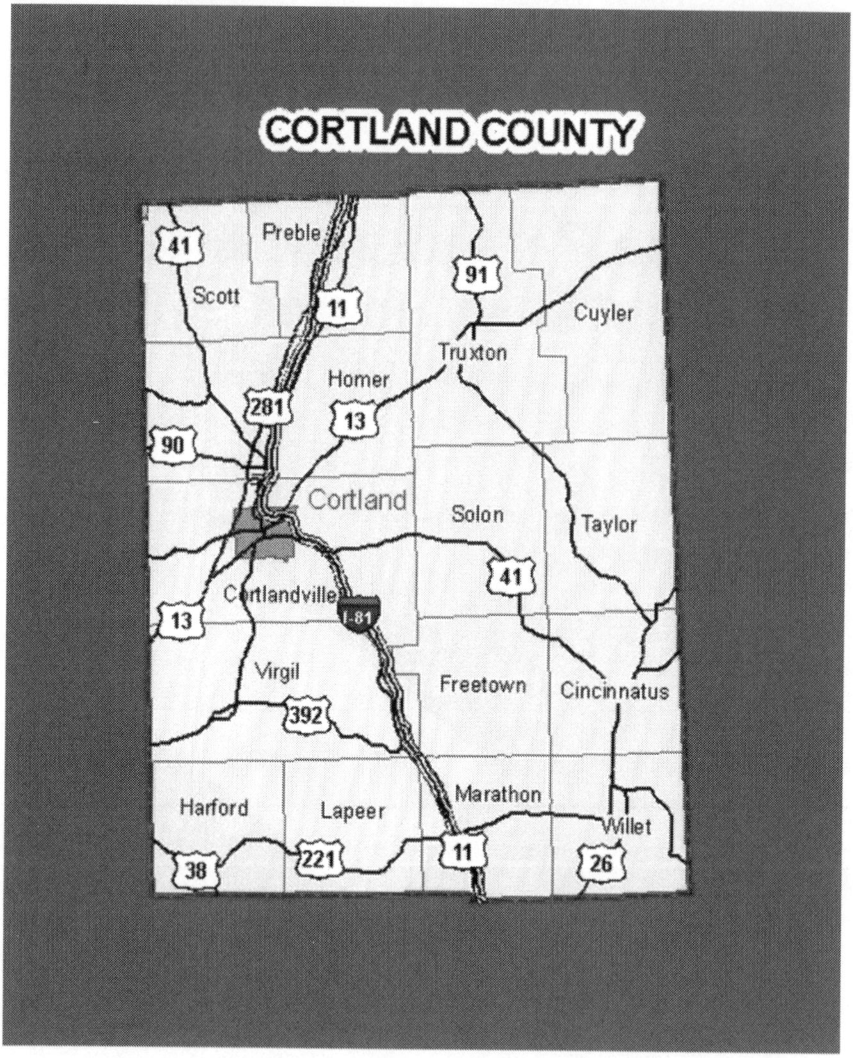

Map of Cortland County. Created by Matthew Vitale for ilovethefingerlakes.com.

The Remarkable Life of Albert Haskell Jr.

The King of Crown City

Martin A. Sweeney

HAMILTON BOOKS
AN IMPRINT OF
ROWMAN & LITTLEFIELD
Lanham • Boulder • New York • London

Published by Hamilton Books
An imprint of The Rowman & Littlefield Publishing Group, Inc.
4501 Forbes Boulevard, Suite 200, Lanham, Maryland 20706
www.rowman.com

86-90 Paul Street, London EC2A 4NE, United Kingdom

British Library Cataloguing in Publication Information Available

Library of Congress Cataloging-in-Publication Data

Names: Sweeney, Martin A., 1946– author.
Title: The remarkable life of Albert Haskell Jr. : the king of Crown City / Martin A. Sweeney.
Description: Lanham : Hamilton Books an imprint of Rowman & Littlefield, [2023] | Includes bibliographical references and index. | Summary: "Using a remarkable cache of scrapbooks kept by Albert Haskell Jr. through his lifetime, Martin A. Sweeney narrates a fascinating story of unwavering dedication to the public good. As a lawyer, politician, civic organizer, and economic developer, Haskell never turned away from an opportunity to do something beneficial for others"—Provided by publisher.
Identifiers: LCCN 2023005435 (print) | LCCN 2023005436 (ebook) | ISBN 9780761873921 (paperback) | ISBN 9780761873938 (epub)
Subjects: LCSH: Haskell, Albert Jr. | Politicians—New York (State)—Cortland—Biography. | Lawyers—New York (State)—Cortland—Biography. | Cortland (N.Y.)—Biography.
Classification: LCC F129.C943 S94 2023 (print) | LCC F129.C943 (ebook) | DDC 974.7/720092 [B]—dc23/eng/20230216
LC record available at https://lccn.loc.gov/2023005435
LC ebook record available at https://lccn.loc.gov/2023005436

∞™ The paper used in this publication meets the minimum requirements of American National Standard for Information Sciences—Permanence of Paper for Printed Library Materials, ANSI/NISO Z39.48-1992.

To all those teachers from kindergarten through graduate school
who instilled in me a love of history
and
to all of the descendants of Albert Haskell Jr.,
especially Colleen Sweeney Stafford and Joseph Haskell Jr.,
who held dear a trove of musty scrapbooks and photos.

Opportunity
We expect to pass
through this life but once.
If there is any kindness we can show
or any good we can do, let us
do it now.
Let us not defer or neglect it,
For we will not pass this way again.

Attributed to William Penn and later to Stephen Grellet, this widely circulated Quaker saying was one of three poems in the booklet young Albert Haskell Jr. helped to prepare for Central High's Junior and Senior Day at Little York Park in 1911, the year he graduated. He may have substituted "we" for the singular pronoun "I."

Contents

List of Figures	xi
Acknowledgments	xiii
Author's Note on Sources	xvii
Introduction	1
Prologue	3
Chapter 1: The Formative Years	5
Chapter 2: The Years of Arts and Letters	23
Chapter 3: A Young, Aspiring Lawyer	47
Chapter 4: The Great Rotary Hijinks	57
Chapter 5: The New D.A. Goes After Bootleggers with Izzy and Moe	69
Chapter 6: Bathtub Gin, Bootleggers, and the Black Hand	77
Chapter 7: The People vs White Slavers, Faith Healers, and a Murderer	85
Chapter 8: Haskell Takes on the Klan	103
Chapter 9: The Tragic Demise of Alton Howe	115
Chapter 10: Tubercular Cattle Scandal	119
Chapter 11: Another Murder Case and Retirement	127
Chapter 12: A Continued Career in the Law	133
Chapter 13: The Political Arena	143

Chapter 14: The Milk Strikes 159

Chapter 15: Civic Engagement 173

Chapter 16: Promotion of Economic Expansion in the 1950s 179

Chapter 17: "Elder Statesman" of Cortland's Industrial Growth 189

Chapter 18: A Man of Faith 209

Epilogue 219

Notes 225

References 231

Index 235

List of Figures

Albert Haskell Jr.'s parents: Albert Sr. and Mary Gibbons Haskell. From the collection of Joseph Haskell Jr. Used with permission. 21

A postcard of the high school in Cortland, NY attended by Haskell. From the author's collection. 22

Little York Lake's pavilion and boat dock. From the author's collection. 39

Haskell cottage near northern end of Little York Lake. From the collection of Joseph Haskell Jr. Used with permission. 39

Haskell's concession stand at the Little York Park Pavilion. Haskell is on the left. From the collection of Joseph Haskell Jr. Used with permission. 40

Albert Haskell's brother, James Haskell, dressed for a sales trip. From the collection of Dan and Linda Sweeney Quinlan. Used with permission. 44

Albert Haskell's nephew, Lester Richardson, at the lake. From the collection of Dan and Linda Sweeney Quinlan. Used with permission. 45

A streetcar at entrance to the Little York Park Pavilion. Courtesy of The Cortland County Historical Society, Cortland, NY. 52

Izzy and Moe reading a newspaper about their exploits in Cortland before departing by train. A clipping found in Haskell's scrapbook. Photographed by the author. 72

Sheriff Henry (left) delivers Eugene Graham to Auburn Prison. A clipping found in Haskell's scrapbook. Photographed by the author. 100

Newspaper artist's depiction of seven cattle dealers changing their pleas. From a Syracuse, NY newspaper clipping in Haskell's scrapbook. Photographed by the author. 123

Haskell seated with a candlestick telephone on his desk. From the collection of Dan and Linda Sweeney Quinlan. Used with permission. 125

Haskell with four cartoons depicting his career path until 1927. From a news clipping found in Haskell's scrapbook and photographed by author. 132

Fred Fadik (on right) with his counsel Albert Haskell Jr. A clipping found in Haskell's scrapbook. Photographed by the author. 136

Jimmie Haskell holds the ball in photo of St. Mary's team 1932–1933. A clipping inserted loosely in Haskell's scrapbook. Photographed by the author. 147

Assemblyman Haskell shakes hands with Speaker Joseph McGinnies as Assemblyman J. Austin Otto of Steuben County stands to the right on December 20, 1933. Photo by Acme News Pictures, Inc. From the author's collection. 150

Governor W. Averell Harriman (left) greeted by Haskell in May of 1957 at the cornerstone laying ceremony for Trinity Corp. of Cortland, NY. A clipping found in Haskell's scrapbook. Photographed by the author. 183

Thompson's letter with Greek Peak letterhead. A clipping found in Haskell's scrapbook. Photographed by the author. 186

Marine Midland Trust Company advertisement touting Cortland. A clipping found in Haskell's scrapbook. Photographed by the author. 197

Acknowledgments

This project would not have been possible without the support of my editor Brooke Bures and the editorial board and production staff of Hamilton Books at Rowman & Littlefield. To them I am most grateful.

Author's Note on Sources

There are three thick scrapbooks and a plastic bag containing news clippings and sundry ephemera pertaining to the life of Albert Haskell Jr. in the possession of his granddaughter Colleen Sweeney Stafford. She is a first cousin to the author and graciously and patiently relinquished this prized primary source material for research that took several years. Colleen's mother, Regina "Jean" Haskell Sweeney, was the author's paternal aunt.

One thick scrapbook labeled CHS kept by Haskell from his Cortland high school days, filled with personal letters and ephemera, is in the possession of his grandson Joseph Haskell Jr., of Cortland, NY. This scrapbook was provided for the author's use after the account of District Attorney Haskell and the Klan in Cortland County appeared in the author's column on local history in *The Homer News*. The author spent hours interviewing Joe Haskell Jr. on at least three occasions. The first was on September 7, 2015, Labor Day, at his home. The second time was much later at the Town Hall in Homer, New York, where the author, a public historian, has an office. The third time was by telephone on February 22, 2022, during the COVID-19 pandemic. Some facts were provided via email.

Unless stated otherwise in the Chapter Notes, the information in each chapter is understood to be derived solely from these scrapbooks. Every indication is that these scrapbooks were assembled by Haskell himself as events unfolded. Additional sources have been noted where the inclusion of historical context was merited. Of course, news accounts sometimes contain inaccuracies, which may mean the reader of this biography may discover errors, but the assumption was made that, at the time, Albert Haskell Jr. would have noted inaccuracies upon compiling his trove of informative news clippings. The dedication shown in compiling several scrapbooks bearing witness to his life's activities and accomplishments makes one wonder if he sensed, starting in high school, that he was destined for greatness and that some future day his biography might be written. The author is grateful that the scrapbooks have been kept by Haskell's progeny and that he was given the opportunity to use them to write this long overdue biography of "The King of Crown City."

Introduction

Some individuals journey through life just below the radar of greatness. They contribute in exemplary ways to the warp and weave of the American social, economic, and political fabric, but their names do not quite find their rightful niche in the history books. Albert Haskell Jr., was such a man. An accomplished lawyer, politician, banker, and civic organizer, Haskell's life spanned the Gilded Age, World War I, the Roaring Twenties, the Great Depression, World War II, the Eisenhower years, and the turbulent Sixties. His greatest legacy was to the people of the City and County of Cortland, in Central New York State.

Cortland has been called "The Crown City," because like the seven spikes radiating forth from the crown adorning the Statue of Liberty, the City of Cortland has seven valleys radiating out from the city. The seven valleys are the West Branch of the Tioughnioga River, the East Branch of the river, the Tioughnioga Valley to Binghamton, Trout Brook Valley, Factory Brook Valley, Cortland-Dryden Valley, and Otisco Valley.

"Mr. Cortland," as some called Haskell, rubbed elbows with some of the movers and shakers of the first half of the twentieth century. As a district attorney during Prohibition, he worked with the likes of the famous G-men Izzy and Moe. He crossed paths with murderers, white slavers, and the Ku Klux Klan. He was the first DA in New York State to haul a Klan Kleagle into court for successful prosecution. He was an advocate for New York State dairy farmers during the violent milk strikes in the 1930s and prosecuted those who were part of a tubercular cattle scandal. He was an avid member of the Republican Party, but he was respected by members of all political parties and a friend of New York State's Democratic Governor Averell Harriman. He was acquainted with Roman Catholic prelates, with a general who helped General Eisenhower in planning the D-Day invasion, and with a fellow lawyer and Rotarian who helped in prosecuting Hermann Goering and other Nazi field marshals at the famous Nuremberg Trials. He was comfortable in the presence of the rich and powerful and those who were poor and powerless. And he got things done. In the heyday of economic growth in the1950s he played a pivotal role in bringing industry to Cortland and Cortland becoming known as "the typewriter capital of the world." He lobbied successfully for Interstate 81 to traverse Cortland County rather than a route further east. A careful reading of the facts of his remarkable life reveals a man determined to take advantage of every opportunity life brought his way to work for the public good. The conclusion reached would be that he merits the title of "King of Crown City," an appellation he would have been too humble to accept. Yet, it remains that his life story challenges each of us to be a better person.

Prologue

Five hundred people packed the cafeteria of St. Mary's parochial school on North Main Street of Cortland, New York. The weather on this Saturday evening of January 25, 1964, was typically chilly, but the atmosphere inside the school cafeteria was warm and festive. Three local business organizations—the Cortland County Chamber of Commerce, its Retail Merchants Association, and the Homer Chamber of Commerce—had deviated from past practice and decided to join forces for putting on "the finest and most remembered banquet we have ever had."

The magnet that drew the crowd was the guest of honor. The man was of medium stature, kindly face, calm exterior, wore glasses, and had a well-known fondness for Robert Burns panatela cigars. To the people of Cortland County, located in the heart of Central New York State, this man was high in public stature and well deserving of the testimonial dinner prepared in his honor. Living and working all his life in the city of Cortland, the county seat, with seven valleys carved by glacial activity emanating forth in all directions of the compass, the man had evolved into a kingpin of political, social, religious, and civic life of the region. By all rights, the man to be feted, Albert Haskell Jr., could be dubbed "The King of 'Crown City.'" But "king" or even "kingpin" would not meet with the approval of the politically and democratically minded gentleman of 71 years. Instead, the newspaper referred to him as "Mr. Cortland."

"Good evening, ladies and gentlemen, and welcome." The toastmaster, Louis Wolner, supervising principal of the nearby Homer Central Schools and acknowledged public speaker par excellence, delivered the words of welcome and began the evening's event. The event would celebrate the life of a friend and benefactor to many in the gathering. Accolades would be poured out liberally upon the man. Morris Noss, Haskell's friend and successor as president of the Cortland County Development Corporation was present. Wearing his distinctive trademark dark-rimmed glasses and bowtie, Noss would correctly observe, "Surely no individual has done more for the good and the welfare of this county than this man we are about to honor. If ever one man could be called 'Mr. Cortland' or 'Mr. Chamber of Commerce,' it would be Albert Haskell."

As the General Chairman of the event, Noss had predicted the event would be "the finest and most remembered banquet we have ever had." That evening he would repeat "The boards of the three sponsoring organizations join in their feeling that this tribute has been earned many times over." Testimonials at a dinner near the end of a person's life are wonderful tributes, but do they fully capture the richness of a life well lived? How does one do justice to a long, productive life filled with outstanding accomplishments by reducing it to three after-dinner speeches? To fully grasp just how remarkable and multi-faceted was the life of Albert Haskell Jr., one must absorb it in its totality; that cannot be accomplished in a couple hours. The best place to start a review of his life is near the beginning. . . .

Chapter 1

The Formative Years

Summer was officially over, but colorful autumn leaves had not yet spiraled to the ground in Cortland, New York. The air was still warm. The date was September 23, 1910, and Albert Haskell Jr., the son of Albert and Mary Gibbons Haskell, would be celebrating his nineteenth birthday in twenty-two days. Actually, the young man may not have been a Junior at all, and no middle name may have been bestowed upon him. His father was Albert Eugene Haskell, and he was always known as Albert Haskell, brother to James, John, and Nellie Haskell. Minus the middle initial, he would travel through life as Albert Haskell Jr. However, census records do show him listed as Albert E. Haskell Jr. It may have simply been a matter of him not liking the name "Eugene."

From the Haskell residence at 123 Prospect Street, young Albert made his way to Cortland's Central School on Railroad Avenue (now Central Avenue) on the eastside of the city. As he rounded the corner of Main and Railroad, the high school senior passed by Burgess' Clothier for Men. Above this purveyor of clothing for males of all ages was the popular Palm Barber Shop. It featured four barbers, and their bold slogan was "We guarantee the best hair cut in the city or no charge."

Up the street and across Church Street was the high school built in 1892. The imposing edifice topped with a cupola was destined to be bought by the County in the 1970s after a new school would be built on the hill south of the city. The former school would be re-purposed as a county office building. Here, in his formative years, young Haskell had been busily honing the skills that would make him a "king-pin" in his adult life: writing, public speaking, legal argumentation, and participation in a host of school community activities.

Before the day was through, Haskell would write in a little black book he kept "Sept. 23 - Elected cheer leader of C.H.S." At this time, organized cheerleading at high school and college sporting events was exclusively a male activity and would remain so into the 1940s. Lads known for their popularity, physical energy, and ability to yell into a megaphone were most apt to be elected to lead spectators in cheering on their football and basketball teams. Little did he know then that he would become well-known later as a cheerleader, so to speak, for development in Cortland County.

Soon, another school-wide responsibility came Haskell's way. The boys of Central had a meeting, took a vote, and organized a permanent athletic association. The idea of having such a fraternal society had been proposed by Prof. Selah E. Northway as had the idea of possibly putting together a football team. Outdoor sports were being pushed at this time across the land as a deterrent to boys engaging in billiards, which was considered a decadent activity. The city of Cortland had the Idle Hour Billiard Parlors, and there was J.D. Sullivan, manufacturer of cushioned billiard and pool tables. Tables were sold, rented, and repaired for family and public use by Sullivan. Billiards was certainly popular. Even the Messenger House, a respectable hotel in Cortland, advertised not only its grill and garage but the opportunity to enjoy billiard pool.

At the boys' organizational meeting, a slate of officers was elected. Haskell was voted to serve as the association's secretary and treasurer and to be on the Advisory Board. At its first meeting, it was decided that a constitution was needed. But to whom should the task of preparing one be given? With his flair for writing and organizing, the boys deemed it fitting to have Haskell do it. At the next meeting, the constitution crafted by Haskell was read, approved, and adopted.

Soon after this, the prospects for a football team were considered, and one was organized, with Raymond Graham as Captain and Ed McAuliffe as Manager. The season of 1910 would see five games played: Groton—won by 16–0; George Junior Republic won by 15–0; old rivals, the Cortland Normal School (around the corner on Church Street) was fought to a tie, 5–5; lost to Binghamton by a score of 12–11. The final game of the season was played on Election Day against the Normals. The Centrals lost by 12–0. The excuse given in the school's paper was that ". . . they were no match for their heartier opponents on the slippery field."

The football season gave way to basketball, and for the first time in its existence the Central High School turned out a team for this indoor sport. The fellows were somewhat handicapped by not having a place to play early in the season. Dillon's Auditorium was rented, and every night the basketball squad attended practice there. The school paper reported that the school's first basketball team had a "fairly successful" season "having lost three games and won one." The team traveled as far away as Binghamton for contests. Traveling there by train took one hour. The Binghamton YMCA hosted the games. Efforts of the early basketball team were described in verse in *The Purple Pennant*, the school paper:

Our basketball team,
Is the bunch that does gleam,
Like a big dipper, high in the sky,
  Their team work is classy,
  Their shooting is sassy,
As they fight for dear Central High.

The Purple Pennant was published monthly by the students at the Central High School. The subscription price was 90 cents a year; a single copy could be had for 10 cents. The *Cortland Standard* newspaper mono-typed and printed the copies. And Haskell was its editor in chief, having been elected to the post on December 23, 1910.

Besides subscriptions, selling ads was the other way the paper funded itself. The student staff secured ads from Burgess Clothiers for Men, the Palm Barber Shop, Idle Hour Billiard Parlors, and the Messenger House hotel. Lyons Bros. of Groton Avenue were custom tailors, and they ran an ad featuring "the Spirit of Youth" which would make the young man of the day "look well in a Made to Order Suit" for one of three price grades: $18, $20, or $22. There was a "ten percent discount to all students," which made the establishment attractive to Haskell and his buddies. The go-to place for footwear was Sarvay's. Practically needing no advertising and located on the same street as the school, the store ran a simple ad. They were only three words and they shared one big "S": Sarvay Sells Shoes. And this they were destined to do well into the 21st century, from their location on Central Avenue and then on Main Street. Charles E. Buck Music House used their ad to promote "School Specialties: 8x10 pads of paper, 4c each; fountain pens at 19c, 39c, and 69c." McGraw & Elliott at 29 Main Street advertised Kodak Cameras and supplies. Two places where students could gather after school were Scharlock's and Zaharis. These competing ice cream parlors advertised their specialties. Besides frozen concoctions, Sharlock's at 13 N. Main Street boasted of their sherbet and punches, while Zaharis claimed they had the best candies and hot chocolate. Other businesses that were solicited for ads included F. D. Smith Hardware Co. and B.T. Jones Jeweler. The latter touted jewelry, watches, clocks, and watch-repairing at "Reasonable Prices."

The first issue of *The Purple Pennant* came out in February of 1911. According to an article in the second issue, the student produced periodical "was given a royal reception" at Central High School. It was reported that "On the afternoon of the distribution of the first issue crowds of students quickly gathered together to read the news. Nearly everyone seemed pleased with the first issue. . . ." Credit was given to Anna Oothoudt of Miss Vosburg's drawing classes for having the design selected for the cover: two lamps of knowledge bookending the entwined letters CHS and the title, *The Purple Pennant*.

Haskell, as editor in chief, was pleased with the initial success and felt motivated to make each issue better than the one before. The trick was to have something in print for everyone to enjoy. This he knew was true from his earliest job as a "newsie" delivering newspapers in the city. The first issue described the school's initial foray into fielding both a football team and a basketball team. Committees were formed to lead each of the four classes in cheers during games. Juniors were reported to have yelled themselves hoarse screaming out from the stands:

> Cicero, Caesar, Romans, Gaul.
> Juniors, Juniors
> Beats them all.

A page and a half were devoted to school songs and cheers that the whole school could bellow forth. The "Short Yell" went like this:

> Rah—Rah—Rah
> Siss boom Bah
> Cort-land Cen-tral
> Rah, Rah, Rah.

For those more interested in intellectual pursuits, there were articles on recent activities involving Kappa Zeta. Founded at Central High on May 8, 1903, as a men's oratorical and debate society, the organization was still thriving eight years later, and Albert Haskell Jr. was its president for the most recent two terms. Haskell conducted the club's business every Friday at 7:30 p.m. in the mathematics room.

On Thursday, December 29, 1910, Haskell was one of eight speakers to offer toasts at the Kappa Zeta Alumni Association Annual Banquet. Held at the Cortland House hotel, the main toastmaster was Jesse H. Phelps. The small, printed program for the evening event indicated Haskell would make a toast to Delta Epsilon, Kappa Zeta's counterpart for Central's female students. Extracurricular oratory and debate were not co-educational yet; the sexes would be segregated. Under Albert's name in the program appeared this verse:

> To ladies' eyes, around boys.
> We can't refuse, we can't refuse,
> Their bright eyes so abound, boys,
> It's hard to choose, it's hard to choose.

This Haskell took from *A Book of Toasts* compiled by William Ramsey, published in 1906 by Dodge Publishing Company of New York City. The chosen verse was attributed to Thomas Moore. At the bottom of the program, Haskell placed another toast he found in the same book:

> May Good Humor preside when Good Fellows meet,
> And Reason prescribe when 'tis time to retreat.

The maxim would serve him well when called upon to preside over business, legal, and civic gatherings as an adult.

On Friday, February 17, 1911, KZ met to elect new officers, mostly juniors to make a smooth transition in club leadership before the seniors graduated. At the meeting a "vote of thanks was given to Mr. Haskell for the manner in which he conducted the club meetings during his two terms as President." Kappa Zeta gave Haskell his early experience in organizational leadership and public speaking, which he would be called upon to provide in the future on more than one occasion.

For those wishing to follow the exploits of the more adventurous, boundary-crossing members of the student body, there would be articles about them in the *Pennant*. One article described an incident in which some students climbed up on a table in the music room to have a good view into the adjoining biology classroom. Upon attaining the desired vantage point, they discovered the teacher was seated in the back of the biology room "calmly gazing at them." Subtle innuendos were scattered through the *Pennant* that would be amusing to students who understood the inside jokes or jabs at classmates, such as this one: "Resources at the public library that are practically unknown to the reading public will be gladly explained by Robert McKinney."

And, finally, the *Purple Pennant* had its own Jokes Editor, Haskell's good buddy and fellow prankster, Edmund McAuliffe. His job was to see that every issue had a few rib-ticklers, such as these little gems:

> Johnny—"Will you make a noise like a frog, Grandpa?"
>
> Grandpa—"What for, my boy?"
>
> Johnny—"Why, papa says we'll get $10,000 when you croak."
>
> Senior to Junior—"What have you got that bandage around your head for?"
>
> Junior—"A thought struck me."

The tall angular waitress at the Trumansburg hotel scuffed around the room and approached the table where the base-ball team was sitting. "Have you frog's legs" asked Tubbs. "Oh! No, sir," she replied, "I'm obliged to walk this way on account of my rheumatism."

An Irishman was sitting in the train station smoking while waiting for a train. The woman next to him finally turned and said, "Sir, if you were a gentleman you would not smoke here." "Mum," said the man, "if ye was a lady ye'd sit farther away." Very soon the woman said again, "If you were my husband, I'd give you poison." "Well, mum," replied the gent, "if ye was me wife, I'd take it."

Another delightful article in the *Pennant* carried the hallmarks of Haskell's wit and gift for imaginative prose. It was simply titled "The Class of 1911."

> The Class of 1911 consists of a bright and shining galaxy of some fifty stars of the first magnitude. . . . So ponderous is the amount of learning that we have acquired in the past four years that there is grave danger that the rostrum will descend as we ascend, therefore we hereby respectfully petition the board of managers to see that the same be properly reinforced. We have at least a half dozen valedictorians and half a hundred candidates for honors. In the professions, we have several embryo physicians and lawyers to whose natural ability and thoroughness of their preliminary training the graveyards and penitentiaries of the future will doubtless bear ample witness.

There was something prophetic in the last sentence.

Central High students had several opportunities in the course of a schoolyear to attend dances. Students of both sexes attending the dances were provided tiny booklets, and each booklet came with a tiny pencil attached by a thin chord. These served as dance cards showing all the dances for the evening—waltz, polka, lancers, and quadrille. Opposite each dance was a space for penciling in the name of someone who expressed a willingness to be one's partner for that dance. After the event the card could be kept as a souvenir of the evening. And Haskell kept his booklets for posterity, pasting them into three pages of a scrapbook. Ten dance cards pasted in reveals Haskell enjoyed an active social life, with just about all spaces filled in with names of young ladies willing to do the two-step or the waltz to music played by live musicians.

He attended the CHS Junior Dance on May 11, 1910, where the only girl he danced with twice was "F[lorence]. Sprague." Then, he went to the Dillon Dancing Academy in Cortland for the First Annual Hop sponsored by the Athletic Association. For one dollar admission on Friday evening, December 16, 1910, he danced from 9 until 1 with 15 different partners. A Dancing Party was put on by Kappa Zeta and Delta Epsilon on April 21, 1911. At this soiree Albert danced four times with Ruth Schellinger, President of the Junior Class, and did the Virginia Reel with sophomore Laura Stilson. His own Class hosted a Senior Hop on May 11, 1911. He danced three times with Florence Sprague. They did the two-step to "Put on Your Old Grey Bonnet," waltzed to "Meet Me To-Night in Dreamland," and another two-step as the band played "Listen to the Jungle Band." Before the evening ended, Haskell danced with eight other young ladies but sat out "Under the Yum Yum Tree." May 19, 1911, saw the Senior Promenade for which Haskell served on the dance committee. He danced all but two of the first ten dances and only three of the last ten. The Promenade's Patrons were listed in the booklet: Principal & Mrs. F. E. Smith (one of the elementary schools in the Cortland Enlarged City School District is presently named for F.E. Smith), Mr. & Mrs. M. E. Sarvay (of Sarvay Shoes fame), and Mr. & Mrs. Louis Winchell.

It would be hard to squeeze in any more extracurricular activities, but Haskell found time to participate in a school play, as well. The three-act play was titled AFTER TAPS, and Haskell had a bit part as the character named "Gibbs." After the performance, he placed the script in his scrapbook with his lines underlined and notes included in the margins for blocking of his character.

The second issue of *The Purple Pennant* came out in March and highlighted the events of the previous month. Many of the same ads from the first issue appeared in this issue, but the noticeable difference was this issue contained the names of ten local physicians. Some had office hours listed as well as the address of the office. Dr. R. P. Higgins of 20 Court Street had office hours from 10 to 12 a.m. and 2 to 4 p.m. while Dr. C. D. VerNooy simply listed his office address as 50 Port Watson Street.

The big social event in February was a Valentine Party hosted by the Delta Epsilon Debating Society. Held on Friday evening, February 10th, games and refreshments were available in the school's library and dancing in the hallway of the main floor. Haskell dutifully pasted the red heart-shaped dance card in his scrapbook, and *The Pennant* noted: "Although no one was allowed to take silverware as a remembrance of the occasion, a very delightful time was enjoyed by all."

Eight days later, on a Saturday, the Delta Epsilon ladies enjoyed a sleigh ride to Miss Rindge's house on the occasion of her birthday. There, the greater part of the afternoon was spent in coasting. Only once did a sophomore cause a big pair of bobs to deposit its riders in a snowbank as it went skimming over the snow. The fun concluded with the presentation of a chafing dish to Miss Rindge with the best wishes of the Society.

The *Pennant's* third issue, appearing in April, included an exterior photo of the school and reported on another social event involving a sleigh ride in which Haskell participated. Under "Senior Class Notes," an article described an "eleventh hour" sleigh ride to McLean (a tiny hamlet seven miles southwest of Cortland) enjoyed by 22 members of the Senior Class on Thursday,

March 1. The reporter noted "the night was ideal and the sleighing was fine." After one hour, the party stopped at the Elm Tree Hotel, where they found members of the Junior Class enjoying a class dance on the upper level. The Seniors partook of "a bountiful supper . . . served by the genial proprietor. . . ." This was followed by games and music and dancing "in the lower dining room. . . ."

The Seniors departed for Cortland by sleigh but stopped two miles out to place a barricade over the road "to waylay their courteous Junior friends." Two hours later, the Juniors headed home by sleigh. Coming upon the heavy obstruction in the road, they tried in vain to move it. Thus, they turned about and made their journey via another route. In the same issue, under "Junior Topics," the Juniors maintained the Seniors were jealous that they could not participate in the junior dance and that is why they blocked the road.

Unfortunately, the Seniors' prank could have had serious consequences for the general public had there been an emergency requiring travel over the blocked roadway. Such is the immaturity manifested by youth. Haskell always showed a great fondness for playing pranks on others, but future stunts were better thought through in his adult years.

Coming to grips with the adverse consequences that can befall the innocent because of the transgressions of a few is a part of growing up, and it seemed to manifest itself in the opening article in the same issue of the *Pennant*. It seems the school library must have been closed for a while, because the article concluded with this observation: "There are always a few people who misuse a privilege, but it would seem that if our library was again opened to the students that some system might be introduced so that all would not suffer because of a few troublemakers."

Another article, most likely penned by Haskell, noted that on the morning of March 30, 1911, "the students of Central High were very much surprised to see high up at the extreme front of the building a large neatly painted '1911' banner. The banner remained unmolested all day for the reason that it was in a very conspicuous yet unapproachable place. Late in the afternoon the banner disappeared as mysteriously as it had come." What the students did not know at the time was that the night before the Seniors had an informal dance in Empire Hall [10–12 Port Watson Street], and after the dance a plot was hatched. Ed McAuliffe, Walter "Spav" Titchener, Ray Graham and Albert Haskell decided to place a "1911" banner on the front of the Central High School. They worked from midnight until 5 a.m. Just as day was breaking, the banner was securely fastened to the building. The night had been windy, and it snowed considerably. Because of the intense cold and the danger of falling from the icy roof, the boys were all glad when the job was done. The Class of 1911 Banner remained on the school until 3 in the afternoon when it was taken down by Haskell and Ed McAuliffe. The banner was cut in two and made for fine souvenirs for the two lads. On the back of his memento Haskell inscribed the story of the banner and concluded proudly "This was the longest time that any class banner had remained on the building at one time—Albert Haskell."

In a year of firsts for the school, this announcement appeared in print: "For the first time in its history the Central High School will place a track team in the field." On May 26, Coach Northway took five men to Colgate University for a track meet with seventeen other schools. Given this was Central's first big meet and the first track team the school had ever assembled, Central felt they performed well coming in 11th out of 18.

In early April, Kappa Zeta and Delta Epsilon announced that there was to be a "Speaking Contest." Entrants would have one week to prepare their "declamations," and a preliminary contest would be held on April 14 to whittle the number of contestants down to five. Haskell and a number of the Kappa Zeta boys set about preparing to show off their oratorical skills. Haskell chose "The American Flag" as his topic, certain that a patriotic speech would impress any judge, especially when it included the closing lines of verse he lifted from "The American Flag: Forever Float That Standard Sheet" (published April 22, 1861):

> Forever float that standard sheet,
> Where breathes the foe but falls before us.
> With freedom's soil beneath our feet,
> And freedom's banner streaming o'er us.

After the preliminary contest concluded, Prof. Northway announced the selection. Going on to the grand finale would be Frank Ryan, Lester VerNooy, Edmund McAuliffe, Harold Munson, and Albert Haskell Jr. On April 21, students and their families gathered in the school's chapel to witness the young orators delivering their best performances. The judges Rev. David S. Curry, Rev. Stephen A. Lloyd, and Professor S. E. Northway listened carefully and made notes as each boy stood and spoke when called. After a brief deliberation, the judges announced that it had been a close contest, with only one point separating the top two orators. Edmund McAuliffe had given a stirring speech titled "With Sheridan at Stony River" but the Kappa Zeta pin for first place was awarded to Albert Haskell Jr., and McAuliffe walked away with a box of club paper as the second-place prize. Haskell walked away with greater confidence in his public speaking skills and a determination to find a niche in life where this talent might serve him well.

For the present, Haskell had to concentrate on getting out the May edition of the *Pennant.* Of course, he made the deadline and wrote the opening piece, a tribute to the school's vice-principal, Prof. Northway. Haskell wrote of Northway in glowing terms, calling him ". . . a young man who has made the Central High School one of the best in the State." Haskell reminded the student body that Northway came to Cortland from Colgate University last fall, set about reorganizing athletics at the school, and "put our Athletic Association in a thriving condition. . . ." It was Northway who conceived the idea that the school should have a school newspaper. "Do we not owe to Professor Northway a great debt?" asked the editor in chief. He concluded, ". . . he has been untiring in his efforts to make school life helpful and interesting. We are grateful to you, Prof. Northway. . . ."

Tied in with these changes must have been a decided uptick in school spirit at Central, which did not go unnoticed by young Haskell. In this issue, he chose to include a piece on "School Spirit." He wrote:

> School spirit is one of the essential elements in the education of the American boy and girl. . . . every intelligent American boy and girl has enthusiasm, and school spirit affords a means of utilizing this surplus activity, and changing the mind of the students from mischievous pranks to work which will enable them to keep up the standard of American citizenship. . . . thus promoting friendship and cooperation in the school.

The issue listed in alpha order all 53 members of the Senior Class of 1911—33 females and 19 males—and announced that their class motto was "Second to None." The Class also announced that a Senior Dance was to be held in Dillon's Dancing Academy on May 19, 1911. The committee of eight seniors included Albert, and they boasted that Kane's Orchestra would furnish music, with "new and original novelty dances."

"On April 22," as reported on page 11 of the *Pennant*, "the George Junior Republic base-ball team journeyed to Cortland to engage in a battle royal with the wearers of purple and white. The team from Freeville were [sic] too confident, for they went home with a good, sound beating to the tune of 8–4. This was a fine start for our team, and it was up to them to keep up their record."

Six days later, Central's baseball team departed for two days of play in Trumansburg and Ithaca. The Sports Editor provided a detailed account.

> They left Cortland at 9 o'clock Friday morning and arrived in Trumansburg in time to play in the afternoon. Our team has been used to playing on a good skin diamond, and when after reaching Trumansburg they were quietly dropped over into a freshly ploughed field. They were, to say the least, bewildered. But that was not enough. Those Trumansburg lads then put in a fifty-cent ball. This together with the ploughed field was our hoodoo and we lost the game by the score, 8–0. From Trumansburg the team went to Ithaca the next morning. The trip between these two places was not made by railroad but by

> stage. It was a beautiful drive, as Trumansburg lies near Cayuga Lake and the road runs along the lake nearly all the way. On the morning of the 29th [of April] we arrived in Ithaca and went at once up to Cascadilla School [a boys' preparatory school for Cornell University founded in 1876. At this time Universities typically required students to be proficient in Latin and Greek. However, students from rural areas often did not have access to instruction in these subjects. Some early members of the Cornell faculty became concerned about the quality of education available to such students and founded Cascadilla School to address this inequity. However, students also pursued athletic activities such as football and crew and created yearbooks to record their activities.] Their team has been playing a great game of ball this season and they were sure of winning from us after our defeat at Trumansburg. Baseball luck was on our side that day and by fast fielding and good teamwork we succeeded in defeating them. The score was 7–2 in favor of Central High.

The winning streak continued. On Wednesday, May 3rd, Syracuse Technical School's strong baseball team came to Cortland and was trounced 6–3 which reportedly gave Coach Smith reason to beam broadly that day. And then Trumansburg attempted a pay-back.

> On May 20, the Trumansburg High School team came to our city and tried to defeat our team as they did at home. They received the surprise of their life. In the first of the second inning "Big Six" Tanner, as he is known by his fans, and called "Doc" by his friends, was hit in the cheekbone by a fast pitched ball. He was so seriously hurt that he was taken at once to the doctor and a new pitcher put in his place. The Trumansburg men by hard work and a few errors on the Central's part forced 3 runs over the plate, but while they were doing that we worked 8 runs across the plate . . .

That final 8 to 3 victory may have been spurred on by the clobbering the Central team received three days earlier when they went up against the "Normals." Central's "old rival" was the Cortland Normal School on Church Street and not the Homer Academy on the Green in nearby Homer. The State University of New York College at Cortland was founded in 1868 as the Cortland Normal School. The original campus would be destroyed by a fire in 1919, and the school rebuilt at its present location on the hill. In time a wholesome, traditional rivalry, especially in sports, developed between the Cortland Enlarged School District and the Homer Central School District. But on this particular day, May 17, the Normal baseball team "whitewashed" the Centrals on the Rambler field 6–0 in a fast, clean, and sobering game.

The Normals were thrilled that they were at least better than Central at one sport, but it was hard to top Central for its spirit. One of the fight songs

Haskell led during a basketball game with the Normal School he recorded for his scrapbook:

> On, Central High, the basketball team is out for glory.
> Fight, Central High, the Normal boys are limp & gory.
> The cry is on, Victory
> We'll raise the banner on high triumphant
> Smash! Bang! We'll beat the Normals.
> Whoop it up for Central High.
>
> Put on your old gray bonnet
> With the purple feather on it
> And get all ready for the game.
> We will lick the Normal
> In a manner informal
> But we'll lick them just the same.

Onto one of the pages of his scrapbook Haskell fastened by a paperclip a gauze-like material measuring 16 inches by 27 inches with cloth numbers "1" and "9" sewn onto it. Is this part of another Class of 1911 banner? It is not the same material as the earlier banner, but it is apt to be the Class banner that graced the school's flagpole on May 11th, "Senior Day." According to the June issue of the *Pennant*, a banner proclaiming "1911" was placed on the flagpole the night before. In the morning, the seniors marched into chapel with colors flying. Several class yells were given, and the class song sung. Then, the class was excused for the remainder of the day.

At 2 p.m. they went to the park in Little York (known today as Dwyer Memorial County Park and actually located in Preble, NY). It was the only resort area between Binghamton and Syracuse. Only five years old, the Main Pavilion at the park had been designed as part of a resort destination by the Cortland Traction Company that operated a trolley line to the park from Cortland. The pavilion was (and still is) a two story Stick/Eastlake style structure, rectangular at the core, with surrounding verandahs and a jutting pavilion at each corner. The central hip-roofed section contained a single large room at each level—a restaurant on the ground floor and a dance hall on the upper floor. It would find itself listed on the National Register of Historic Places in 1979, and since 1972 it has been the home of Cortland Repertory Theater's summer stage productions. Besides the Pavilion, the park housed several boathouses, an observation deck above a water tower, and amusement rides.

The afternoon of May 11 found the seniors wandering about the woods, taking pictures, and rowing on the lake. Around 6 p.m. a delicious supper was served in the pavilion overlooking the lake. This followed with toasts and short speeches. Dancing was to follow, but then suddenly everything went black. The lights went out. It was soon discovered that the nearby village of Homer was also in darkness and that it was due to a lack of electrical power and not to the tricks of the Juniors, as they tried to make the Seniors believe before they stealthily departed on the next Cortland-bound Cortland Traction Company streetcar. Not to be thwarted, two kerosene lamps were borrowed from a local cottager. Perhaps the cottager was Haskell's father, since he owned three parcels of land on the lake, and a cottage near the pavilion with a 43-foot lake front was on a parcel he had purchased in September of 1904 when Albert was entering his teen years. And, thus, dancing that night by romantic lamplight was enjoyed by the Seniors.

Eight days later was the annual Senior Dance at Dillon's Dance Academy. The hall was decorated in lavender and white, the class colors. Seventy-five couples were present. There was no intermission, and the young people "tripped the light fantastic" until 1 a.m. to use the expression made popular from the American song "Sidewalks of New York" (melody and text by Charles B. Lawlor and James W. Blake) in 1894. Everyone knew the chorus: "Boys and girls together, me and Mamie O'Rourke / Tripped the light fantastic / On the sidewalks of New York."

One of the last issues of *The Purple Pennant* devoted two pages to a listing of the Seniors in a column and for each a humorous description of his/her "Appearance," "Needs Most," "Favorite Book," and "Future Occupation." Albert Haskell Jr. was described as "Modest" in Appearance and most in need of "Assistance." His "Favorite Book" was the "Purple Pennant." "Senator" was predicted to be his "Future Occupation." Given his penchant for debate and oratory, the prediction seemed possible. It was not going to be too far from the mark. He would be elected a member of the New York State Assembly in 1932 and would be considered later for the New York State Senate.

June, the last month of school, was a whirlwind of activities for Central's graduating seniors. It commenced Wednesday evening, June 7, when the Senior Class was entertained at an informal reception at the home of Dr. and Mrs. VerNooy. Their son Lester was in the graduating class.

The afternoon and evening of Friday, June 16th was devoted to an informal dance and banquet for the Senior Class put on by the Junior Class at Little York Park. Each senior and junior was given a small souvenir booklet clad in purple, the school's color. "Your Day and Mine," a poem by David Starr Jordan, appeared on the first page. At the time, Jordan was the first president of Stanford University. He was a native-New Yorker and a Cornell graduate inspired by Louis Agassiz to study ichthyology. He went on to teach natural history at several Midwestern colleges. His poem seemed to speak to the new opportunities awaiting both the outgoing seniors and the juniors entering their all-important, final year at Central.

Today is your day and mine,
  The only day we have,
The day in which we play our part.
  What our part may signify in the
Great world we may not understand.
  But we are here to play it,
  And now is our time.

The next page contained a letter indicating the reason for the gathering . . .

Little York, N. Y.
June 16, 1911

The Junior Class of 1912,
Central High School,
Cortland, N. Y.

Dear Friends:
We, the members of the Class of 1911, wish to thank you for your kind invitation to attend a reception and dance at The Little York Pavilion June 16, 1911. The object of this little booklet is to present to you a small token of our esteem and regard, and to cement the bonds of friendship between the two classes of 1911 and 1912. Wishing you the best of success in your Senior duties and hoping that the friendship formed in Old Central will continue throughout life, We are,

Very Sincerely Yours,

THE SENIOR CLASS OF 1911
Editors: Albert Haskell
Leah Sprague

This was followed by a listing of the members of both classes and their respective class officers, three poems, and a word of "Farewell."

For Haskell and his classmates, Commencement Week began on Sunday, June 18, at 7:30 p.m. with the Class gathering at Cortland's First Congregational Church for a sermon delivered by Rev. Stephen A. Lloyd. The next day, a Class Reception was held from 8 to 11 p.m. Engraved invitations to the graduating seniors indicated the hosts would be Principal and Mrs. F. E. Smith of 15 Lincoln Avenue. The following evening, Tuesday, June 20, at

8 p.m., Commencement was held at the Cortland Theater located on Groton Avenue. The final event would be the Alumni Banquet at the Cortland House at 9 p.m. on June 21.

Thus, Albert Haskell Jr., in gown and mortarboard, marched in and received his high school diploma and was one of nineteen graduates selected for special roles in the commencement exercises. As he noted with pride in his little black book, "May 2, 1911—I took part in the Senior Competition for Commencement and after a hard struggle won first place as Class Orator of the Class of 1911." His topic was "The Great Northwest." It gave him the opportunity to establish early on a glowing reputation as a public speaker. He placed a copy of the "oration" in his scrapbook, along with the small commencement program and two admission tickets.

He, also, included a copy of the satirical program the Class of 1911 distributed at their graduation—a spoof of the more solemn event—to entertain those in attendance. The program's title was "Grand Blow-Off of High School Gas." The sub-title was "Lavender Burlesque." They referred to themselves as "The Prof's grand collection of zoological monstrosities consisting of 33 --- BLUSHING BEAUTIES 19 --- DUDES." With tongue-in-cheek, they announced that "Seven (7) trained parrots will appear assisted by nine (9) fanatical monkeys, exactly as advertised. The Grand Boss has finally decided that the amount of talent represented by the assemblage of scholastic ignorami [sic] is not sufficient to cover two evenings, so the public will have but one evening to be tortured."

"Elder Dowd" referred to the Class President, Louis R. Dowd, and the program offered readers this caution: "The enraptured listeners will please hold onto their seats as his rasping voice pierces the auditorium. Underclassmen have thoughtfully ordered an extra supply of burdocks, cabbage, and lemons in case of more than one encore."

Margaret McSweeney was to deliver a Poem at commencement. The spoof program made this comment: "Before she gets thru, the audience will probably wish that her place in the history of this night had been in Pokeville [a take-off on the eastern portion of the Town of Cortlandville, correctly known as Polkville]."

While a "Debate" between Frank J. Brown and Frank J. Ryan was to be showcased, the students' program referred to the debaters as "Buster Brown" [of shoe fame] and "Mr. Dictionary Ryan." Of the latter it was noted "Ryan's arms won't come off. They always act that way when he declaims." Though Haskell was not involved in the actual "Debate," he probably followed along with some interest, given that its topic would prove to be quite prophetic for him: "Resolved, that the Best Interests of Cortland County Would be Subserved by the Erection of Suitable Buildings for the Business of the County."

Another student in the comical program was said to have a mouth "as a perfect facsimile of a Massachusetts bivalve," and the audience was told to expect to "Hear the rattle of pots and pans" during Louisa Jones' piano solo.

As for Albert Haskell Jr.'s "Oration," he was listed as "Zeac Haskell" followed by this commentary: "Hear ye! Hear ye! The phenomenal boy orator cometh forth to shout. Listen carefully ye denizens of Summer Hill and Groton City [small rural communities several miles west of the city of Cortland], for ye will hear nothing." Haskell clearly learned in school to not take himself too seriously and to give vent to self-deprecating humor. This stayed with him all through his life.

The evening after graduation was the fifth annual Alumni Banquet. Haskell and his fellow graduates dined at the Cortland House on chicken fricassee with rice, mashed potatoes, wax beans, cucumber salad with French dressing, and cake and ice cream for dessert. Eight attendees offered "Toasts" that evening, and Haskell was one of them. His topic was "Central High School," and in the printed program after his name and topic appeared a quote: "Be not too tame, neither, but let your own discretion be your tutor." It seems in retrospect to have been advice he took to heart going forward.

In a little black book, Haskell devoted a page to a poem he must have written and most likely delivered as his "Toast" at the Alumni Banquet. It marked the bitter-sweet end of school for Haskell and the Class of 1911:

June times at hand
We hear the distant call
Welcome to thee her sons and daughters all.
Once more we're gathered
A song to sing
And then we will be parted
Perhaps never to meet again
And when we think of times spent here of yore
We will remember for ever more.

Just a song at parting
When our hearts are sad
But for dear old 'leven
Still we must be glad.
All our treats are over
Here in Central High
Good bye friends and schoolmates
Farewell to Central High.

Albert Haskell Jr.'s parents: Albert Sr. and Mary Gibbons Haskell. From the collection of Joseph Haskell Jr. Used with permission.

A postcard of the high school in Cortland, NY attended by Haskell. From the author's collection.

Chapter 2

The Years of Arts and Letters

During his high school years Albert Haskell Jr. had given thought to his plans for the future. His heart was set on going to college next. Colgate College in Hamilton, New York, attracted him and Prof. Northway hoped his student would attend his alma mater, but because Haskell fancied himself becoming a lawyer, he needed to consider applying to schools granting law degrees. He narrowed the possible law schools to consider to four: New York University, Albany Law School, Brooklyn Law School, and Jefferson School of Law. Though he lacked a credit for Intermediate Algebra and had taken only two years of Latin instead of the requisite four, he was granted a scholarship at Colgate for the science division but not for the arts. At the last minute he opted to attend Cornell University and would spend the next four years in Ithaca, New York earning a law degree.

Haskell continued in college the practice he started in high school of keeping several small black booklets that contained calendars and were made available by the businesses stamped on the covers. In high school, on several pages, he recorded aphorisms for living a good life that he found especially meaningful. On one page he penciled these:

> "Life is a battle, and the successful soldier is he who wields the sword of knowledge."
> "Right sometimes sleeps but never dies."
> "Of all things by which mankind are cursed,
> Their own bad tempers
> Surely are the worst."
> "Recollect that trifles make perfection, and that perfection is no trifle."
> "Ill habits gather by unseen degrees,
> As brooks make rivers,
> Rivers run to sees (sic)."

On the next page he penciled in fifteen items for an agenda for a club meeting he was to chair, including roll call, reading of previous minutes, a treasurer's report, and an election of officers. He filled the next page with more aphorisms, including this one:

"Diligence is the mother of good luck."

And the next page listed more pieces of advice for building good character traits:

"Books are friends which every man calls his own. The friendship of books never dies."
"He is truly great that is great in charity."
"Our deeds determine us as much as we determine us."
"Knowledge is power."
"Debt is the worst poverty."
"He who is good at making excuses is seldom good for anything else."

On the next page Albert wrote down a Kappa Zeta debate topic: "Resolved that the Panama Canal should be fortified by the U.S." He had to take the affirmative, along with classmates Willis, Broburton, Bowdich, and Ryan.

Then, even more aphorisms followed:

"True worth is in being, not seeming. In doing each day that goes by some little good, not in dreaming of great things to do by and by."
"He who wrongs his friends, wrongs himself more."
"Life is not so short. There is always time for courtesy."
"He who is honest is noble whatsoever his fortunes or birth."

Another debate ensued, and for this topic he was on the negative team: "Resolved that Texas was unfairly taken from Mexico by the U.S."

One page is taken up with a poem in German, since in addition to Intermediate Algebra and English, his classes included German II. The last entry in this booklet reads like a diary entry: "Sept. 9 – 1911 Miss Regina Schonessy 11 Gifford Street Binghamton, N.Y."

This Miss Schonessy was destined to become Haskell's first wife. Her name was actually spelled "Shaughnessy," but when it comes to the beloved's last name another famous aphorism tells us "Love is blind."

The next booklet Haskell used was inscribed "Compliments of E. B. Baxter, 'The Quality Shop,' One Price Clothier & Furnisher, 150 E. State St., Ithaca, N.Y." 1911 is the date recorded inside. He started using it September 21 with this notation: "Today I started reading law in Jas. Dougherty law office." As a Cornell student residing at Ithaca's 519 East Buffalo Street, Haskell used the little black booklet as a handy assignment pad for classes—law, English I, psychology, and political economy—and for recording reminders of important things, such as paying room and board by the end of the month. He listed a few friends' names and addresses and made one observation about Ithaca weather: "The past week has been one of the worst weeks of winter which I have ever experienced. We have had fierce blizzards, deep snow, and zero temperature." Scattered throughout are important points he thought worthy of remembering, such as: "Volenti non fit injuria means That to which a person assents is not esteemed in law an injury or in brief the injured person has assumed the risk."

When not busy attending classes and studying for exams at Cornell, Haskell carried on a brisk correspondence with former Central High classmates, friends, and relatives. Though no letters written by him exist, the ones he received he kept in his scrapbook. They reveal much about life in the early 1900s and even more about Haskell's relationships with others and what they thought of him and were willing to confide in him.

For example, this letter dated October 24, 1911, was sent from Cortland and signed "Your C.H.S. friend, Leland [Singer]": "I was up to Mr. Howe's last night for supper and we were talking about you and he said you would never make a lawyer because you were too honest for that. He said it took a scoundrel to make a good lawyer." Time would prove Howe to be wrong. In another letter from Leland, the Central High senior described how the "club" election went. The election of the club treasurer was very close. Not until a fourth ballot was Leland Singer elected, and he could not wait to tell his friend Albert.

> Here it is midnight and I have just come home and got my coat and hat off. My pen wouldn't write fast enough. . . . I want to thank you from the depths of my heart for this success. You are laughing, and wondering how you did it. Well, you were the one, and the only one who gave me a good sound basis to stand on. You, I know it was you, that got me in the club. You have done a lot besides for me. The truth is that of the two years that we went to school together, mornings and noons, I learned more going up and down Prospect Hill than I have in all the books of my four years high school work. You made me see success that cannot be gained by cramming books. And, Albert, (oh, I wish I could get a hold of your hand) I want to thank you again, and again, and again for what you have done for me. Perhaps someday I can return the compliment by deed rather than by sheer thanks.

Haskell's good friend "Ed" McAuliffe went off to Syracuse after graduation but not to college. On October 22, 1911, he wrote to Albert.

> Al, old man I am heartily glad you are "In" so well over at Cornell and I hope you will like your work. I started work in the Solvay Mach. Shops two weeks ago tomorrow morning and I didn't stick there very long believe me the man who was working next to me got knocked out of commission the first day I was there and two days later I saw an other guy get his, so I bid farewell to Solvay and started for another job. They say a man a week looses (sic) his life in the shops on an average. So last Tuesday morning I started to work for The Hunter, Tuppen Co. in the receiving room.

Ed gave his opinion of the college football scene: "I see Cornell is playing classy foot-ball. Syracuse boys are rotten to say the least." He signed off quickly by saying it was 7 p.m. and he had a date for 8 p.m. "I go up on E. Laurel St. any old time I feel like it, that's where my friend lives I met up at the [Little York] lake. God, boy, she's some class."

Bob Hull, another Central graduate and Syracuse University student wrote a letter dated October 25, 1911, from 422 S. Crouse Ave., Syracuse, NY. He told Haskell he took in a play but was strapped for cash: "Believe me, I am pushed for money so hard I had to borrow enough to show the girl a good time after the show." The best part of the letter described the adventures of a mutual acquaintance.

> Deac Doyle is still on hand at the Law School. Did you hear of his trip to the Fresh-Soph Reception a few weeks ago? He got wise to some dame and took her up to the Reception. Deac got as far as the edge of the campus with her. A bunch of Juniors and Seniors nabbed him just as he got off the[street]car. They turned his pants clear up to his crotch, unfastened his garters from around his legs and tied them together. Then they ripped off his collar and tie and fastened his tie over his soft hat and under his chin. With his suspenders hanging down behind they sent Harry to the Reception.

As Hull told it, before Doyle was let go, his assailants exacted thirty-five cents from him for last year's program to the Reception. "After Deac got inside he had to buy a paper collar from a kid who sold them." Hull reported that "College work is going on as usual. Haven't flunked anything yet." He complained about his math professor, however:

> By gum, but that course is hell. The old cuss stands at the board and works the theorems out; and if anybody asks a question he winks at them over the top of his specs and goes to work again. The fellows raise the devil all the time with him.

The next month a letter arrived in pencil dated November 18. It came from Walter "Titch" Titchener at 94 Clinton Avenue, Cortland. He started out by stating he is writing the letter during English class while "your old friend

Marlea [Mary L. Fairchild, English teacher] is dictating some questions." He explained that he had read over the Athletic Association's constitution to find out about changing it to allow the girls to have membership. He wrote that it was discussed "strenuously" at the first regular meeting of the year and might be put to a vote at the next special meeting. He doubted the Association would pass an amendment, and he added he had mixed feelings himself: "it would be a good thing in some ways but in others it will be punk." He noted he had seen "Eddie" [McAuliffe] in Syracuse but had some concerns about him. "I think that something is wrong somewhere." He said the young man did not go out much and was "quieter than he used to be." "He acts just the way he did last year when he had trouble with his Father." He goes on to tell that

> Yesterday was Laura Stilson's birthday and I invited her in to a little luncheon just for two which I gave in my private office. We had cider (with foam on top), Nabisco wafers, some dope that they call chocolate rocks that were purchased at Coon's Bakery and bon-bons. The chocolate rocks were all that the name implies.

During his first semester of college, Haskell wrote to the teacher at Central he most admired, but Selah E. Northway did not respond until December 14, from his residence at 68 Madison Street in Cortland. Northway admitted to being delinquent in responding to Haskell's letter but went on to show he was still able to "read" his former student well.

> You have probably found a new world unfolding before you. The people you mix with are older and have different ideas and ambitions than the people you knew in High School. What a difference! I could see that you realized it when you made us a visit the day before Thanksgiving. I knew then just how you felt.

Northway brought his former student up to speed about life at Central High since he graduated:

> Things seem to be going along very much smoother this year and it is due to the fact that there is no new teacher to distract people by starting things [like clubs and an athletic association]. I feel quite content with working with everything that has been started.

Northway explained that Katharine Stoppard was the next "administrative successor to our last year's editor," and he complimented Haskell when he added she had imbibed something of the same spirit that he had "in making things move along and be successful." He closed by writing that he hoped to see Haskell sometime during the Christmas break and wished him success in his "new life." If Haskell had a "leg-up person" during his formative years, it was clearly Professor Northway.

Letters from Cortland included a few from home. The ones from his mother indicate that she was not well educated but was a doting parent. She always opened her letters with "My der dearst albt" and closed with "my dear little Boy take good care of yor self. . . . from mothr to my dear Albt Boy I due mis you so much." She left no doubt that she loved him unconditionally.

> Wll dear take good care off your self albt dear and due the Best you can and dont fret and you are bound to come out all write trust in God and make the Best off your time Whitch I no dear you due. . . .

And it is clear why Haskell included this aphorism in his booklet: "Make most of it while yet you have that most precious of good gifts—a loving mother."

On January 15, 1912, a handwritten letter went out to Haskell on stationery with a letterhead indicating a slight name change in his high school. "Cortland High School" appeared at the top with the names of the all-female faculty listed along with Principal F.E. Smith and Vice-Principal S.E. Northway. The letter was signed "Your friend, S.E. Northway" and the return address was his residence at 35 and a half Charles Street, Cortland. The letter was an official notice: "You are welcome to take the Int.[intermediate] Algebra examination the morning of Jan 20th. I will be glad to see you and possibly to congratulate you on passing the examination." Apparently, Haskell had requested the opportunity to re-take the final exam in the course to either pass it or to attain a higher score. Whatever the reason, he obviously was not content to let the record stand about his mastery of the subject. And was there not something recorded in his little black book about "Diligence is the mother of good luck"?

Haskell was in communication, too, with relatives in New Jersey. His sister Nellie Haskell Richardson and her son, Albert's nephew Leslie (called "Lester"), lived in Ridgewood. They frequently summered at the Haskell cottage on Little York Lake. In a letter dated March 7, 1912, Nellie indicated how much she enjoyed last summer at the Lake and was anticipating another great summer. Then she wrote about Lester and a masquerade dance he attended.

> He dressed like a girl and no one knew him. He wore a pink dress and cap with a braid of hair down his back with a big pink bow and pink stockings and black slippers. He looked just fine, and if you could have seen his big legs in those pink stockings. And his dress came to just a little below his knee. He takes mandolin lessons all the time and he plays very fine all the new songs, so we will have music this summer with his mandolin.

"Lester" sent letters from 15 Walnut Street to his uncle the Cornellian. He attended Ridgewood Grammar School and shared a glimpse into his young life. Six years away from graduating with the Class of 1917, he would complain about the "punk football team we have." Or he would write that he was practicing his mandolin and ask his "Dear Uncle Spare Ribs & Gravy" to send Cornell songs. Like his mother, he looked forward to summers at the lake and to rides on a boat that was named after him.

If "Ed" McAuliffe in Syracuse had seemed depressed in earlier letters to his buddies, that was not the case in his letter of March 20, 1912, to Haskell.

> A week ago Tuesday night a bunch of us went over to the Auto show and I got my glims on a peach of a looking little head. She was game all right but I couldn't shake the bunch so I had to pass it up. I ran across her up street tonight and she was with some fellow. . . . I walked around awhile and later I ran on to her all alone and I braced it. I spoke and she says, "I don't believe I know you sir"; I says, "Cheer up. Plenty time to get aquainted (sic)," and she said "I don't believe I care to." I says, "Perhaps you'll change your mind." Then she told me she liked my nerve. I says Thanks God there's something about me you like. . . . I stopped and says we may as well fight it out right here what's the matter don't you like the looks of me and she politely told me she wasn't the kind of a girl to pick up with any thing (sic) she met on the street. Then I apologized for butting in and told her I liked her looks and would like to meet her if it was convenient for [her] and if not I'd quit so she gave me her address and invited me down Friday night so then I made my get away and the other guy she was waiting for picked her up and away she went. I'm wondering what kind of a reception I'll get but certainly my god she's some doll.

If Haskell reciprocated and shared accounts of his dating on campus or off, there are no records.

McAuliffe, also, wrote that he received a letter from Raymond Graham saying that "you can't be a medical student in N.Y.C. without drinking beer and smoking. . . ." He also indicated he had sent "a defiant challenge to F. M. Titch[ener] to an all-night session with beer bottles and cigarettes." He closed by suggesting a reunion of "the old rounders" at Easter time at Hall's "or some other dam[n] good place. . . ."

For a course he was taking in political economy, Haskell solicited the assistance of Congressman John Wilbur Dwight, a Republican representative of the 30th District of New York, a native son of nearby Dryden, New York, and at the time the House Minority Leader. The topic was the Payne Aldrich Tariff of 1909, which had had only a slight economic impact but an enormous political impact. The so-called insurgents felt tricked and defeated and swore vengeance against Wall Street and its minions Taft and Aldrich. The insurgency led to a fatal split down the middle of the Republican Party in 1912.

On April 12, 1912, Congressman Dwight sent a typed message on U.S. House of Representatives stationery indicating that "some documents on the tariff question" Haskell had requested should arrive in "ten days or two weeks."

To help defray his college expenses, Haskell operated the summer concession stand and boat rentals at the Pavilion at Little York Lake. His nephew Lester in Ridgewood, New Jersey had written, asking his uncle to give him a job behind the counter from the 25th of June to the 1st of September. Later he sent another letter: "I received you[r] telegram and was glad to hear that you have give (sic) me a job I will show you I can." On the back, Lester included a sketch of a sign on a post: "BOATS FOR RENT A HASKELL." In the spring of 1912, Haskell's mother sent him a letter with a comment about the Little York Pavilion job he had landed: "A good meny peple thinks it is yor fathr that is going to run the place."

Haskell was involved in debating at Cornell as he had been at Central High, and he invited "Ed" McAuliffe to come to Cornell for a visit in May. Ed acknowledged receipt of the letter, congratulated him on his success in debating, and wrote "It is very kind of you to ask me over 'Al' and I'm going to try hard to do it but you know my job is the worst kind of one to get off on." He confided to Haskell about a dance he wanted to go to:

> . . . . it ought to be good up at the lake but I'll be dammed I'm sort of shy. I don't know whether Catherine would go with me or not I suppose she's [not legible] by this time. . . .

A letter dated October 2, 1912, on stationery of the office of Frank E. Young, Counselor at Law, arrived in Haskell's mailbox. It was from a friend named "Chat," who was a law clerk at the office and a law student at S.U. He wrote about his life:

> I have been on the jump almost all the time since I have been back, between work in the office and the rushing season [inducting new fraternity brothers] up at the house and . . . renewing a few old acquaintances about the city.

He described how he and another clerk were given sixty surrogate court orders to serve for which they received a dollar and ten cents for every one they served just as soon as they made out the affidavits. He said he planned on being back in Cortland on October11th to register to vote. He suggested that on that weekend they drive up to the lake to "get a few chestnuts and maybe fish a little." "The chestnuts must be ripe," he stated, "as the market here is full of them." Then, he went on to explain:

> This is a big week for Syracuse. The Democratic State Convention is being held here this week and the city is full of Democrats and most of the Democrats are

> so damned full of Syracuse booze that the navigation is bad especially on the choppy sea on a stormy night.

Stationery of another Syracuse law firm, Gregg Brothers & Rulison, in the Kirk Block, was used on October 24, 1912, to communicate to "Dear Haskell." It was from Harry J. Doyle of Irving Avenue, Syracuse, the same Doyle that Ed McAuliffe had written about earlier. The envelope was addressed "c/o Gama eta Gama Chapter House, Ithaca, NY":

> I had quite a visit with Edmund McAuliff (sic) the other night and why don't you urge him to come to Cornell? He was feeling quite blue and reminiscent—said he wished he had been able to go to college when you did etc. If you would write him perhaps he would save the money and eventually grad from Cornell. You certainly have a great amount of influence over him. I think it very probable he wouldn't succeed very well in Syracuse University. Saw Titchener last time I was home. He said he was rooming with [Walter] Tubbs [of Central Class of 1911]. We have quite a number of Cortland High grads up here now, and I can say with some pride that the Class of 1911 is pretty well represented. . . . I have a quiz in Quasi-Contracts tomorrow.

Doyle explained that he was directing this letter in care of Haskell's frat house because he had mislaid his address. One can only wonder what Haskell thought of Doyle's opinion of Cornell's academic rigor compared to that of Syracuse.

Doyle was not the only one to misplace Haskell's Ithaca address. Bob Hull sent a letter from S. Crouse Avenue in Syracuse on October 30, 1912. It was mailed to Haskell's frat house.

> I am enclosing a notice of a meeting of the Junior law class which shows that Judge Harry Doyle is still popular with his classmates. Perhaps he will show some of us up yet.

A news clipping was enclosed. It stated that Doyle had been elected class treasurer in a mock convention by a unanimous vote after he excitedly reported that the treasury had a deficit of ten dollars. Hull went on:

> Of course you will be in Cortland Tuesday to vote. The Cortland crowd here will be there too unless [Theodore] Roosevelt dies before then. If he does there won't be any use for me to come home. I haven't seen Chat for about a week. Guess he is working hard or else is doing the "society stint." Syracuse [football] managed to come back last Saturday in the game with Michigan. Rochester plays us here next Saturday: Colgate next. What is the matter with Cornell? Can't she "hoove" [slang for move, as in "to hoof it"] at the right time?

Hull complained of not having enough money—only 11 cents in cash—to go to an outing of the forestry club.

> It's no disgrace to be poor but it sure is mighty inconvenient sometimes. I've got a job Friday morning beating rugs and Saturday morning some work at the nursery. If I can live until then I will be rich.

He informed "Al" that the Athletic Association of Cortland High School was hosting a dance December 20 and asked, "Can't you gather up a skirt somewhere and go?" He told his pal to be prepared to come back whenever "the K.Z. alumni spread will be held" and closed with "As ever Bob."

Soon after November 7, 1912, a letter arrived from "your old Pall[sic], Ed" in Syracuse. McAuliffe wrote that he had a chat with "the Hon. H.J.D. [Harry J. Doyle]." Doyle had said he was going to write Haskell and have him tell Ed to "go back to school." Ed gave his opinion: "I imagine it would be a hell of a place for me now." But he thanked Haskell for inviting him over for a visit at Cornell. He advised that it would have to be some Sunday since it was too difficult to be allowed time off from work. "Yes I am still in the same old rut and I like it except when I catch hell which is nearly every other day." He indicated that he had written a letter to "Titch" in Flint [Michigan] and was looking forward to seeing Haskell on Thanksgiving Day.

Two days later a letter was sent out by Lester Richardson in Ridgewood, N.J. He joined in with the universal lament that "Cornell has some bum [football] team." He wrote that he planned on going to Princeton next Saturday to see Yale beat Cornell. He boasted that Ridgewood High's team beat a Brooklyn team 39–0. And he announced he was in the high school's mandolin club. "I can read any piece of music you put in front of me." The club planned on traveling one hundred miles north during the winter to perform and then have "a twelve course dinner for nothing." The best part was "We are going up in an auto." He let his uncle know "They have some fine moving [silent] pictures here." He wrote of the Lake and pavilion job next year but indicated another job was more likely. "I will work for you maybe if Mr. Corbin don't (sic) give me a job, but I think he will." On the back of the last page of the letter, Lester drew a picture in pencil of himself playing the mandolin and listed six "new songs": "You're my Baby," "Row! Row! Row!," "Waiting for the Robert E. Lee," "That Mellow Melody," "I've Got the Finest Man," and "Pareasene." He meant "Parisian," and drew an arrow from the word "French" to the song title, in case his uncle did not know. Then, as an afterthought, he wrote "Extra!!! We got a phonograph." He noted that "mama is playing a march on it." Obviously, Lester was enjoying all the latest technology available: the automobile, motion pictures, and the phonograph.

What arrived next was a letter of November 10, 1912, from Leland Singer postmarked Genoa, NY. Having graduated from Cortland High School, Singer informed Haskell that he was now a teacher "trying to let my purse grow a bit." Located about eight miles north of the Cornell campus in the Sage District, he was teaching fifteen pupils, covering primary through grade 7 "besides Regents and algebra and Latin in High School." "Talk about work! Well you just bet I earn my $10 per all right. And it's no joke either. You needn't laugh about it." He wrote that he was on the Cornell campus the previous month for a teachers' conference at Barnes Hall and the Ag College. He described it as "a full day of dry talk, etc. with all the old-maids of Tompkins Co."

Right on the heels of this letter arrived another. It was written on stationery of a hotel in Patchogue, New York to Haskell from his 32-year-old brother Jim, a traveling sales representative for the Cortland Cart & Carriage Company of Sidney, New York. Jim expressed how glad he was to hear from his brother [by letter] and that he was "very thankful you still like the study of law." Offering brotherly support, Jim reminded his younger sibling "It won't be long before your college days will come to an end, as two more years after this year won't be long in closing in on us." Jim wrote that he had spent some time at their sister's in New Jersey and found the Richardsons to be "so very attentive to a widow who I believe is teaching him [Lester] on his mandolin." Jim told Albert that their mother had written in her last letter to him that Albert had taken her to the movies. He added, ". . . and [I] am always glad to hear of you putting yourself out to please her." He closed by saying he had to catch a train but was "looking forward to the time when I will see you again." Though he was on the road traveling much of the time, Jim managed to send out "best wishes" on picture postcards from places where business brought him: Seventh Avenue Hotel in Pittsburg; Fort Sumter from the Battery at Charleston; Fayetteville, North Carolina; Washington Park and Music Hall in Cincinnati; and a hotel in Augusta, Georgia. Neither brother knew that the fraternal closeness they enjoyed was going to end tragically before Albert completed college.

One month later a typed letter on stationery of the Cortland Cart & Carriage Co. of Sidney, N.Y. arrived in Haskell's mail. It was signed by a stamp bearing the name of L. I. Hatfield, President & Treasurer. Addressing "Friend Albert," the employer of both Haskell's father and brother explained that a check was enclosed for $50—$30 of which was charged to his father's account and $20 to Jimmie's. The Haskells had received a favorable report about Albert's performance in a recent debate and wished to reward him. And Hatfield assured him "that we are very glad to include it as requested."

At the same time as these December letters, Ed in Syracuse mailed one. The former "Joke Editor" for the *Purple Pennant* was finding little humor in life. "I am sitting alone in our little flat with my feet against the radiator and the wind is blowing a good stiff breeze around the corners." There was no snow yet but it had been "a cold day." ". . . the north train was one hour late. The messenger said they were stuck in the snow at Pulaski." He said he swore and threw a package today into the driver's pile when he saw it was marked with "please don't open until Christmas." He received a card from "Titch," who was coming through the 20th. "I guess he means to stay home now." He said some fellows from the [S.U.] hill put on a play and he "heard someone remark that it was pretty punk." One of the leads was played by Francis Kane, a Cortland High School graduate. "I met him on the street with a straw hat under his arm." Ed took some comfort in thinking "It will seem better when you come home now to see old Titch around." He confided that he had received a depressing bit of news from his sister. She had written that the family was in temporary housing on West Main Street in Cortland. "It made me feel rather hard when I think of the old place gone the only home we ever knew you might say, but I guess it is all for the best it will be easier for all. Give my regards to any of the fellows you may see."

In early January of 1913, "Chat" sent a letter on stationery of S. G. Daley, Counselor at Law, Syracuse. The letter was a follow-up to a tiff the old gang from high school was having with Harry Doyle.

> Last Sunday morning Harry came over to the house and wanted to see me alone and I suppose you know about the line of stuff he handed out. He was sorry for what he said the night before and didn't want me to take offense as he knew what he said to you effected (sic) me just the same and a whole line of that damned bull. I told him that the 3 of us [Albert, Bob Hull, and Chat] had always hung together and probably always would, that we had never sought his company and would be more than pleased not to have it. The best thing he could do was to keep away from us and the less his sore-headedness stuck out all over him the better off he would be and to keep his mouth shut. I gave him particular hell and told him if that was all that I had work to do and that the interview was over. I don't know as it will do any good but it may. If it don't, we will have to raise him one under the tail.

Bob Hull weighed in on the brouhaha on January 18. In the midst of six final exams at Syracuse—with the four hardest done, including Botany—Hull took the time to inform his friend about his recent interaction with Harry Doyle:

> Judge Doyle tried to give me the glad hand [a warm and hearty, but often insincere, greeting or welcome, as from a politician] yesterday noon. He thought I was mighty choice of my selection of friends because I didn't shake [hands]. He sure is about as dense as they make them. You know that now as well as I do. Believe me, he'll never get any more change from here.

Hull sent another letter from Syracuse on March 5, which started off with an update on Harry Doyle, who had not been to see him since the verbal altercation. "Yesterday the 'Judge' passed me on the street and didn't say a word. I can hardly blame him but I am rather glad to be rid of him." Hull wrote that he planned on being home again in Cortland around March 19 for a week's vacation, and he inquired if Albert would be around then. He suggested that "Perhaps the Temple [movie theater on Groton Avenue] will have something exciting?" He explained that every Friday, one of the classes goes on an all-day fieldtrip. His forestry class went to the woods on a Monday, and he was with the ax and saw crew. "Believe me Al, when 4 o'clock rolled around for $0.10 I would have quit college and shoveled shit for a living. Yesterday, my back was so sore I could hardly get out of bed." He confided that he was not looking forward to the class' "experience trip" scheduled for June 15 to Aug. 15 in Tannersville in the Catskill Mountains. It was going to cost each Sophomore and Junior in the forestry class $100. He said he would rather work in the summer to earn some money.

Then, Hull closed with an interesting question: "How is your friend in Binghamton?" This was a reference to Miss Regina Shaughnessy of Johnson City, New York. The daughter of Frank and Sarah (Reardon) Shaughnessy, she was Haskell's love interest with a very Irish last name. If they exchanged letters, none of hers were placed in Haskell's scrapbook. Clearly, he had referred to her in correspondence with Bob Hull.

Haskell found time to correspond with his close friend Ed in Syracuse, and on March 10, 1913, Ed wrote back. He expressed gladness that Haskell got through his third semester exams. ". . . we were always so glad when they [exams] were off our minds in C.H.S., myself anyhow. You know how they used to bother me?" He informed Haskell that he was back at his old job checking in the freight for more money and a potential raise.

> I have to meet two trains with my squad of four or five men and sign for the money and values with a gun tied to my belt. The other day I carried $160,000 out of the depot in a bag on my back as though it was so much mud. You should see me stand on the platform and yell at the men to hurry up and get the freight out of the train. Some guy what!

Ed asked to get together with Haskell again on the Monday after Easter, if both of them should be back home in Cortland. "I haven't seen you in so long I forgot how the hell you look."

Haskell's friend Leland Singer attended the presidential inauguration of Woodrow Wilson in the nation's capital. On March 11, 1913, from North Lansing, N.Y., he penned a letter describing for Haskell his experience.

> We certainly had a fine journey. I guess we saw everything to be seen. We saw all the public buildings, parks, historic places, statues; in fact everything. We sat only a few yards from where Wilson took the oath and when we were in Philadelphia coming back we recognized ourselves in the moving pictures. I especially wanted to tell you of the big men whom we shook hands with. We met Mr. Taft while he was President; Mr. Wilson, Secretary of Agriculture under Mr. Taft; Uncle Joe Cannon, that grand old man; Speaker Champ Clark; [NY] Gov. Sulzer [impeached earlier in the year]; Capt. Hobson who sank the "Merrimac" bottling up Santiago in the Spanish War. . . . We saw all of Taft's old Cabinet; and Wilson's new Cabinet, besides governors from ten or twelve states. We were in the House of Representatives and watched . . . debating on the appropriations bill permitting two new battle ships to be built. . . . they got one battleship, but not two.

Leland said he felt "boiling over" with political spirit and enthusiasm "all the while I was there."

Palm Sunday 1913 fell on March 16. After attending church, young Lester Richardson sat in the new office of the Bergen Aqueduct Company of Ridgewood, New Jersey where his father, George B. Richardson, was employed as Superintendent. The office window permitted a view "way down the avenue," and the office stationery permitted a means of corresponding with his Uncle Albert. Showing much improved handwriting, he informed Albert that "Papa is going to bid on a water job down to Asbury Park" and if he should get it, "Mother is going down there for 6 weeks this summer but I am going to the lake [Little York] to stay with Grandma." Eagerly, he asked, "Are you going to have the boat delivery this summer [at the pavilion]? When will you know? I hope you do have it." He closed "with love for all the family," and imbued with his surroundings, he chose to sign in a very business-like manner: "L. J. Richardson."

On another Sunday, this time in April, brother Jim Haskell was in a room of the Grand Union Hotel "Opposite Grand Central Station" in New York City. Using hotel stationery, he penned a supportive letter to Albert, expressing appreciation for a letter from him that was enclosed in a letter he had received from their mother.

> While I don't spend very much time in corresponding with you, my thoughts and heart are with you the same as if you were a son of mine. It is with pleasure I feel in being a link in the chain of your success which is bound to come, if you follow the standards and principles which you have followed in the past.

Then, waxing philosophical, Jim continued,

> . . . . my business was pretty poor on this southern trip. I suppose if everything came easy for us all the time we would be bound to get careless. It is the ups and downs that keep us ever lastingly plugging. Time is drawing closer every day to the time when we all [the family], I hope, will be together again.

He closed by asking Albert "to kiss Mother Dear for me when she comes over. . . ."

This letter from Haskell's brother was followed by a letter from "your loving sister, Nellie" in Ridgewood, N.J., postmarked April 10, 1913. She was putting in a pitch for Lester to be hired at the pavilion in the summer.

> [Lester] says no Asbury Park . . . he wants to work for you and I guess you could use him for he is a little boy no longer. He says when his work is done he will dress up in white pants and play his mandolin and get the girls. You will have to throw Romeo into the lake if he springs white pants. . . . next summer will soon be here and Little York will sure look good to us all.

Nellie enclosed a little separate note about their mother's upcoming visit to New Jersey. It warned, "Don't let Mama see this." On the inside she wrote "going to surprise Mother with presents from us all so send me a kerchief or some little thing before she comes. I wrote to Julia about it and Jim knows."

Whatever travel plans Mother Haskell had were cut short by illness. Dr. Higgins came to the house by bicycle on a Thursday night in a pouring rain and determined she was on the border of pneumonia. He gave her two medicines and instructions "to keep turpentine and lard fresh every 15 minutes." He said if she did not get better to call him, and he would come back. He returned on Sunday and said her fever was gone. Haskell sent a letter to express his concern and she responded on April 14 that she was upstairs with "Gillia" [Julia, her daughter-in-law] and John [her son] caring for her. Doc Higgins had called from his office to see how she was improving. She said she would come over next Saturday [to Ithaca] if nothing happened. She told him not to worry. She claimed she was "a hundred times better" and "so thankful to be alive as I was so sick."

"Chat" was next to write—a handwritten letter on stationery of Frank E. Young, Attorney and Counselor at Law at the Onondaga County Bank Building, Syracuse, dated April 20, 1913. He was finishing up at S.U.'s Law School and preparing for the bar exam. He wrote that he had read in the paper that Haskell had "rented the pavilion for the summer," and that "There is no reason why a person cannot make money there if it is run right. . . ." He asked, "When are we going to get at those yellow-bellied perch?" He was quite eager to fix up a time when they could go up to the lake together. He told his fellow angler that he had come across very effective fishing bait and would be glad to tell where the bait is found. He explained that he had taken a room at 332 West Onondaga Street so he could be alone to study in quiet solitude for the bar exam to be taken on the 24th and 25th of June after commencement on the 10th. Being a good friend of the president of the senior class, he had been made a member of the Cap and Gown Committee. They had managed to order 400 fine caps and gowns free of charge. He closed by saying Haskell should have attended the great party at Gamma Sigma. 143 couples were there. Dancing began at 8:30 p.m. and finished at 4 a.m. He added, "The next day I felt like (that proverbial material) looks when struck with a club."

Haskell and his fellow classmates finished up their second year of studies at Cornell and dispersed in different directions to their summer jobs. Haskell headed to the family cottage near the northern end of Little York Lake and to his summer job at the Pavilion. There, at his concession stand, one could get a sandwich, pie, and coffee for 15 cents. For an extra nickel it could be topped off with an ice cream soda. Here, too, one could rent canoes, rowboats, and bathing suits. In a scrapbook, Haskell posted a menu. A hamburger cost 10 cents, a sliced ham sandwich 5 cents, pies of seven possible fillings for 5 cents a slice, and drinks for 5 cents: coffee, tea, milk, lemonade, birch beer, root beer, and cream soda. Orange, strawberry, ginger ale, sarsaparilla, moxie [a carbonated beverage of bitter flavor originating in 1885], and grape juice were available to slack a summer's thirst. Ice cream—be it plain, in sodas, or cones—cost 5 cents. Flavors included vanilla, chocolate, maple walnut, and strawberry. If none of these treats struck the fancy of a visitor to the park, Haskell also sold Schrafft's chocolates, peanuts, cigars, cigarettes and tobaccos, "and a complete set of the latest souvenir post cards of the park." It was an enviable situation for a college boy in the summer, especially when compared to the summer jobs of his peers.

One of Haskell's fraternity brothers wrote him a letter on July 27, 1913, from Rochester, New York. He indicated he wished he could spend a few days at the lake, where he suspected Al was "doing a big business." Instead, he had been busy "working for a surveyor 6 days a week for 9–10 hrs. per day." He had Sunday off, but the crew was so tired "we want to sleep about all day." They had just finished up New York State, and were leaving that night for Cleveland, Ohio. "We have surveyed Ontario, Wayne, Niagara, Monroe and Orleans counties in that order. We get up against all sorts of people, of course, and we are seeing a lot of country and getting some valuable experience as well as making a little money. Will spend 2 weeks in Ohio and then on to Virginia."

Not all of Haskell's fellow Cornellians felt the need for summer employment, however. "Piff" from Brooklyn made no mention of needing to work. His letter of July 27 stated that he passed all of his exams and his time at home had been "very pleasant." As for what he had done that summer, he

Little York Lake's pavilion and boat dock. From the author's collection.

Haskell cottage near northern end of Little York Lake. From the collection of Joseph Haskell Jr. Used with permission.

Haskell's concession stand at the Little York Park Pavilion. Haskell is on the left. From the collection of Joseph Haskell Jr. Used with permission.

wrote: "some I don't dare tell and the rest is too numerous." But "Piff" did tell of going with his father on two deep sea fishing trips and spotting "a whale off Sandy Hook" on one of the excursions. He asked if fishing was any good at Little York and if there was a hotel there "where I could stay for a week or so" in August. He expressed a wish to see Haskell "for a few days at least." It smacked of a self-invitation to the lake.

Not all of Haskell's campus buddies had the good fortune of "Piff." One of his fraternity brothers had the opposite experience. His letter of August 8 was addressed to Albert Haskell, Little York, N.Y., Cortland County. It was delivered to the Pavilion. The return address was Mt. Mongola House, Ellenville, N.Y., where the young man was working for the summer. He told of not faring well on "Procedures" and would not be returning to Cornell for the next schoolyear. Instead, he had accepted a contract to act as Principal of the school at High Falls, N.Y. "I have three teachers under me," he wrote "and teach, myself, the Seventh and eighth grades, give Regents exams, and also teach German I and Algebra." He expressed interest in how Haskell had fared on his examinations and asked if he was going to move into the new frat house in the fall. He said he would be coming to Cornell the week of

Sept. 22nd to take the make-up in "Procedures" and hoped to see "most of the boys" then.

Haskell had written back immediately to "Piff" in Brooklyn, describing "some good fishing and boating" at the lake, and on August 9, "Piff" wrote how pleased he was to receive the message. He said he was sorry that Haskell was among those who did not do well on "Procedures." "It's nothing more than hard luck," he wrote, "and you've certainly had your share of it this year. You better change your name from McNutt to something else for next year." "Piff" hoped Haskell would be in Gamma and reside in the house with the other boys in the fall. Among the attractions at the lake, Albert must have included the girls, because "Piff" commented ". . . as for the girls I've seen enough of them already. Haskell had sent him postcards of the pavilion. "Piff" said they were much appreciated and observed "you have a dandy little place there and it certainly looks up-to-date." And he added a compliment: "Well, look who's running it!"

"Procedures" must have been a challenging course and exam. Another lad from Haskell's fraternity wrote him in August from a summer house in the Shawangunk Mountains, Ellenville, N.Y., that he, too, had scored a big, fat C in "Procedures" and would be seeing him in the "Make-Up." Attesting to Albert's popularity, this fraternity brother also hoped that Albert would be able to be in Gamma's new house—a better house and rid of "the 'rough neck' bunch. . . ."

Charles P. Coffey, called "Cabbey," also corresponded with Haskell that summer. Haskell had admitted to him that he had "conditioned" the course in "Procedures" and had to take a make-up exam in the fall. "Cabbey" wrote, "It is funny that you conditioned 'Procedures,' for we studied that together and I got my highest mark in that." Yet, the scholar confessed he had "conditioned" in "Property" and "Agency" and would have two make-ups in the fall. Another classmate named "Coleman" had fared worse on his exams, according to "Cabbey," and he added, "so you see we are not bad at all." Also, he informed Haskell that "Logan" passed the bar exams, and he and "Morasco" intended to set up a law office in Croton-on-Hudson. "Cabbey" asked if "Al" would care to study "Property" with him when they got back on campus. He offered to send Haskell his notes on "Procedures" or to get Coleman's set of notes and send them. What he communicated was the real sense of teamwork the students were learning they needed to successfully pull themselves through the rigors of law school on an Ivy League campus. Indeed, Haskell and the others were learning the necessity of teamwork in accomplishing anything in political, social, and economic life.

Furthermore, in law school and through his correspondences, Haskell was acquainting himself with a cross-section of humanity. On the socio-economic spectrum he found there were fellows who were better and lesser than himself. He was learning how life's circumstances were affecting each of his friends and, thus, preparing him as an adult to be comfortable in the presence of people from all walks of life.

Being told you have to take an exam over again is not pleasant news, but neither is it the most terrible news a student can receive. Actually, it is quite common when it comes to the bar exam in New York State to have to take it more than once. Much more tragic news can interrupt your life, and it did for Haskell in his junior year at Cornell. Albert Haskell Sr., in 1914, was in his fourteenth year with the Cortland Cart and Carriage Company. In January of that year, he was traveling with his son James on a business trip through the Southern states when an eleventh-hour change of plans occurred. Albert's father canceled his passage on the steamship *Monroe* to make a sales trip through Pennsylvania while his 34-year-old son Jim was to continue on alone. Sailing for the Old Dominion Line on its northward trip from Norfolk, Virginia, to New York City, the *Monroe* entered foggy waters. At 2 a.m., Friday morning, January 30, 1914, the steamship was hit by the southbound steamship *Nantucket*. The *Monroe* sank.

Albert Haskell Sr., was the first to receive the tragic news. He phoned his son John of 123 Prospect Street, Cortland, who then notified his mother, who was making her home in Ithaca at the time to be of help to her youngest son, a law student at Cornell. At first the news communicated was not that dire. Jim was first reported to have been saved by either the *Hamilton* or a revenue cutter. Then, all the family's hopes were dashed. The steamship line informed the Haskells that the body of James A. Haskell had been lost at sea along with forty others.

Newspapers of the time were prone to dabble in yellow journalism, and tragedies at sea could be especially sensationalized to sell papers. One reporter commented "How James Haskell faced his last moments in life must forever remain as a sealed book that none may read." That was true enough, but it did not stop the paper from printing a conjecture offered by Jim's boss, Louis I. Hatfield, president of the Cortland Cart and Carriage Co. of Sidney, N.Y. Hatfield, "who loved him as an own brother," imagined that in the last few moments, Jim Haskell "gave no heed to himself, but died while trying to save the lives of others." Though not substantiated by any facts, this account of heroism was viewed as in keeping with "the noble character of this young man who was always eager to help others." The news article went on to publicly extoll the virtues of the lost man and his family: part of a family "highly esteemed and universally respected"; "like his father, was a self-made man"; ". . . what they lacked in capital, they more than made up in good character, fidelity to trust and perseverance"; and "The family was a united home circle" known for "family reunions [that] were held every year in Cortland."

What brother would not be proud to have his deceased brother eulogized in the paper with these words: "It would be difficult to find a person so free from selfishness, so manly and upright in his dealings with his fellow men; a loyal, devoted son and brother. . . ."? The same words could be and were later used to describe Albert. His brother was the proverbial man of few words, but "what he had to say was always brief, concise and to the point." A member of the Cortland Elks Club and of the Cortland Council of United Commercial Travelers, Jim was considered "the soul of honor"—a character trait that his youngest brother would strive to emulate. Since 1912, the Cortland Cart & Carriage Company had been experimenting with the production of a motorized commercial vehicle. A limited number were produced, but with the loss of the company's star salesman production was put on hold for eighteen months.

Of course, the Haskell family grieved, and it was good for both Albert and his mother that they resided together in Ithaca when tragedy befell them. As heart-wrenching as the event was, they realized it could have been worse. Though likely steeped in some survivor's guilt, Albert Haskell Sr., realized he could have shared the same fate had he decided to accompany his son home by ship. And where would the family have been then? So, following the aphorisms inscribed in his black booklet, Albert Haskell Jr. forged on with his studies. He was determined to persevere and to graduate from Cornell's Law School as part of the Class of 1915 and to wed Miss Regina E. Shaughnessy of the Binghamton area on June 29th of that year.

Haskell returned with his bride to Cortland, New York, where they would make their home for the rest of their lives. Over time, Mr. and Mrs. Haskell would have three sons: James Albert (named after his brother lost at sea; 1918–1933), Joseph Charles (1923–1993), and Charles Kelly (1925–1954). And there would be one daughter, Regina Mary, known as "Jean" (1928–1995).

In July of 1914, the Great War in Europe commenced after the assassination on June 28 of the Austrian Archduke Franz Ferdinand and his wife in Sarajevo, Bosnia. Brought on by the mounting pressures of militarism, alliances, imperialism, and nationalism, the Allied Powers entered into combat with the Central Powers. Like others across the nation, the community of Cortland, New York, followed the events unfolding across the Atlantic and tried to calculate what the war's impact would have on them.

Albert Haskell's brother, James Haskell, dressed for a sales trip. From the collection of Dan and Linda Sweeney Quinlan. Used with permission.

Albert Haskell's nephew Lester Richardson at the lake. From the collection of Dan and Linda Sweeney Quinlan. Used with permission.

Chapter 3

A Young, Aspiring Lawyer

Now, back in the summer of 1914, before his college graduation and marriage, when great war clouds were looming, Haskell returned to his job at the Little York Pavilion, but the job blossomed into more than just operating the concession stand and boat rentals. The ambitious young Haskell had entered into the catering business for the summer, and in doing so he was introduced to an organization that would have a future impact on his life, and he would impact the organization. The annual Cortland Chamber of Commerce dinner of August 26, 1914, saw 250 citizens of Cortland gathered at the Little York Pavilion. The newspaper touted it as "a highly successful affair" with a "fine dinner served by Albert Haskell Jr." Imagine catering a dinner for that number using the refrigeration and cooking appliances of that era.

The gathering that summer evening was presided over by Chamber President Edward Dalton. Dalton spoke of how an organization's success depended upon the enthusiasm of its workers. He said, "The people of most communities may be divided into two classes, the lifters and the leaners. There are usually twenty leaners to one lifter, but in Cortland I am glad to say that this is reversed and we have twenty lifters to every leaner." By listening into the speech or reading excerpts in the newspaper, young Haskell was likely exposed to Dalton's talk and inspired to be one of the "lifters." Dalton extolled the advantages Cortland enjoyed, such as its centralized location in the State and railroad routes. He said,

> We have many things of which we may be justly proud. We have the best Normal School in the State, a Traction [street car] Company which for service and cheapness of rates is unequaled in any city of the size of Cortland or in many larger cities. We have a most efficient system of public schools. We are a city of good roads and good streets. We have beautiful homes which are owned by the people.

Dalton spoke of Cortland as an exceptional business city and praised the Chamber of Commerce for its efforts to bring in new industries, such as the new factory of Gonley & Edmonds which was now being built to manufacture mill machinery and tools. He spoke, too, of the good work of the Farm Bureau at fostering closer ties between urban and rural folks. Little was stated by Dalton that Haskell would not be espousing himself before audiences at a future date.

The principal of the Normal School, Harry DeWitt DeGroat, spoke of a carnival to be held in November to coincide with Cornell's "Farmers' Week." This would be bringing in New York State Commissioner of Agriculture Huson and Commissioner of Education John H. Finley and would draw the attention of the whole state to Cortland. He said, "Let Cortland be known as a leader in agriculture and dairy products and thus create a demand for our products."

Haskell absorbed these comments, along with those offered by C. P. Seymour of the Wallace Wall Paper Company. This businessman spoke of the need for "Optimism" during the Great War that had broken out in Europe the previous month and was causing a slackening of trade with foreign markets. "We must all work to keep things moving," he said, "to make long pay rolls instead of laying off men. We must try to keep the working classes from suffering during the coming winter." He expressed, too, the hope that the Wickwire Brothers, local makers of wire mesh products, would be able to "give steady work in spite of conditions." "Let us do our best," he urged, "to prevent depression of trade and closing of factories."

A Mr. Briggs was introduced next to talk of his desire to see Cortland as the site of a factory to make his new invention, a machine for sorting mail that had been successfully tested in Syracuse and would likely be adopted by the government for leased use in post offices across the nation. It was probably best for this entrepreneur that he left unmentioned how this automation would replace four men in the sorting process, which would mean unemployment for postal workers at this critical time. But it would mean jobs in manufacturing and leasing in Cortland, if it came to fruition and, as he added, "if sufficient funds can be raised to get it here." He pointed out that four hundred machines would be needed in New York City alone. Such a market should be an incentive for investment. Haskell took in all the elements that were needed to promote a vibrant economy for a community like his hometown, and he would not forget the lesson imparted. The informative evening at the Pavilion closed with the attendees singing a stirring rendition of "America." Haskell finished up his labors that night and walked the short distance to the Haskell cottage with a check in his pocket, ideas to ruminate upon, and a feeling of readiness to finish up his final year at Cornell.

Life for Haskell was not all work and studies. He made time for swimming and fishing and boating at the lake. He enjoyed taking in an occasional [silent] picture show in Cortland, and he most likely enjoyed a show at the Cortland Theatre owned and operated by the Dillon Brothers at 8–10 Groton Avenue. The theater was only in operation for a dozen years—1907 to 1919. It hosted vaudeville performances by "road attractions" with matinees at 2:30 p.m. and evening shows at 8:20 p.m. and silent movies, when available, at 2:15 and 7:15 p.m. Judging by one of Haskell's scrapbooks, he attended at least one live performance. Inside the scrapbook was inserted a 24-page Program for "Cortland Theatre." On its cover, in color, was a stylized profile of a bust of a female in a circle frame. Outside of this was a smaller profile bust of a jester.

Besides two undertakers, other local merchants ran ads inside the program. W. A. Ryan did "Horseshoeing and General Repair" at 86 Homer Avenue, while H. P. Hollister's Maple Avenue Garage and Livery had automobiles for hire day or night and reminded the theatergoers "We make a specialty of repairing Ford cars." The Chocolate Shop, the newest and most up-to-date confectionary store, made its own candies and ice cream and claimed that the corner of Court and Main Street was "The place to meet your friends."

The featured program was a musical performance by Al G. Field Greater Minstrels with a cast led by Bert Swor, the "Dean of Minstrel Comedians." Field's real name was Alfred Griffith Hatfield (1850–1921), and he was one of the best-known minstrel impresarios in America. Since 1866, his troupe had made an annual tour across the nation starting with a kick-off at the Ohio State Fair in Columbus. Field would be remembered as a consummate showman. His shows were of spectacular proportions, and unfortunately this genre of entertainment with performers in black face contributed to the fostering of racial stereotypes.

It is quite possible that Haskell did not attend the show alone, for it was near the end of his college education that he was courting Regina Shaughnessy. He would find that the show, in the words of *The New York Herald*, knew how "to make the world forget its cares and troubles." He would get to see one of the premier comedic singers of the era, Bert Swor, and "A Sumptuous Scenic Spectacle" titled "The Minstrels of the Nations."

The first scene depicted a camp of U.S. soldiers in Panama and the assembling of soldiers of all nations to celebrate the opening of the Panama Canal with 23 musical numbers performed by 13 different vocalists. Songs included "You Made Me Love You" and "Mother Machree." Next, there was a Patriotic Tableau, "Old Glory Shelters All," with flags of the nations displayed. An intermission followed, consisting of ten minutes with Thomas Roper's Orchestra. Then there was "The Days of '61" featuring Johnny Dove's Dancing Delights doing a medley of dances in three scenes. White performers in black face (an acceptable practice in theater of the times) portrayed such characters as Uncle Amos, Uncle Remis, Uncle Tom, and Aunt Eliza. A comedy sketch set at an aviation field delighted the audience next, followed by "3 Lyres," who were "Late from their European Triumph" of "Tinkling Tunes To Tickle The Taste of Tired Theatregoers." The grand finale was a "Tropical Travesty" in Panama, a burlesque on the "Movies" in five scenes, involving a motion picture crew, actors, actresses, Hawaiians, and sailors.

The theatrical extravaganza provided a good revenue for the Dillon Brothers and some respite for Haskell from the world of war and studies in which he labored. After Law School he was hired in Cortland as a clerk to Clayton R. Lusk for a year and admitted to the bar in 1916.

It was at this time, as a young lawyer, that Haskell began to solidify his reputation as a public speaker. He found himself increasingly called upon to speak at Columbus Day observances, St. Patrick's Day dinners, and affairs put on by the local Elks Club, which he joined, and which counted Attorney Lusk in its membership. Haskell became known as an articulate and entertaining toastmaster for various occasions and a deliverer of stirring patriotic speeches during the war in Europe.

It began when the 25-year-old lawyer was first invited to be one of five speakers at the nineteenth annual St. Patricks' Banquet of Division No. 1 of the Ancient Order of Hibernians. The affair was held in Cortland's Empire Hall on March 16, 1916, the day before St. Patrick's Day. There was much singing of popular songs, led by William P. Walsh with Floyd Stanton at the piano.

William Nix, the first speaker, spoke of "Preparedness." The Great War in Europe was advancing toward its second year, and Nix reminded the banquet guests "Our first duty is to protect ourselves," and "Our second duty is to assist Europe in staving off a yellow peril." Unfortunately, this was an anti-Asian sentiment that was inserted into a program whose topic had traditionally focused upon the Irish as immigrants who had contributed to America socially, economically, and politically.

Some of this expression of intolerance was mitigated by Principal James A. Shea of Lincoln School in Syracuse and his talk on "Citizenship." Shea made a forceful appeal for "the elimination of social, religious, and political lines which might instill into the hearts of men, women and children any thought of class or clan." He asked the audience to "Put yourself in the other fellow's place, and give him credit for his point of view."

Father Joseph Cameron of Binghamton spoke of "The Church and Human Liberty" and Edward Ryan of Syracuse, grand secretary of the Catholic Mutual Benefit Association, spoke of "Ireland the Nation." The latter focused on the Irish struggle for home rule, to be free of England and to be an independent republic.

But the newspaper said that it was Albert Haskell Jr., who delivered "one of the most inspiring and pleasing toasts of the evening." The paper credited him as "the young man [who] held the closest attention of his hearers throughout his discourse." His topic was "Americanism." He spoke eloquently of the Irish who came to our shores for freedom and bled here for the country and benefited it by their accomplishments. He said that we should have in us a feeling of pride for their deeds and for what it means to be an American:

> The word American inspires all who come to our shores and we should be proud of our country and its greatness. We have a right to be proud of our peace and prosperity and glory in the advantages which our country offers to us. Let us be Americans in every sense of the word and nothing else. Let us be strong and upright men, ready to defend the land we love and ever cherish its memory.

His conclusion was powerful in its delivery and content: "The past is across the sea; the future is here. Let us so live and do that we may hand down to the coming generations a rich inheritance." The speech left an impact on the listeners, and others decided that here was one whom they should have speak at their events, too.

Three months after this, when things seemed to be going so well, Haskell could not have expected what was to happen next to the Haskell Family. On Monday afternoon, June 19, 1916, Haskell's sixty-three-year-old father was out on Little York Lake in a motorboat. He was alone, and Albert Jr. later noticed the boat was not moving. Albert Jr. hurried out in a rowboat. He found his father unconscious and managed to get him back to shore. His father was then transported to Cortland via the trolley car that made regular stops at the Pavilion. Albert E. Haskell died two days later at midnight at the hospital. The press said he succumbed "as a result of a shock [sudden drop in blood flow through the body] while out on the lake." The funeral was at St. Mary's Church and burial in Cortland Rural Cemetery. Haskell's mother took up residence with John Haskell in Cortland for the next ten years.

There is an emptiness within when a beloved parent passes, but life moves inexorably on and sometimes presents opportunities to engage in matters that would have made that parent proud. And so it was for Haskell. Division 1 of the Ancient Order of Hibernians invited him back for the next year's event but this time as the emcee. The *Syracuse Herald* of March 20, 1917, reported on the 20th annual banquet of the day before and commented on Haskell's performance: ". . . his opening remarks and references as he introduced the several speakers were a pleasing feature of the occasion." Haskell explained that since the Great Famine of 1846, the population of Ireland had decreased

A streetcar at entrance to the Little York Park Pavilion. Courtesy of The Cortland County Historical Society, Cortland, NY.

by 47 percent and the number of Irish people in the U.S. had risen. He lauded their loyalty to the U.S. but pointed out "if you strike from the heart of a Celt love for his native land you take away his dearest possession."

After a meal of roast Cortland County turkey and dressing with all the fixings came the dessert: pistachio and vanilla ice cream with assorted cakes, coffee, cigars and cigarettes. What followed was a lengthy program that did not end until the wee hours of the morning. One gentleman from Syracuse, Francis J. Lynch, spoke of how the country was "passing through a terrible crisis" and characterized Germany's submarine campaign as "murder." He closed his remarks by saying, "the American flag shall float unsullied as long as a true Irishman lives to hold it aloft."

The banquet table that evening saw high school youths rubbing elbows with lawyers and clergy. For many of the students, this was their first experience at giving public oration. Haskell could relate to any youthful nervousness they were experiencing, and as the Toastmaster for the evening he modeled for them how it should be done. The *Cortland Standard* said, "Seldom have the people of this city had the privilege and honor of enjoying as fine a toast list as was presented last night." It joined the Syracuse paper in reporting that Haskell "proved to be an ideal toastmaster." To keep the affair light and celebratory, scattered through the program were ten songs for all to sing, including one ditty that finished with "But if I knock the 'L' out of

Kelly, Sure he'd knock the 'L' out of me." And a good time was had by all, especially by Haskell.

Establishing a reputation as a talented toastmaster was a gateway to a career in politics. Working for the likes of Clayton Lusk, who was to become Republican State Senator in 1919, did not hurt any either. Connections could be made if one was interested in entering the political arena. So, on Thursday evening, December 14, 1916, at the Messenger House in Cortland, there was a Republican County Committee Dinner. The first speaker to be called upon was Albert Haskell Jr. He stood and a news reporter noted that he "gave a few of the reasons why he personally was in favor of Charles E. Hughes" for President. He liked Hughes' pro-stance on a protective tariff and his record as both the Governor of the state and as a member of the U.S. Supreme Court. Hughes resigned from the Supreme Court on June 10, 1916, to be the Republican candidate for President. He was also endorsed by the Progressive Party, thanks largely to the support given to him by the former President Theodore Roosevelt for whom Haskell was especially partial. Other Republican figures such as former President William Howard Taft endorsed Hughes and felt as Haskell did that the accomplishments Hughes made as Governor of New York would establish him as a formidable progressive Republican alternative to Woodrow Wilson.

Thus, Albert Haskell Jr. became active in the Republican Party. He would remain a stalwart member for the rest of his life. His first political appointment came in February 1917 when he was named Secretary of the Civil Service Board in place of Cashier E. H. Richards who resigned. Mayor Hoagland was at the helm of Cortland's city council meeting when the appointment was made. The public was informed by the press that a decision had been made that the paper heartily endorsed: "Haskell is a bright, promising young attorney . . . who will . . . someday make his mark in the world of law. It is a splendid appointment, Mayor Hoagland."

Two months later and five days after the U. S. Congress declared war upon the German Empire and joined the Allied Powers, Haskell distributed business cards announcing that Mr. Albert Haskell Jr. "who has been associated with Clayton R. Lusk for some time past," would, as of Wednesday, April 11, 1917, "engage in the practice of law at the offices formerly occupied by Dickinson & Duffey, sixty-nine Main Street, Cortland, New York." Officially, on the second floor of the Second National Bank, the Cortland native son was entering the practice of law independently with the potential for a greater political role if he so aspired.

In the same month, Edgar Mayette, president of the Oriental Furniture Company of Canisteo, New York, had his bookkeepers send out notices of debts owed the company. Included on each statement was a piece of clever verse composed by Mr. Mayette:

Way Past Due

Say neighbor! We're needing some money and we're writing to ask some from you.
Please send us enough to cover that invoice of ours that's past due.
To make us wait any longer, you know in your mind, is a sin;
So make out your check while you're thinking, and let Uncle Sam bring it in.

One recipient of this notice was the McEvoy & Hartnett Furniture Company of Cortland, New York. Their affairs were reposing at the time in bankruptcy court, and the notice of the overdue bill was brought to the attention of the lawyer representing the bankrupt firm, Albert Haskell Jr. Haskell knew that a response to the furniture manufacturer was in order. Not to be outdone by the company president-turned-poet, Haskell took matters in hand and responded in kind:

Gentlemen:
Received your letter of recent date,
Am writing this—so you'll know your fate,
Am sorry to say, your rhyme of hope
Found McEvoy-Hartnett Co. "BROKE."

In Bankruptcy they were forced to go,
And a Trustee was elected to look after their "dough."
The "dough" is short—but if a claim you file,
You can expect a "dividend" after a while.

In the future, all rhymes regarding your bill,
Please send to George S. Tarbell, Referee in bankruptcy, at Ithaca, on the hill.
And if you hope, and if you pray,
Perhaps—a portion of your "invoice" will come, SOME DAY.

Very truly yours,
ALBERT HASKELL, JR.
Attorney for Trustee of Hartnett Bros.
In Bankruptcy, No. 7809

This unique exchange of business correspondence came to the attention of the press. Two newspapers published an article on the subject, but it was *The Canisteo Times* of Wednesday, May 1, 1918, that introduced more humor:

A Muse Sings of Bills Past Due

And asked the debtors to pay;
Come across, he said, or we'll have to sue,
For we've waited many a day.

Then to Mr. Mayette the attorney spoke,
As he smiled with a lawyer's glee,
The company that owed you has just gone broke,
And is now in bankruptcy.

The news article concluded that Mr. Mayette expressed a desire that a dividend on his claim might "come in time for the twelfth or fifteenth Liberty Loan."

The Liberty Loan to which Mr. Mayette referred was a war bond that the U.S. government sold to raise money to support the Allied cause in World War I. Congress' April 24, 1917, Emergency Loan Act authorized the issue of $5 billion in bonds at 3.5 percent. Interest on up to $30,000 in the bonds was tax exempt. A symbol of patriotic duty, buying bonds became very popular with Americans who were watching their young men go off as "doughboys" to "make the world safe for democracy." Buying bonds introduced many to the idea of financial securities for the first time. It was a great way for the government to raise funds for the war effort and a great way for citizens in Cortland and across the nation to invest in a reasonably secure instrument.

America's entrance into the global conflict tipped the balance of power in favor of the Allied Powers. On the "eleventh hour of the eleventh day of the eleventh month" of 1918, an armistice was signed between the Allies and Germany at Compiègne, France. This marked the cessation of hostilities on the Western Front and would continue to be celebrated as Armistice Day in the U.S. until 1954 when it became known as Veterans' Day.

The years 1919 through 1921 found Haskell actively involved in Cortland's civic and social life. He was then the Exalted Ruler of the Cortland Lodge, No. 748, of the Elks Club, a member of the Cortland Lodge of the Loyal Order of Moose, a founding member of a chapter of the Rotary Club in Cortland, and a member of the Cortland Country Club. His active roles in these organizations allowed him to engage in the kind of networking required to have name recognition for political aspirations. For Haskell, as a trained lawyer, the post he aspired to was District Attorney for Cortland County.

At age 30, having easily gained the support of the local Republican Party, Haskell secured his name on the ballot for DA. With all of his civic credits and his position of treasurer in the Cortland County Bar Association, he was well positioned to campaign. A campaign article in a November issue of the *Cortland Standard* touted him as "one of the most promising and capable of the younger members of the Cortland County bar, of good natural ability,

[and] excellent legal mind. . . ." Though he admittedly had no previous connection with the office of District Attorney, the newspaper claimed that he had "thorough legal training and years of successful miscellaneous practice" that made him "unusually fitted to take hold of the duties of the prosecuting attorney of the county" and able to "master every detail connected with the office." The election in November saw Haskell receiving 7,928 votes and his opponent 258 votes. Clearly, it was a landslide victory for the young lawyer.

Chapter 4

The Great Rotary Hijinks

Since its founding in 1919, the Cortland Rotary Club [now the Cortland Noontime Rotary Club] has become the gold standard for local and international service clubs, and Albert Haskell Jr. was a charter member and remained active all his life. The Cortland club came into being because of Dr. Daniel Kelley, Superintendent of schools in Binghamton and president of the Rotary Club in Binghamton. Edward A. Brewer, known as "Ted," was a member of the Binghamton Rotary Club when he moved to Cortland from Binghamton in January of 1917. With Kelley's assistance, Brewer talked up the possible formation of a Rotary Club in Cortland, but World War I caused further action to be postponed until April 22, 1919. With some interest generated among Cortland's businessmen and professional executives, a dinner and informal discussion was held at the Cortland Country Club on May 29.

An organizational meeting at the Cortland Country Club followed on June 4, 1919. Haskell took the minutes of that June 4th meeting and placed an onionskin copy in one of his scrapbooks for posterity. He recorded the following questions raised that evening: Is it likely members will be willing to meet every week? Where do we meet? How many missed meetings vacates membership? What is the Club to do as an activity? Will there be an adverse feeling on the part of those who are not eligible for membership? [Rotary excluded women at that time] Could they muster the 25 charter members required in order to organize a local club? With those issues satisfactorily resolved, a resolution was then drafted calling for the organization of a Cortland Rotary Club with a constitution and by-laws created in conformity with those of the International Association of Rotary Clubs. The nomination was carried calling for a temporary chairman and secretary: "Ted" Brewer and Al Haskell, respectively. The permanent organization and election of officers and directors was accomplished one week later at the first Rotary meeting. Merton Sarvay, Dr. Paul T. Carpenter, William Walsh, E. Warren Smith, Edward Alley, and Randolph H. Miller were elected to serve on the first Board of Directors. "Ted" Brewer was elected as president, Dr. H. Dewitt

DeGroat as vice-president, Edmund W. Ott as treasurer, and Albert Haskell Jr. as secretary.

Singing was a common part of Rotary Club meetings, and the Cortland Club had a booklet of "Rotary Hymns." Though sexist by later standards, one of the club favorites was titled "Can You Tame Wild Women?" Another song, "By the Old Tioughnioga," boasted of the Club's geographic location and its welcoming of visiting Rotarians:

> By the old Ti-ough-ni-oga
> Where the valleys meet,
> Our Crown City—good old Cortland,
> Waits, her friends to greet.
> Busy—happy- healthy- clean,
> There she stands for aye,
> You'll be welcome, brother Rotarians
> When you come that way.—Yell.

The next meeting was on September 16, 1919, at the Cortland Elks Club. Charter Night was held October 3, 1919, at the Messenger House with the requisite number of twenty-five charter members present. Photographs of these and subsequent Rotary meetings shows a rather staid-looking Haskell, an appearance belying the fact that he had a sense of humor that tended to manifest itself in some elaborate and memorable pranks. An inclination toward pranks was apparent back when young Haskell climbed up on Central School's icy roof to hang a class banner.

The first of the Rotary hijinks spearheaded by Haskell was focused on Rotarian James A. Farrell, the Buick distributor in Cortland. Farrell had built a large showroom connected to his service garage on South Main Street in the city. He departed for Buffalo with Fay G. Parsons to drive back with a new Buick, and Haskell, along with Chris Tyler, "Ted" Brewer, and Ralph Bennett, decided the new showroom deserved a proper grand opening and Jim Farrell should be given a special welcome upon his return from Buffalo.

So, electric lights were installed in the show room, along with decorations in Rotary colors. Tables were arranged, food prepared, and Rotarians from Syracuse invited. And there was one more preparation made. Next to the Cortland Savings Bank at the other end of Main Street was a vacant lot. Here a platform was erected. Secretly, an item was raised up and placed on the platform and then covered with a canvas so no one could see it until the grand unveiling. Only five Rotarians were orchestrating the event. Other Rotarians were not told anything other than to be at the Cortland Savings Bank by 6:15 in the evening on Wednesday, October 20, 1920.

A large crowd was on hand by 6:15 when a new Buick arrived driven by Parsons and Farrell. Immediately, they were escorted to seats of honor, and Rotarians moved in close to the platform for the "ceremony." Randolph H. Miller delivered a speech to present the honorees with a special automobile. He stated that the motor oil used in this car was "concentrated bull." Thereupon, the canvas was lifted to reveal the "Mazuka"—a 1913 Buick with no tires that had been in a wreck. There was much laughter and applause.

The "Mazuka" was tenderly lowered to the ground, and Farrell and Parsons were seated within. The car was drawn out to the streetcar tracks, and 52 Rotarians, pulling on a huge rope, formed a torch-lit procession that made its way down Main Street to Farrell's garage. There, supper awaited at the showroom.

Pancakes and sausage were served. Maple syrup was served in oil cans. Butter was served in grease cups. Rotarian Farrell was first to be served a pancake, and it was a big one. He bit into the griddle cake, only to find a large steel ring cooked inside. Doughnuts were on the menu. A few had piston rings inside; others had rubber bands. Fifteen Rotarians from Syracuse were introduced, and two new Rotarians were inducted, J. Leon Beaudry and Lew Winchell.

Haskell made a point to write by hand "The Unveiling of the Mazuka" and to place it, two transcribed copies, and three news clippings of the event in a scrapbook. This newsworthy escapade, no doubt, served as an elaborate public relations stunt and attracted more members to the Club. By September 1, 1921, the club roster listed 82 members. But an even more elaborate prank by Rotarian Haskell followed a year later with some interesting consequences.

This prank took place on the evening of September 28, 1921. Just as no respectable woman would be seen in public without the fashionable straight-line chemise and close-fitting cloche hat over bobbed hair, no Rotarian of the Twenties would dare leave his house without wearing a fedora, especially when going off to a Rotary Club meeting. However, this was to be no ordinary meeting of Rotarians. Members were instructed to put on old, worn-out clothes, to leave stiff collars behind, and to report to Rotary President Tyler's dry-cleaning establishment on Court Street in Cortland by 6:15 p.m. Entry was to be gained upon giving the password: "Kalzuka."

Shortly, Club members boarded one of twenty automobiles. The "Tin Lizzies" headed down Tompkins Street to the city limits, where all but the drivers were asked to put on blindfolds. The blindfolded Rotarians were transported along the Virgil Road, then a right turn and up a hill a short distance and then to the left and onto a farm road. Unknown to them, while the motorcade was turning onto the Virgil Road, a Ford had cut in, and the last four or five cars followed the Ford to Virgil. The main motorcade ended up on a back road. The cars came to a stop.

The Rotarians were ordered to get out and to remove their blindfolds. As they did, trumpets blared, and standing in front of them were seven men in the white hooded regalia of the Ku Klux Klan. Two were mounted on horses. The ghostly figures led everyone into the woods by torchlight—oil-soaked cattails set ablaze. They marched for half a mile. An occasional gunshot could be heard. Several Rotarians mumbled displeasure with associating with the Klan as they stumbled through the woods.

They came upon a clearing and a small hunting lodge. Food awaited. Sitting around a campfire, everyone was invited to partake of hotdogs, pickles, doughnuts, and hot coffee served in tin cups. They realized they were surrounded by dark woods, and every once in a while, the night air was punctuated by the sound of a gunshot. Apprehensively, they noticed Klansmen lurking in the woods around them.

Suddenly, someone realized that some Rotarians were missing. Nineteen of them had been part of the motorcade. Where are they now? Should we look for them? A search party is organized and sent down the road. The "lost battalion" is found, escorted back to the clearing, and offered food.

Bang! Bang! Guns go off again. Everybody looks up the hill. Through the woods seven or eight Klansmen are approaching. One of them is holding a burning cross. They march right up to where the group is sitting, and the leader begins to read an Imperial Proclamation by order of Colonel William J. Simmons, Imperial Wizard and Emperor of The Ku Klux Klan of Atlanta, Georgia:

"Gentlemen of the Cortland Rotary Club: Believing that you gentlemen are interested in the principles of true Americanism and are aware that the principles of our order are similar to the principles of Rotary, a delegation is here this evening to solicit your interest and cooperation in our cause. We believe, as did our forefathers, in maintaining white supremacy. We believe that the Jews of this country are an overwhelming menace to capital business. We believe that the greatest threat to our beloved country comes from the Roman Catholic Church. Now, my friends, I want you to listen while I conclusively prove to you these contentions.

"In your own community, consider for a moment the insidious influence of that hideous, creeping, crawling, hissing, pie-eating Parsons, better known as 'Pa.' What more safe and sure method could be devised to forever banish from your midst this miserable specimen of humanity? I answer—the Klu (sic) Klux Klan!

"Personally, I know you would welcome the opportunity to rid your club and community of a certain wooly haired, foul-mouthed, blatting Hebrew of musical comedy fame. Though he bears the name of the Apostle Paul, he is but a sheep in wolf's clothing. You know who I mean—'Old Carp.'

"Do you approve of the way 'Pop DeGroat' gives hand-in-hand with the Bootleggers, with a gun on one hip and a pint bottle on the other? Can the law reach this man? No!! The Klu (sic) Klux Klan is your only remedy.

"Haven't you noticed of late how chummy Charlie Wickwire, Ed Stilson, 'Ted' Brewer and Doc Scovel have been? They meet regularly on pretense of perfecting plans for the new Presbyterian Church annex. Are you blind? Remove the cataract from your eyes!! It's wine, women, and song! Call in the Klan and clean them out!

"Do you know that 'Chris' Tyler, who is a neighbor of 'Al' Haskell, positively knows that said Haskell is secretly a Catholic and has recently installed and purchased a wireless outfit for the sole purpose of communicating with Rome after January 1st, when he becomes District Attorney? How can you expect justice under these conditions? Down with his wireless program; let him beware of the Klu (sic) Klux Klan!

"Think what it would mean for you to silence forever 'Bill' Walsh. Will you endure forever the discords which this whiskey soaked, cigarette smoking, card-playing, nasal toned, would-be Caruso thrusts upon you? Leave him to the Klan!

"Do you know that Floyd Wood, Harold Helm, and Ben Hilton, known in police circles as 'The Hill Gang,' are terrorizing the community and must be wiped out before your Normal School [on the hill] is completed? Why not introduce them to a coat of tar and feathers at the hands of the Ku Klux Klan! How much longer will you allow 'Tookie' Newcomb, that mellow toned fat Irish hypocrite, to persecute the unfortunate element of this beautiful valley? Do you not know that he drags down thousands of dollars in private contributions to the Cause of the Poor? What does he do with this vast wealth? Poker, is the answer! Call out the Klan!

"Finally, is there an 'honest' physician in your fair community? If so, we would like to know who. These uneducated parasites are lopping off the lives of your healthy wives and children at an outstanding rate. Would you consult 'Higgins' on a case of diphtheria? Or 'Kelly' with his keen edged sword, when life is so sweet? Protect your lives, and call on the Klu (sic) Klux Klan!"

With that last statement—"Bang! Bang!"—gunfire is heard again, and into view come three deputies of the Sheriff's Department. They bark out, "Alright, you're all under arrest." The police were part of the hoax, but when the unsuspecting Rotarians saw Officer Franz, they thought they were headed for jail for sure.

Some Rotarians stepped forward immediately. They explained that the whole sordid affair has been a hoax. They owned up that Rotarians Lloyd S. Ingalls, Merle S. Nye, and Albert Haskell Jr. had secretly planned this burlesque Klan meeting for weeks. The "Klansmen" were members of the Ithaca Rotary Club, except for the men on horseback who were local farm boys dressed up and hired for realism. The nearby rustic cottage was owned by Rotarian Ray Wiltsie.

Then followed the Club's business meeting and the adoption of a new by-law, in accordance with Rotary International, that a member is to be automatically dropped if at the end of six months, his attendance record falls below 60 percent. Attendance is one of the cardinal rules of Rotary. The only excuses accepted are illness and absence from the city. What comes next is an hour of entertainment and a running line of laughter furnished by the Ithaca Rotarians. What Rotarian would not want to attend a meeting as unique as this one?

Then all made their way back to the cars by lantern light, concluding that the monthly evening meeting of the Cortland Rotary Club had tried the members' nerves at the beginning but turned out to be one of the most enjoyable they ever had. And Haskell took the KKK Proclamation he had written by hand on large sheets of paper and consigned it to history in his scrapbook.

The newspapers published full accounts of the elaborate prank, but the Binghamton and Syracuse papers reported that all had been arrested. Sheriff Chrisman found it necessary to publish that it was really a hoax. But the story did not end there. Quite the contrary, Haskell just had to keep it going. As DA-elect Albert Haskell Jr. later wrote:

> We had enjoyed so much fun during the episode that I couldn't let it die . . . so I conceived the idea to have a little more fun. A nephew of mine resided in Ridgewood, N.J., a few miles from Patterson, so I began writing letters to him purporting to come from the Klan. He [in turn] would mail the letters in Patterson so they came [to Cortland] in a regular way through the mail. Being secretary and a member of the Board of Directors, I was in a position to keep the pot boiling which I did for about three weeks. . . .

The first letter to the secretary of the Cortland Rotary Club was dated October 1, 1921, from the "King Kleagle of the Klu (sic) Klux Klan of Patterson, NJ."

> Dear Sir: We have just received [news clippings] which we believe has tended to subject our wonderful organization to ridicule and disgrace. . . . In the spirit of fairness, which is one of the dominant characteristics of our great organization . . . we will hold this matter in abeyance for five days. . . . You must realize that your members individually and collectively are liable to damages . . . for libel and slander. . . . Unless we hear from you within five days we shall refer the matter to our nearest attorney to proceed at once against the members of the Cortland Rotary Club . . . Yours for fair play. . . .

The *Cortland Standard* for October 1, 1921, reported: "Rotary Club hears from the Ku Klux Klan."

> Coming like a bolt from a clear sky was a message received by the Cortland Rotary Club from an official of the Ku Klux Klan in Patterson, NJ. The bomb dropped right in the middle of the weekly luncheon program when it was read by the secretary. That some of the members took it seriously was evident when one of the members stood up and announced that he washed his hands of all blame and declared emphatically that he would shoulder none of the responsibility. Merle Nye took some flash pictures of the Klansmen. He put them in his drug store window. His landlord, a Rotarian, ordered him to move the pictures or lose his license. Some of the members sought legal advice. Paul Kelley who is attorney for the Brockway Company contacted the Brockway representative at Patterson to verify the box number and check on the Kleagle.

The Club's Board of Directors authorized Secretary Haskell to send a letter on October 7th disavowing the Klan's charges. The next day the "Klan" in Patterson sent Albert Haskell Jr., attorney at law, a letter stating, "we consider your letter vague, indefinite, evasive, and an insult." The letter specifically charged Professor M. W. Samson of Ithaca "did knowingly and willfully and unlawfully impersonate our esteemed imperial wizard. . . ." He read "at the request of the [Cortland] Committee . . . to members of your Club what purported to be an official proclamation of the . . . principles and the secrets of the Ku Klux Klan. You also appropriated to yourselves and used in your ceremony the official insignia of the Klan, viz, 'The flaming cross,' and also used our official Ku Klux Klan robes, which are protected by copy right . . . under the laws of the State of Georgia. . . . Now you Yanks can see that . . . we mean business. No more evasion or hot air, or we will take matters in our own hands."

Now Haskell documented that "there was considerable excitement for a few weeks" until President Chris Tyler noticed that the "official" Klan letters had an odd spelling error—K*lu* instead of *Ku* Klux Klan—and suspected Haskell. For club history, Haskell wrote "[President Tyler] traced the letters to me and I confessed to him and together we prepared for the grand finale." One more letter was arranged to come from New Jersey. For this, a letter dated October 1, 1921, to Mr. Lester J. Richardson of 19 Walnut Street, Bergen County, Ridgewood, NJ, stated:

> My dear Lester:-
>
> I am enclosing herewith a letter which I wish you would mail from Patterson not later than Monday next, and if possible, I wish you would get it in the mail sometime Sunday. On last Wednesday night we had a burlesque on the Klu [sic] Klux Klan at the Cortland Rotary Club, and you will see from the enclosed clipping that we had quite a time. The newspaper account of this event was published in the Syracuse Herald, and the Syracuse Herald is one of the papers

> that has been publishing all of the information in regard to the exposure of the Klan. My idea in sending this letter is to have a little fun with the boys here as some of them are afraid the Klan may make them trouble. You can read the enclosed letter, and send it by special delivery in the enclosed envelope. Do not fail to get it in the mail so we will surely have it somewhere late Monday night or early Tuesday morning. With kind regards to your mother, father and yourself, I am
>
> Sincerely yours,

In Haskell's fashion, the scrapbook he was keeping received the envelope that was addressed to Albert Haskell Jr, Attorney at Law, Second National Bank Building, Cortland, N.Y. It, also, became the repository for the phony letters Haskell had typed to appear as if it was an actual exchange of correspondence between the Cortland Rotary Club and J. Charles Moore, King Kleagle of the Ku Klux Klan, Box 779-C, Paterson, N. J.

The fake letter dated Paterson, N.J., October 8, 1921, addressed to Albert Haskell Jr., threatened violence. It stated the Klan planned to take matters in their own hands and would appear at the next meeting on Tuesday at 8 p.m., October 25, 1921 . . . in lodge rooms over Sarvay's Shoe Store [on Central Avenue].

For the grand finale, two Cortland Rotarians arranged for a dozen Rotarians from Syracuse to be outfitted with hoods and masks. Promptly, at 8 p.m., they were knocking at the door above the shoe store. The Klansmen marched in, and the leader demanded an apology from Chris Tyler. Tyler refused. Discussion became heated. The Klansman pulled out a gun and aimed at Tyler. The lights went out, and "guns blazed." When the lights were restored, most Rotarians crawled out from under tables. The costumed guests were introduced, and the great Rotary Klan Hoax came to an end.

Rotary charter member and grand prankster *par excellence,* Albert Haskell Jr., became the District Attorney for Cortland County on January 1, 1922, and was the Rotary Club President for 1922–1923. By 1924, the actual Ku Klux Klan would be very active in New York State, and almost every town in the County and the City of Cortland had branches of the intolerant Klan under the auspices of a Col. Robert L. Rice, the grand kleagle of Cortland County. In April of 1924 a serious incident in Marathon, NY, would, ironically, pit Rotarian Haskell against the Klan.

At the Cortland Rotary Club's 90th Anniversary Gala Dinner at Tinelli's Hathaway House in Solon, New York, on April 14, 2010, the author gave a presentation recalling Haskell's KKK prank of 1921. At the conclusion, a hooded Klansman entered the banquet hall shouting words to the effect "This is a big lie! The Rotary Club continues to badmouth the Klan. Good luck trying to get back to Cortland tonight." The author shouted, "I demand you unmask yourself!" The Klansman removed his hood to reveal Albert Haskell Jr.'s Rotarian grandson Tom Haskell. Thus, the Haskell Rotarian tradition of pranking continued.

The Cortland chapter of Rotary International from its start has been far more than a fun-loving, fraternal organization. With a motto of "Service Above Self," the Cortland Rotarians have considered ways of raising money for worthy causes. Big projects started in 1923 with a Rotary Ball for the benefit of crippled children. Held at Crescent Corset Company, the dance netted $2,325. Another ball in 1926 brought in $7,007 profit for the American Legion Endowment Fund. Succeeding years saw other successful dances and fundraising events to support community enterprises.

The serious side of Club president Haskell was evident when he gave a well-received ten- minute talk at the 1923 Rotary District Conference held in early March in Montreal, Canada. Titled "Carrying Rotary Ethics into Business," Haskell stressed the need for employers to not treat their employees as commodities but as human beings. At its close, the speech was met with a great ovation from the one thousand Rotarians present, and *The Cortland Democrat* of March 8 reported the presentation was "one of the biggest hits of the Rotary district conference at Montreal."

Early Rotary luncheon meetings continued to be marked by fellowship and mirth, and Haskell was frequently the impetus. At his beloved cottage on Little York that he inherited from his father, he had a bass and a gold watch mounted on a wall. Of course, this was one of Haskell's favorite tall tales. He enjoyed regaling folks with the story of the time he was fishing on the lake and lost his watch overboard. A lake bass swallowed his gold watch and dutifully came up to the surface from time to time to have it wound. Then, he caught the fish and had it and the watch mounted.

Through the years, Haskell's fish story lived on. Around 1954, a fellow Rotarian, at a luncheon meeting, presented him with a 3 x 5 card with this poem:

> Al Haskell claims to own a bass
> That has a lake "stem winder,"
> He now can eat this chicken breast
> And send Uncle Mert its hinder.

Spin-offs of the tall tale evolved over time. A typed letter dated July 1, 1957, was sent to Haskell from Philip S. Nason, PhD, the esteemed minister of the First Methodist Church on Church Street in Cortland. It contained a great tale about a diamond ring being lost overboard in a lake. Haskell's advice was sought on how to hook the bass with the ring on its fin.

Another amusing episode became forever connected to Rotarian Haskell. At the Rotary meeting on July 29, 1958, Haskell was photographed "dramatically unveiling his famous 'besum' plant." The photo appeared on page twelve of the Club's 45th anniversary brochure with this explanation:

> This plant with its secret ingredient, developed by Al, is said to enable its discoverer to develop a master brand of mosquito[e]s for guarding Preble Swamp and also is used for domestic purposes to get rid of unwelcome visitors in his home. The besum also produces "walking" and "jumping" bass as well as the miracle liquid used for the snow machine at Greek Peak.

A tradition of Rotary is for members to take turns being responsible for inviting interesting guest speakers to their meetings. One of Haskell's turns came on Tuesday, October 7, 1952. At the noon luncheon at the Hotel Cortland, he introduced Major General Ray Barker, Superintendent of the Manlius School, which was a military academy at that time east of Syracuse. Barker, a native of Elmira, New York, had served as a former Governor of the post-World War II American Sector in Berlin, Germany, and before that had been part of the group that planned the D-Day invasion of Nazi-occupied France. No doubt, Haskell and his fellow Rotarians learned much from conversing with this prominent figure who had a front row seat to military history.

Because of his longevity, Haskell's involvement with Rotary was noted and honored on more than one occasion. On October 6, 1953, the Cortland Club celebrated Past Presidents' Night and its 34th anniversary at the Cortland Country Club. Musical numbers were provided by the legendary jazz trombonist Spiegle Willcox. February 21, 1955, marked the Golden (50th) anniversary of Rotary International. The Cortland Club was then one of 8,400 Rotary clubs. Meeting at the Hotel Cortland, its gold-colored souvenir program listed Haskell as a founding member and past president (1922–1923). Lou Wolner, Superintendent of the Homer Central School District, was the emcee and assisting him with the program were Dr. Ralph C. Lankler, Porter Bennett, and Albert Haskell.

The Rotary luncheon at the YMCA on Court Street in Cortland on September 29, 1959, celebrated the 40th anniversary of the club's founding. Haskell and Edward H. Clark, publisher of the *Cortland Standard,* were honored as the only surviving charter members. Haskell said, "Over the years our hopes, our ambitions, and all we desired for Rotary have been more than fulfilled." The two honorees were presented sets of tie bars and cufflinks by Ted Fenstermacher, a prominent Cortland attorney who served as a chief prosecutor of Nazi field marshals in the famous Nuremberg war crimes trials following World War II. One can just imagine the conversations Haskell had over the years with Fenstermacher about his experiences in Germany, listening to him describe what it was like to be a 26-year-old interrogating a star defendant, Hermann Goering. Goering was convicted for his role in the execution of innocent Jews and war prisoners, but on the day he was to be executed he committed suicide by swallowing a cyanide pill that he had kept hidden from the guards.

1963 marked the 45th year of the Cortland Rotary Club. Reflecting on "What Rotary Means to Me," Haskell observed that Cortland Rotary means "over two thousand luncheons and dinner meetings, each meeting requiring at least an hour and a half listening to a speaker or being entertained. . . ." "Has it been worthwhile?" he asked. If confined to one reason, he said it is this:

> . . . . the opportunity for new acquaintances and the friendship which membership in Rotary makes possible. Rotarians who work together, unselfishly in community service, in furtherance of the Rotary ideals, soon get to know and understand and appreciate each other. With understanding and appreciation comes tolerance, good will, team effort and friendship. . . .

And Haskell pointed to benefits for the community, too. There had been aid to crippled children, contributions to Community Chest and to the hospital, and other community activities. "Benefits for the community and friendship for its members" is what Rotary meant to Albert Haskell.

On March 5, 1963, at a Rotary luncheon, a "presentation to Albert Haskell" was delivered by Rotarian Walter W. Grunfeld, an editor and publisher from Marathon and a Holocaust survivor. Typed on "Independent Newspapers" letterhead, these moving words were handed to Haskell afterwards and placed in his scrapbook:

> To many of us, you represent all the good things that Rotary symbolizes. . . . you are ever helpful to others . . . ever mindful of the joys and sorrows of your fellowmen . . . ever willing to lend a helping hand to someone in need of your guidance. . . . you are utterly devoted to Rotary and have, over the years, exemplified the highest ideals of service and unselfishness. As our president in 1922 and 1923, and charter member secretary, we honor you today, and express to you our sincere appreciation for all you have done for Rotary during the past 44 years.

Chapter 5

The New D.A. Goes After Bootleggers with Izzy and Moe

Albert Haskell Jr. was not too far into his new job as District Attorney when he was called upon to enforce the Eighteenth Amendment of the United States Constitution. Known as Prohibition, the amendment made it illegal to make, transport, or sell any alcoholic beverage. The law would prove to be the most unenforceable in American history and would be repealed later in 1933 by ratification of the Twenty-first Amendment—the only instance in the nation's history that a constitutional amendment was repealed in its entirety.

Undaunted by the task at hand, Cortland County's newly elected DA and newly elected Sheriff, Frank M. Henry, started off with a roar into the "Roaring Twenties" with intent to enforce the law locally. They organized raids in early February of 1922 on eight suspected sites in the Italian and Russian neighborhoods of Cortland. Haskell obtained search and seizure warrants from Judge George M. Champlin, and around 8 p.m. on February 7 Cortland Mayor Hollister arrived at police headquarters and requested the officer on duty to telephone all city police officers and summon them to report for immediate duty. Meanwhile, the county law enforcement officers—the sheriff, deputy sheriffs, and patrolmen—were gathering at the DA's office. At the appointed time, Haskell telephoned City Police Chief Bowker and gave the word to launch the coordinated raids.

Armed with the search warrants, DA Haskell, Sheriff Henry, and the deputies headed for the city's south end. The other police officials took the east side of the city. At the Dominick DeVico place on Port Watson Street, four barrels and a cask suspected of containing wine were secured and removed but not without overcoming some resistance. DeVico straddled the cask in hopes of preventing its removal. As the newspaper described it, ". . . under persuasion of Officers Keeling and Slocum, not exactly the babies of the force, DeVico left the cask and the cask went aboard the truck like so much cotton batting." Another incident involved an individual who attempted to block a cellar door with his body while telling the sheriff he could not go through. The sheriff was reported to have gained access. The impeding individual was said to have "moved fast and far."

All told, the raids through the night and into the next morning found a great quantity of wine, hard cider, and whiskey stored at six locations in the city. The net value was believed to be $2,000. In addition, at one site an individual already convicted in federal court and awaiting trial for indictment in supreme court was found to be harboring two loaded revolvers, wrapped in rags, and hidden in boots, and a long dagger. The beverages seized were removed to the basement of the courthouse as evidence of a federal crime. The downside of the items placed under lock and key was the place reeked like a brewery.

The newspaper interviewed Haskell and on February 8 made a favorable report:

> The district attorney is determined to stop the sale of intoxicants both in public places and in private houses and says he will spare neither time, pains nor money to accomplish that end. He feels that a good start has been made.

Haskell's initiation into the world of law enforcement was a huge success, but six days later he was to find himself working with two of the country's most famous G-men on a couple more noteworthy raids.

On Valentine'February 14, 1922, a man walked into the David Harum Hotel on Main Street in Homer [where the fire station is now] and presented himself to the man behind the bar, Harry Cortright. He introduced himself to Cortright as a traveling tobacco salesman and said that he had some fine cigars for sale at a reasonable price. Being of an affable nature and genial in conversation, the salesman was able to convince Cortright to agree to purchase an allotment of cigars that would be delivered at a later date. To seal the deal, the salesman offered to buy drinks, and Cortright produced the requested libation.

What Cortright did not know was that this was no salesman. This was Prohibition Agent No. 1, Isidore Einstein, a federal agent sworn to enforce the 18th Amendment. By selling liquor to Einstein, Cortright had committed a crime.

The next day, Einstein reappeared at the David Harum Hotel. With him was his partner and fellow agent, Moe Smith. The pair had obtained a search and seizures warrant from U.S. Commissioner Wickham of Binghamton, and they had local law enforcement personnel with them. Stepping behind the bar, all they could find was a solitary pint of liquor. They then proceeded to conduct a thorough search of the premises, which included the upstairs. There the pair came upon a room with a placard on the door. The placard read "Quarantine for Influenza." Unfazed, the pair ordered Cortright to open the door. He refused. So, the pair broke it down. "Inside was enough 'evidence' to convict a few hundred," Einstein later told reporters.

Before the day was over, based upon a lead they were provided, the pair visited the Central Tire store on Port Watson Street in the city of Cortland. Behind a pile of tires and inside some of them, they found a large quantity of liquor. The pair claimed the store had been a distribution center for booze for some time. As a result of the two raids in Cortland County, three men were arrested and set to appear before United States Commissioner Wickham in Binghamton on Thursday, February 23, 1922.

District Attorney Albert Haskell Jr. was enthusiastic about the success of these raids and complimented Einstein and Smith for their accomplishment. They, in turn, spoke highly of Haskell's efforts in the operation. Haskell and Sheriff Henry had requested the assistance of the two G-men and were pleased with Einstein's assessment that "conditions in the city and county, as to the observance of the dry law, are pretty good" but he would be "ready to come to Cortland again at any time."

Working under the direction of Chief Field Agent John S. Parsons of Oswego and in conjunction with DA Haskell, Einstein and Smith had arrived in Syracuse by train and then swept down upon Cortland without prior announcement of their arrival in the county, even to other local law enforcement officers. Einstein and Smith were able to use the element of surprise to their advantage. By the time of these two raids, Einstein and Smith, known in the popular press as "Izzy and Moe," had become household names. Mere mention of their names put fear and a healthy respect for the eighteenth amendment into the hearts of men and women engaged in bootlegging. Once on a train ride from Monticello to Port Jervis, the pair were recognized, and upon arrival at Port Jervis, the engineer, in true Paul Revere fashion, hopped off and ran from gin mill to gin mill yelling, "They're coming. Izzy and Moe is [sic] coming!"

By early 1922 the agents were well on their way to becoming famous for using guile and jovial geniality to best the bootleggers in sensational operations. With well over 1,800 arrests and convictions to their credit, Izzy and Moe kept coming across new challenges. Even they had to smile about the novel way proprietors in Homer and Cortland had tried to conceal their booze.

"Few bootleggers have shown the brains evidenced by the proprietors of 'David Harum's' place in hiding the stuff," declared Izzy to a reporter. "It was the first time we've been faced with a quarantine sign, duly authorized by the board of health. I've never seen liquor quarantined before," he added, smiling. "Well, Izzy, bootleggers seldom put the stuff in automobile tires, notwithstanding the movies," Moe interrupted, "and that's what we found at

Izzy and Moe reading a newspaper about their exploits in Cortland before departing by train. A clipping found in Haskell's scrapbook. Photographed by the author.

Cortland." Izzy explained, "You just unscrewed the tire valve and drew your own drinks at 50 cents a clatter. . . ."

The pair of booze sleuths traveled north to Oswego next. There they conducted a raid on a hotel known as the Hanley House and arrested its proprietor, John Musicko, and an employee, Sam Desanto. Both were jailed with a $1,000 bail. Izzy and Moe had planned to focus next on the city of Syracuse but were unexpectedly summoned back to New York City. They departed by train after making this warning: "We didn't strike Syracuse this time, but we'll be back!"

Back in New York City, the newspapers interviewed them about their activities Upstate. They did not speak highly of the February weather "up at the North Pole in Cortland County." Izzy said that if you want to travel up there you must go by horse-drawn sleigh "and when you get there they have to carry you in and lean you up carefully against the wall, because if they should bend you anywhere you would break, just like that." They explained that they first had gone to Homer, which, with tongue in cheek, they said "is named for Babe Ruth." What they discovered there and in Cortland, they said, was "the most terrible hooch—positively" compared to whiskey made in the City.

How did these two men happen to embark on a career as G-men armed with a sense of humor? The ratification in 1919 of the amendment to establish Prohibition required federal and local police forces to recruit new members rapidly in order to enforce the law. With no background in law enforcement, but speaking several languages (Yiddish, Hungarian, German, Polish, with a little Russian, French, Spanish, and Italian) in addition to English, Izzy Einstein, a 1901 immigrant from Galicia, signed up as Prohibition Agent No. 1. In a short time, he invited his friend Moe Smith to join him as a partner. Though both were personally indifferent to temperance, they felt the law must be upheld, no matter how hard it was to enforce. Besides, it was good employment, and they were good at it. According to the February 28, 1938, issue of *Time,* in their joint career they made 4,932 arrests, of which 95 percent (around 4,680) gained convictions. They confiscated 5 million gallons of liquor, worth an estimated $15 million, and thousands of bartenders, bootleggers and speakeasy owners were sentenced to jail.

In late 1925, Izzy and Moe were "laid off" in a reorganization of the bureau of enforcement. A report in *Time* magazine suggested they had attracted more publicity than wanted by the new, resentful political appointee heading the bureau, although the press and public loved the duo. By 1930, both men had moved on and were working as successful insurance salesmen.

Izzy died in 1938 after a leg amputation for diabetes, and Moe died on December 16, 1960. The New York *Herald Tribune* called them "the only prohibition agents whom the public liked." "Their exploits and disguises touched America's funny bone," stated the paper. To root out bootleggers, they posed as vegetable vendors, conductors, churchgoers, and grave diggers. They raided stills in cemeteries, basements, garages, and once in the backroom of a church.

Izzy, wearing a fake goatee and posing as a delegate from Kentucky, and Moe, wearing a cowboy hat and posing as a delegate from Montana, even infiltrated the 1924 Democratic National Convention in the old Madison Square Garden in search of illegal alcohol. They came up short. Only soda pop was available. One sting operation involved the pair crawling up onto the beach at Coney Island, shivering with cold and demanding of a suspect enough stimulant to save their lives. Another sting had the two coming forth from a car barn and informing a suspected bootlegger that they had nearly frozen to death in the line of duty during the long, cold night and pathetically inquiring if a little alcohol might not be had to revive them. When the liquor was provided, the pair provided another arrest to record.

Moe claimed that the accounts of their disguises were overdone by the press. In a 1933 interview, he said, "We didn't disguise none. If we went to a golf club to make a pinch, and put on golf knickers, the papers said we were disguised." The real agents looked nothing like the handsome G-men in the movies. Moe looked more like an affable, prosperous automobile salesman. Izzy, in need of a shave, tended to be scruffier in his sartorial appearance, with buttons missing on his vest. Both were a bit overweight and gave no outward sign of being physically fit federal agents. And, more remarkably, neither ever carried a firearm, not even during arrests.

Nevertheless, the successes of Izzy and Moe became legendary. The two who passed through Cortland County but once were described in a November 23, 1925 *Time* article as having experienced thrilling adventures comparable to those experienced by Robin Hood "adventures as thrilling as those of Sir Launcelot, as those of Richard Cœur de Lion, as those of Don Quixote de la Mancha." And Albert Haskell Jr. had the good fortune of collaborating with both men in his capacity as the young and newly elected District Attorney for Cortland County. Raids in conjunction with the notorious Izzy and Moe were surely viewed as a feather in his cap, but could Haskell be successful at prosecuting more than bootlegging cases in the courtroom? He would have more than ample opportunities to find out.

At the same time Izzy and Moe were raiding Homer and Cortland, Haskell had his first chance to prove his mettle as a prosecuting attorney in the case of The People vs Arthur Butler. Butler, a young man of Homer, was charged with assault in the second degree. In August of 1921 Butler had been hired to work for a man named Williams of McGraw. Williams alleged that Butler feigned illness on the second day, but Williams allowed him to remain in the house. For the next ten days, Butler did no work. Next, Mrs. Williams disappeared, and Butler suddenly got well and quit as the hired man. In court,

Williams claimed that he tracked his wife to Syracuse and then to her sister's home in Little York on November 28. Finding Butler there, Williams accused the hired man of adultery. Butler responded by using metal knuckles to beat up the offended husband. Haskell brought this, his first case as a DA, to a successful conclusion when, on the afternoon of February 14, the jury returned a verdict of guilty.

Haskell's first trial case was rendered additionally unusual by the fact that the court ordered Butler to be examined by physicians to ascertain his mental state. Butler's attorney, George H. Metcalf, told the judge that he believed his client was "mentally irresponsible." When brought into court to hear his sentence, Butler was asked if he had any reason why sentence should not be passed. He cried out, "Yes, sir. I have not had a fair trial and, further, I had no confidence in my attorney." Butler insisted that he had "a perfect right to try to lead any woman from the path of shame and save her." He admitted that he had been married twice and that his last wife had refused to live with him. His "peculiar answers, and in such unusual verbiage" caused County Judge George M. Champlin to defer sentencing until Butler had been examined by physicians.

The testing was a challenging experience on February 17. The physicians reported they had to put off the testing until the next day because their initial efforts were checked by "the young man's brilliant and confounding answers." They claimed that Butler used so many uncommon words—"medical terms and such intensely intellectual phraseology"—that they had to continually interrupt the examination to look up the man's words in a dictionary. Though the newspaper reported the "Homer Subject Is Too Learned For Physicians," the conviction was upheld and sentence delivered on February 25. Haskell had no time to celebrate his victory, however, because the next day he had to prosecute the case of The People vs Dan Patrioco on a violation of the excise-liquor law and after a considerable time had been taken in securing a jury. Between enforcing Prohibition and prosecuting a case of assault, the new DA was very busy.

Chapter 6

Bathtub Gin, Bootleggers, and the Black Hand

DA Haskell's case load for much of 1922 involved matters of extortion and violations of the anti-liquor laws. The trial of Dan Patriarco and Gasper DiOrio generated considerable interest and was well attended. Haskell adequately proved the men had violated the Prohibition enforcement law. Patriarco denied the charge, but Haskell had a private detective from Binghamton take the stand and testify that, disguised as an Italian-American workman, he had purchased a pint of wine from Patriarco in the Arlington Hotel in Binghamton on New Year's Eve, 1921.

On February 17, 1922, before passing sentence on the convicted Patriarco, Judge Champlin explained that he felt the defendant had been "a tool in the hands of a criminal band of violators" and did not fully realize his behavior was unlawful when he sold the liquor. Yet, the judge said that punishment was required because "a slight penalty would only be the means of encouraging the violators to continue the practice." Thus, Patriarco was fined $200 or 200 days in the Onondaga County Penitentiary. In addition, he would have to serve thirty days in the Cortland County jail. If the fine was not paid, then the thirty additional days would be served at the penitentiary.

As for Gasper DiOrio, he, too, was convicted on a Prohibition enforcement charge on the same day. When he stood before the judge for sentencing, he explained that he had previously been convicted in a federal court in Syracuse for a similar offense and had paid a heavy fine for his experience. Judge Champlin then closely questioned DiOrio. What was his knowledge of the enforcement law? What were his past experiences? What did he intend to do in the future?

The judge admonished DiOrio. "You are standing close to the danger or dead zone, between fine and imprisonment."

The defendant interjected, "But I promise, sir. I will cut out the liquor business entirely for the sake of my wife and five children."

The judge said he would give DiOrio a chance to make good on his promise because of his family. The sentence meted out was $300 or 300 days in the penitentiary.

While Haskell acquitted himself well in these two cases, at the same time the jury came in with a verdict of not guilty in a third Prohibition case. It took the jury nearly nine hours to deliberate in the case of Claude Pickert. On the first ballot the decision was eight to four for acquittal. On the next, it was ten for acquittal. After a time, the jurors were unanimous for acquittal. Pickert, a restaurant owner on Orchard Street in Cortland, had been charged with selling a half pint of whiskey and two glasses to two roof painters, Fred Anson and Frank Bush. The trial on February 16 and 17 had drawn quite the audience because Anson and Pickert had been war buddies overseas in the recently concluded Great War, and the case was the most bitterly fought of all the Prohibition cases Haskell had to prosecute. Several times the judge rapped his gavel to restore order in the courtroom. At one time he threatened to clear the room. "This court is not putting on a vaudeville performance," he announced.

The cause of the entertainment was, unfortunately, Haskell's chief witness, Fred Anson. The case fell apart when Anson was under cross-examination by Pickert's attorney, Elmer Thompson, for whom Anson had worked the past three years. Severely grilled by Thompson, Anson testified that the police commissioners of Cortland had offered him either the office of Chief of the City Police "or something as good" if he succeeded in getting evidence against the defendant. Merriment ensued in the audience, the jury went into deliberation, and Haskell had to watch as Pickert walked free. And Anson received nothing but laughter for his troubles.

Ten days later, another bootlegging incident was brought to District Attorney Haskell's attention. This time a tip from Syracuse was received by Sheriff Frank Henry early on Saturday night, February 26. Booze runners were said to be headed toward Cortland County, and law enforcement was urged to be on the watch. A description of the vehicle was provided—a Brockway "speed wagon."

According to plans, at 11 p.m. the officers took up positions along Route 11 north of the village of Homer. Under-Sheriff Chrisman and Officer Slocum camped out at the stone bridge north of the village. Frank Miller, on foot, took up a post about a quarter of a mile further north on the highway, and Sheriff Henry went to the intersection of Route 11 and Little York Crossing Road. The men waited one hour . . . then two hours . . . and then three.

Around 2 a.m., Sunday morning, a vehicle matching the description drove past the Sheriff. The sheriff's car pulled out. At a respectful distance, the sheriff trailed the suspect to prevent any possible retreat. The vehicle in question then passed Mr. Miller. As planned, Miller signaled ahead to the men at the bridge, and the men set up a roadblock by positioning the big police truck crosswise at the bridge. The booze runner would be hemmed in.

The south-bound truck driver was surprised. Forced to stop, he asked, "What's the trouble?" Chrisman answered, "I'm broke down." At this point, the Sheriff and Miller pulled up behind the booze runner. Escape would be futile. The trucker was found to be unarmed, and a search was made of the truck. Under the truck covering, the officers found some fruit baskets and other articles. Under them was found ten big bags of sugar. At least, that was the label on the bags. Further examination revealed that each bag was disguising a twenty-gallon cask suspected of containing liquor. Later, the casks would be determined to hold a total of 200 gallons of high-quality Canadian whisky.

The driver gave his name as Denny Bender of Buffalo, New York, and claimed he was driving the truck for a man named Strauss, also of Buffalo, who was ill. Bender said he had no knowledge of the cargo he was hired to deliver. "I'm just the driver; that's all," professed Bender as he was promptly arrested. He, the truck, and the cargo were taken to the sheriff's office in Cortland, and Bender was jailed overnight. The Brockway truck and half the casks were confiscated.

On Monday morning, Bender was brought before Homer's Justice of the Peace for arraignment. Bender still maintained he was innocent of wrong-doing and refused to tell the Justice the origin or destination of the contraband, though the arresting officers believed the booze was headed through Homer to the city of Cortland or Binghamton. He gave his age as 30 and said he was married. He asked permission to make a phone call to a friend in Buffalo about his plight and to request his friend to not tell his wife of his arrest because she was ill in a Buffalo hospital. Bender was returned to the County jail to be held for the Grand Jury. Bail was set at $1,000.

District Attorney Haskell was informed that the illegal alcohol was "the largest quantity ever seized at one time by an official of the county." For County Sheriff Henry it was the fourth raid made by him since he assumed office the first of January. The exciting event had all the makings of a future Hollywood movie about Prohibition bootleggers in the "Roaring Twenties" minus the use of "Tommy Guns."

The next major action took place in Truxton, New York. At 6 p.m. on March 2, 1922, Haskell, with several members of the Pellerin Detective Agency, swooped down on a hotel in this rural community. Two deputy sheriffs posing as "bootleggers" had arrived fifteen minutes earlier at the hotel for a sting operation. The hotel proprietor, Daniel Buckley, took them to a nearby garage to negotiate "a purchase" with two men from Syracuse, Clifford Rogers and Albert Sobey. The latter had only one leg and got around on crutches.

A few minutes later, Haskell, Sheriff Frank M. Henry, and several deputies and private detectives arrived on the scene. Armed with a search and seizure warrant, they surrounded the hotel and entered through different doors. Noting the arrival of the other members of the raiding party, the deputies at the garage pulled their guns and placed their quarry under arrest.

Meanwhile, Mrs. Buckley spotted Sheriff Henry when he entered the hotel. She ran down the hall and into the dining room, slamming the door behind her and locking it. A moment later, an officer ran outside and found Mrs. Buckley dumping the contents of a pitcher out on the cement walkway. The officer told a reporter, "She all but threw it in my face." The officer retrieved the pitcher and seeing it still contained some liquid handed it over to the Sheriff for analysis.

Another deputy posted outside saw the bartender come out on a porch and drop something into the snow. It was a half pint bottle of whiskey. The bartender was later taken out to see if his feet fit the footprints in the snow. They matched exactly.

Finding no more contraband at the hotel, the officers went to a nearby barn. There they discovered a quart of whiskey under an old couch. Then, they proceeded to the garage where Rogers and Sobey were being detained. A touring car belonging to Rogers was found to be harboring fifty gallons of grain alcohol in five-gallon cans, two of which were packed in saw dust in each of five iron-bound wooden boxes marked "olive oil." Rogers tried to worm his way out by saying, "I have nothing to do with this. Sobey hired me and my car; that's all." But the two men had been under federal surveillance for over a month. The two men, the car, and the confiscated booze were taken to Cortland. Rogers and Sobey refused to provide the names of "two Binghamton men" who had been transporting booze originating in Brooklyn into the "Triple Cities" of Binghamton, Johnson City, and Endicott, New York, by means of Oswego, Syracuse, and Truxton.

Hotel owner Buckley was arrested. He was already under a suspended sentence for violating the law against the sale of intoxicants in the previous month. He had pled guilty in county court and was fined $300. In lieu of a one-year prison sentence, he was placed on probation for one year. He had promised the judge, "I will not break the law again." Now, two weeks later, here he was behind bars.

For District Attorney Haskell and Sheriff Henry, this raid was a significant coup. The local press reported that within one week, with the cooperation of federal authorities, they had "seized approximately 125 gallons of alleged whiskey, two automobiles valued at more than $1,500 each and a large Brockway truck valued at $1,700." The second car and the truck were confiscated when a Scranton bootlegger's car, filled with a load of whiskey destined for a cockfight in the Cortland area, broke down. The booze was transferred to the truck transporting the birds to battle, and the car was taken to a garage for repairs. The garage workmen detected the odor of whiskey and notified the sheriff. Officers found copper containers in the car and some liquid within. A trap was then set to successfully catch the car's owner and eleven gallons of whiskey in copper containers that returned from that night's cockfight.

Virgil, New York was the next location of a raid in Cortland County. As a newspaper for March 4, 1922, reported, DA Haskell obtained a search and seizure warrant from Judge Champlin for law enforcement officers to conduct a raid on the property of Harry Kolton. Upon an officer threatening to use a poker to force open a cabinet in Kolton's house, Mrs. Kolton produced a key. The door was opened to reveal a copper wash boiler, a worm, a washtub, and a final container. Seeing that the jig was up, Mr. Kolton showed the officers how the still operated. He admitted that he had been producing six gallons a week with the paraphernalia. The mash consisted of corn, wheat, prunes, oranges, lemons, sugar, and other ingredients kept in a barrel and a milk can near the kitchen stove. Burnt sugar was added for coloring. Sheriff Henry said he had been searching for the location of this operation for six weeks. He told the press this raid was a success "for his department, the district attorney, and the police."

The biggest booze bust in Cortland County came at the end of July in 1922 when Sheriff Henry and three separate squads of deputies hit three different locations in the same evening. The Bennett Hotel in Cincinnatus was searched thoroughly, but the officers came away empty handed. The Kinney Hotel in Truxton, owned by the recalcitrant bootlegger Dan Buckley, was next to be visited. A hen house there was hosting five gallons of what was allegedly wine. At the same time, another hotel, the Connors Hotel, was raided. The officers were just about ready to give up their hunt when Clarence Slocum, known as "Cortland's Izzy Einstein," ordered an investigation of the cellar. Stashed below were 125 gallons of wine and 300 bottles of home brew. The suspicious Slocum noticed a locked toilet and ordered it unlocked. Twenty gallons of whisky awaited discovery. This third raid was described by the press as "the largest haul taken from one place since the beginning of the enforcement of the 18th amendment in Cortland county."

In April of 1922 a case of extortion was brought to DA Haskell's attention, and additional crimes came to light. A letter dated February 23, 1922, was received by Charles Sardo, a grocer of 114 Elm Street in the Italian section of the city of Cortland. Written in Italian and postmarked Utica, New York, the letter demanded $500 and threatened his life if he failed to comply. The letter instructed Sardo to bring the sum on the 28th of February to "the new bridge between Cortland and Homer" at 1 a.m. The letter reminded him that he had been fortunate once before but would not escape again. This was a reference to an attempted burglary at Sardo's store back in late December. He was reminded to keep his mouth shut and make full payment; "otherwise you are dead." In the place of a signature was a drawing of a heart pierced with a dagger.

Sardo was frightened. He did not go to the police. Instead, "another source" went to Haskell, and Sardo was called in. Haskell convinced him to hand over the letter. The letter had all the signs associated with an extortion letter from a "black hand society." The Black Hand was a method of extortion brought to America by Italian immigrants in the 1880s. Typically, it involved sending a letter to a victim threatening bodily harm, arson, kidnapping, or murder. The letter would demand a specified amount of money to be delivered to a specific place. It was decorated with threatening symbols such as a skull, hangman's noose, smoking gun, or a knife dripping with blood or piercing a heart. Because it frequently was signed with a handprint or drawing of a hand in thick black ink, it became commonly known as a "black hand letter."

Haskell recognized this and took the threat against Sardo seriously. Sardo never kept the appointment to hand over the $500. Police monitored the overpass at the appointed time, but nothing materialized. Meanwhile, arrangements were made for an Italian-speaking detective in New York City to come to Cortland and work himself into the Italian community on the east side.

Over a period of weeks, the detective did just that and made the acquaintance of Alexander Carbone, a cobbler from Homer, and Dominick Militona, a prosperous appearing man with no known employment. Gaining the confidence of Militona, the detective managed to infiltrate a plot to pull off a payroll robbery. The heist was planned at Carbone's shop on Main Street in Homer. It called for holding up Dr. F. R. Thompson the next Saturday in Cortland on Railway Avenue [South Avenue today]. Thompson, as the company treasurer, would be carrying the $7,000 payroll of the Brockway Motor Truck Company from the Homer National Bank to the plant in Cortland.

Carbone, however, balked at participating in the holdup. He said he did not want to be "mixed up in any trouble." Militona said he would get a friend in Utica to come to help do the job if Carbone wouldn't. Besides, the friend had an automobile, and a get-away car was needed for the heist to be a success. A letter was drafted and mailed to the Utican. The detective planted inside the group knew all of this.

Saturday arrived, but the friend from Utica was a no-show. No heist occurred, but to be safe the payroll bag had been filled with iron washers and some loose bills on top. At this point, the law decided to move in on Militona. On Saturday afternoon, Militona and the detective from New York City were about to cross the intersection of Cortland's Main Street and Railroad Street. Suddenly, Sheriff Henry pulled up to make the arrest. Hardly anyone noticed a man being swiftly handcuffed, deprived of a loaded automatic tucked in his hip pocket, and slid into an automobile headed for the county jail.

With Miltano secured behind bars, Sheriff Henry, Undersheriff Chrisman, and the New York City detective headed north to Homer. Their mission was to arrest Alexander Carbone and search his shop. Carbone was taken into custody, and his cousin, Dominick Natonio from Utica, was nabbed in Cortland along with a loaded revolver. Two loaded revolvers and a shotgun were found in Carbone's cobbler shop, along with two boxes addressed to Carbone and indicating they were from Militano in Utica. The officers opened the boxes. Inside they found men's underwear—about one hundred union suits of different grades—mostly sizes 34 and 36. The labels had been carefully removed. Carbone said he had no idea what was in the boxes—only that they came from Militano addressed to him. Utica authorities were notified to determine if the goods were stolen property, and local authorities were to compare the items with a list of inventory stolen the previous fall from the Merrill Clothing Company in Homer.

The Homer cobbler and his cousin were carted off to Cortland, charged with being part of attempted extortion. Having unlicensed firearms in their possession meant they would have to answer for that at a later time in Homer. Of immediate concern was the matter of the "black hand letter." The reason Carbone was charged with extortion was because Militano claimed Carbone had written the "black hand letter."

At this juncture, a handwriting expert was brought in. Both Carbone and Militano were asked to make copies of the content of the letter Sardo received. It was evident at once that Militano lied. The letter was not in Carbone's hand. An analysis of the heart symbol on the letter to Sardo revealed pencil had been used first to make the symbol and then traced over with ink. In addition, it was too perfect to have been a free-hand drawing. Searched at police headquarters, Militano was found to be carrying a postcard marked with a red, heart-shaped symbol. It was similar to the one appearing on the death threat to Sardo, and it showed signs of a tracing.

The detective from New York City explained that his work revealed the well-dressed Militano had approached a number of the youths in Cortland's Italian community about forming a local "Black Hand Society." His proposal was met with indifference by some and much fear by others. The latter welcomed with much relief the news of Militano's arrest. On April 11, 1922, Militano appeared before City Judge Dowd with his lawyer George Metcalf. He was remanded to jail to await the grand jury the next month. The newspapers reported that Haskell and others in law enforcement "have made an important arrest and that they have nipped in the bud what may have otherwise become a serious matter."

As for the Homer cobbler, Carbone was held overnight in the Cortland jail and released the next day of the extortion charges. On April 3, 1922, he was arraigned before Justice Miller in Homer. He pleaded guilty to possessing revolvers without a permit and was fined $25. The sentence of six months at hard labor in the Onondaga Penitentiary was suspended on grounds of good behavior. The judge noted "he is a first offender, a former soldier, a citizen, a hard worker and was married only a short time ago." A newspaper concluded, "While not actively mixed up in the attempted extortion, or the planned hold up, [Carbone] is not entirely free from blame, but has been pretty badly scared, and the authorities believe, has thoroughly learned a lesson." It was left to the public to determine if District Attorney Haskell agreed with that assessment, but no one questioned the service rendered Cortland and Homer by thwarting an invasion of the "Black Hand."

Chapter 7

The People vs White Slavers, Faith Healers, and a Murderer

Albert Haskell Jr. served as the District Attorney of Cortland County for three terms, starting on January 1, 1922. Besides trying bootleggers and a Black Hand gang leader, he prosecuted white slavers, a negligent faith healer, and a murderer. It was a most interesting time to be the District Attorney in Cortland and likely not what young Haskell ever expected while studying at Cornell Law School.

The case of the white slavers was described by the press as "one of the most sordid in the annals of Cortland County." On October 19, 1923, the *Cortland Standard* reported that 45-year-old Truxton, New York farmer and widower George Shaw forfeited $1,000 bail by his failure to appear before Judge Rowland Davis for arraignment on charges of buying a 15-year-old girl and her 8-year-old brother as slaves. A bench warrant was issued for his arrest. He was thought to have fled to Pennsylvania. A blind relative sent the bail bond for $1,000 and risked losing everything he possessed if Shaw was not apprehended.

It seems a neighbor, Lark Thorington, sold his children in exchange for a decrepit horse, a suit of overalls, a calf, a dress, and 50 cents in cash. Thorington was not arrested immediately, but an infant was to be taken from his custody by the authorities. Months earlier, Shaw had acquired an older daughter, aged 23, from Thorington.

Early in the summer, neighbors reported concerns to authorities. For three months, Farmer Shaw had kept the girls as his mistresses and forced the boy to do farm chores far beyond his years. The boy had been beaten into submission. The press reported the following: "Half-starved and poorly clad the girls and boy were fast losing their reason when found by the officers." The two females registered no complaints about Shaw's inappropriate relationship with them. The newspaper noted "The two sisters were not bitter but regarded Shaw much as two hound dogs kept about the place."

The older sister was sent to an institution in Rome, New York for the feebleminded. To the authorities, the younger girl appeared to be an idiot but was sent to a girls' home and reportedly showed remarkable improvement in a changed environment and with proper food. However, it was thought she would never reach age-appropriate mental development. The boy, too, was sent to an institution.

Shaw had a reputation for being "a lawless, cruel, burly ruffian." When his wife was still alive, "he beat her terribly a day before she gave birth to a child." Neighbors were asked why they did not report his behavior to authorities earlier. They were afraid to complain, they said, fearing he would retaliate by burning their barns or poisoning their livestock. District Attorney Haskell told the press he was "loath to forfeit the bail bond of Shaw until every effort has been made to find the missing man," and the case was to be "held open until the next term of Supreme Court."

The next clipping from the *Cortland Standard* to find a home in Haskell's scrapbook was from January 28, 1924. It was the obituary for Judge Joseph E. Egglston, a longtime county judge since 1890, who had grown up on a farm next to Alton B. Parker, the Democrat who ran for President in 1904 against Theodore Roosevelt. It is quite likely Judge Eggleston was Haskell's role model. The parallels between the lives of the two men are remarkable. Eggleston was an active Republican. He was much in demand as a public speaker. He was a charter member and past president of the Tioughnioga Club. The tributes paid to Eggleston would apply just as readily to Haskell at a future date: "one of the oldest best known and most distinguished citizens of Cortland County . . . friendly, kindly, honorable, public spirited. . . . a learned lawyer. . . . No one ever questioned his integrity. . . . He was the trusted advisor of a large number whose confidence he had won while in office. . . ." The former County Judge and a former District Attorney, James F. Tobin, died within two days of each other, and the committee of the Cortland County Bar Association appointed to prepare and submit the tributes probably included Haskell: "Both held a high place in our affection and respect," and their passing is a "profound loss" to the Bar and the community.

This was followed by yet another extreme case of child neglect in Cortland County. The trial on December 19, 1923, saw Grove Congdon of 118 South Pendleton Street, Cortland, defending himself of charges of endangering the life of his son. Eighteen-year-old Clifford Congdon was ill with pneumonia in November of 1923. Dr. A. C. Knapp was summoned. Dissatisfied with the doctor's care, Congdon turned to Pastor Clark, a faith healer in Philadelphia. By telegram, the faith healer instructed Congdon to dismiss the doctor. Congdon demanded the pastor come to Cortland to anoint his son. The pastor said that was not possible. The doctor, seeing the teenager was in critical condition, persisted in offering medicine but Congdon refused it. The distraught doctor, upon being discharged, filed complaint, and Congdon was arrested, and his son received life-saving care.

The trial that ensued was most unusual. Thirty-eight-year-old Congdon demanded a jury trial and the right to represent himself. Haskell represented the People, but fairly and frequently during the trial he gave Congdon assistance, explaining what a lawyer would probably do for him had he employed one. Haskell pointed out that under the laws of the State a wife could not be compelled to testify against her husband. Nevertheless, Congdon asked for Mrs. Congdon, the mother of twelve children, to be called to the stand. She testified as to how she lived in eternal fear of the man she described as "a devil-possessed religious maniac." She laid bare the home life of the Congdons and the grip the Philadelphia religious cult leader had on her husband. Of each witness Congdon asked, "Do you believe in the Bible and the divine power of healing?" Every time the court sustained the objection raised by Haskell.

While not advisable for the defendant to take the stand in his own defense, Congdon insisted on doing so. He based his defense on the Bible and its teachings and his firm faith in a faith healer he admitted he had never met. He only knew Pastor Clark through pamphlets and sent him ten percent of his weekly income while living on the town dole. Under cross examination he stated he had been committed to the Binghamton State Hospital seven years ago and remained there for seven months. He insisted he was being persecuted for something he believed to be right.

In his summation, Haskell asked the jury for a verdict of guilty but showed compassion and asked for clemency. "It is too bad," he stated, "that we haven't Pastor A. Clark on trial in court here instead of poor Grove Congdon. If that boy had died this man Clark and Congdon would both be facing you men [of the jury] on charges of manslaughter. . . . Congdon was merely a dupe of this crude fakir." The six jurors found Congdon guilty of "having willfully corrupted the peace and tranquility of his home and jeopardized the health of his son." Congdon, who said he did not want clemency, was sentenced to thirty days in the county jail.

While news clippings about the white slavers and the Congdon case took up one page of Haskell's scrapbook, fourteen pages were devoted to clippings about the most spectacular matter to come before him as the district attorney—a case of homicide. Since its establishment in April of 1808, Cortland County had not seen many cases of murder. The earliest recorded was in 1843 in Virgil when Lydia Edwards killed her 76-year-old father, Jonathan Edwards. It was brutal. She struck her father several times with an axe and then took the man's razor and slit his throat. Lydia was sent to the Lunatic Asylum in Utica. Patrick O'Donohue of Truxton was hanged in the county courthouse [not the present courthouse] in August of 1853 for a double homicide. On September 3, 1852, he clubbed to death Amanda Jane Kinney and her 12-year-old daughter, Jane Kinney. Then there is the mysterious case of the bludgeoning death of Patrick Quinlan of Homer on December 22, 1894. Two were arrested, tried, and acquitted. No one was ever convicted of that heinous crime. And then there was the case of Daniel Salisbury, who was sent to prison for life for killing his wife.

In 1924, public attention inside and outside Cortland County was riveted upon Eugene "Gene" Graham of Truxton, who was charged with the murder of John Reale of Cortland. On October 14, the 62-year-old farmer stood before Justice Rowland L. Davis. That morning, the grand jury indicted the man for murder. Through the defendant's attorney, George E. Metcalf, a plea of not guilty was entered. The grand jury trial would be the last held in the courthouse on Church Street [where the Cortland Public Library is today]. A new three-story courthouse in the shape of a Latin cross built of Indiana limestone was just completed, and Graham would have the honor of being the first to be tried in the new imposing facility.

This was not Graham's first appearance before the bar of justice. At least forty times already he had been in supreme, county, and city court in the city of Cortland. This time, the charge was the most serious. On the evening of Saturday, June 28, 1924, a Lehigh Valley Railroad man, John Reale, was hoeing a patch of potatoes along the Lehigh tracks traversing a farm northeast of the city. The farm, along the East Homer Road, was owned by Mrs. Helen DeEtta Cowan, known as "Ettie." Eugene Graham was the manager of Cowan's farm and reputed to be "her sweetheart." A companion working alongside Reale, Dominic Colasurdo, testified that two shots were fired from the direction of the Cowan farm buildings. The second shot struck and passed through Reale. The pair managed to get to the hospital, but Reale succumbed there of his wounds the next morning.

A lad who was fishing nearby corroborated the account of Reale's companion. Others swore to seeing Graham around the farm buildings with a gun in his hand. A Mrs. Lula Van Schaick heard a gunshot and looked in the direction from which it came. She said she saw Graham "stoop down and raise the gun" and then she heard the second gun shot. Other evidence at the coroner's inquest pointed at Graham. He was detained in jail since the second day after the shooting. He repeated his innocence with such frequency his pet parrot he was allowed to have with him in his cell learned to squawk "There must be a mistake. There must be."

After hearing the grand jury's report, the next thing came as a shock to Graham and to everyone in the courtroom. District Attorney Haskell stood and asked, "Is Helen D. Cowan in the room?"

"Yes, sir," came the answer from in the back.

Mrs. Cowan was asked to come forward. Judge Davis asked if she had counsel. She said she had none and declared she needed none. DA Haskell proceeded to read three indictments against Mrs. Cowan.

The first charged her with falsely swearing in county court last June when Graham was charged with driving while intoxicated in the town of Cuyler the previous January. She had testified to meeting him on the road, talking with him for several moments, and that he was sober. None of it was true. To this charge Mrs. Cowan pleaded not guilty.

The second indictment read by Haskell charged Cowan with attempting to suborn a witness. He said she had endeavored to get one James Sutton to falsely testify to sitting on the riverbank at the Cowan farm on the night Reale was shot and that he had seen a man shoot a gun toward the west. In a later affidavit Sutton contradicted his testimony in numerous respects. When asked how she wished to plead, Cowan defiantly responded, "Not guilty. I don't even know the man."

The third indictment was then read. This charged Cowan with attempting to persuade a married couple, Otis and Margaret Avery, to testify they were at her farm on the day and hour of the fatal shooting fixing an automobile tire and heard three or four shots off toward the river. Again, Mrs. Cowan pleaded "not guilty." Through the reading of the indictments, she stood solidly firm and defiant in attitude and tone of voice. A newspaper reporter stated, "the color of her face matched the mahogany of the surroundings."

The court then allowed Mrs. Cowan to attend the 2 p.m. funeral of a relative but in the custody of Attorney George Metcalf. At 4 p.m. she was returned to the court for the fixing of her bail. Attorney Metcalf requested small bail. DA Haskell asked for heavy bail, and then he suggested no bail at all because of the seriousness of the indictments. Judge Davis set bail at $5,000 for each indictment.

Unable to produce the $15,000 bail, Cowan turned herself in that evening at the sheriff's office. Thereupon, she was locked in a cell in the women's quarters of the new county jail next to the new courthouse—the same facility then holding Graham. She had been a daily visitor to Graham's cell until her incarceration. Requests for permission to talk with each other were now denied. She refused to eat the prison food and to use the blanket, sheets, and pillowcase provided. Instead, she ordered out for her meals and had her own bedding brought in. In his cell, Graham kept muttering, "I don't know why they brought her into this; there sure is some mistake."

Jury selection took two and a half days and concluded on November 19, 1924, at 12:15 p.m. The twelve jurors and alternates were all men, and the majority were farmers. Those excused from jury duty expressed opposition to capital punishment or knew the defendant quite well. One juror, William

A. Stockwell of Cortland, was excused because he was celebrating his fiftieth wedding anniversary.

Those selected were to be quartered on the third floor of the sheriff's residence for the duration of the trial. They were free to attend the movies if accompanied by an officer. They could attend church in groups of two or more, but the sheriff had to assure the pastor's sermon made no reference to the trial. Any newspapers provided the jurors had to have reports of the trial clipped out.

In the courtroom, Graham, clean-shaven and nattily dressed in what the newspaper described as a "blue suit and a neat little blue-bordered handkerchief in his upper left-hand pocket," sat with his attorneys. He had three representing him. There was David F. Lee of Norwich and his associates, Levi R. Chase and George Metcalf.

During the selection of jurors and the rest of the murder trial, the courtroom was jam-packed with spectators. Among those crowding the balcony was Mrs. Reale, widow of the murdered man, and two of her children. Joining her were members of Cortland's Italian community. The press noted that sentiment against Graham and Cowan was strong among the group. It was reported "that if Graham was not severely dealt with the Italians would take the matter in their own hands."

During a lull in the proceedings, a spectator kept gazing up at the skylight with the county seal in stained glass. This attracted the attention of one of the deputies on duty, who inquired as to what was causing the man to be so fixated on the skylight.

"Whoever heard of pineapples, oranges, lemons and bananas representing the fruit industry of the county?" the spectator asked the deputy.

The deputy took a look, wiped his eyes, and replied, "They sure look like them, but they must be pumpkins, apples, and grapes."

By now, the entire gallery had their eyes focused on the skylight above, and the deputy and the sky-gazer quickly slipped out to report their discovery to the Board of Supervisors meeting on the floor above.

With Supreme Court Justice James P. Hill presiding, the trial of Eugene Graham for first degree murder opened at 2 p.m. on Wednesday, November 19, 1924. While the defendant had three highly capable lawyers, District Attorney Haskell prosecuted the case singlehandedly. Seated near him at his table was one of the sons of the murder victim. He opened by stating he intended to present the facts fairly and impartially through twenty or more witnesses and to leave it to the jurors to judge.

After briefly outlining the occurrences at the Cowan farm on the afternoon of the shooting, Haskell called as the first witness County Superintendent of Highways William J. Dwyer. During the months of exhausting investigation by DA Haskell and the Sheriff, Dwyer was called upon to study the lay of the land at the Cowan farm. Using maps, Dwyer showed the jury how the ground was essentially flat between the point where Graham was seen with a gun and Reale's potato patch near the railroad tracks.

Haskell's second witness was 50-year-old Dominic Colasurdo. He described how he and Reale were hoeing potatoes beside the train tracks when he heard the whiz of a bullet and the report of a gun. Frightened, he ran onto the track to look around but saw no one. He then went back to hoeing. Ten minutes later, Reale, who was a few feet ahead of him, threw up his arms and exclaimed, "They hit me." Colasurdo ran to his friend and opened his trousers at the waist. He saw bleeding from wounds on both sides of his abdomen. The two men sat down and cried together. Colasurdo testified the gunshots came from the direction of the Cowan barns. He then related seeing little boys on the track coming home from fishing and Mrs. Cowan in the lane leading to her farm. He assisted Reale along the lane and saw Mrs. Cowan again, but the Defense objected to his sharing any conversation that took place with Mrs. Cowan. A passing car was stopped and Reale was taken to his home and then to the hospital where he died.

The third witness was George Rogers, a 13-year-old schoolboy. He told how he and two younger lads had been fishing that day and saw only two men in the field. They heard two gunshots but saw no one shooting. After passing the two men, they saw a woman in the lane and over at the Cowan farm they observed a man hurrying around the corner of the barn. Under cross-examination, the boy was asked if the noise he heard could have been like a tire blowing out. He maintained that it was not.

Next, Haskell called for one of the other boys, 10-year-old Albert Cole, to testify. The Defense immediately objected, maintaining the child was too young to be a reliable witness. After Judge Hill conferred with the boy, he deemed Cole could be sworn to testify. Cole corroborated George Rogers.

The fifth witness to be called was Adelbert Stevens. He told of being at work in a field on higher ground across the river when he heard two shots fired. When cross-examined, he admitted that brush and foliage obstructed his view of the river.

The last two witnesses of the day were Charles Johnson of Marathon and Sheriff Henry. The former admitted the gun admitted as an exhibit was a 25–35 rifle he had sold to Graham twelve years ago. The Defense successfully objected to Johnson explaining the carrying power, but he was allowed to state he had fired it on a range of one hundred yards. The sheriff finished the first day of testimonies by saying the rifle exhibited was the one he seized at the Cowan farm and that Graham had admitted ownership.

Testimony resumed the next morning, Thursday, November 20, 1924. Charles E. Davidson, a Lehigh Valley train engineer, was first to take the stand. He stated the train had passed the Cowan private crossing at about one minute before 7 p.m. Under cross-examination he could not recall seeing any men along the tracks.

According to the press, the "star witness for the people" was next. Mrs. Lulu Van Schaick described what she saw on the afternoon of the shooting:

> After supper sometime around 6:30 o'clock I went into the sitting room of my home. I started to write at a desk, and I heard a report. I got up and looked out the east window. I saw Graham and Mrs. Cowan standing near the barn on the Cowan farm. Mr. Graham had a gun in his hand. I sat down again to write. A little girl, Martha Ames, visiting us, came into the house and asked me to play a game of croquet. I then went out and played a short time, when I happened to look over to the Cowan farm and saw Graham going into the house. He came out again and went down between the barns. I saw him squat down, aim and shoot.

Thereupon, Mrs. Van Schaick proceeded to crouch down and show Graham's position with a firearm upraised. Attorney Lee bounded to his feet.

"I object, your Honor, to this demonstration."

The objection was overruled. Mrs.Van Schaick concluded by stating, "I paid no more attention to Graham after I heard the shot."

Attorney Lee then cross-examined. He endeavored to get Mrs. Van Schaik to testify as to the clothing Graham had on. She could only recall a white shirt. And she placed the time of the shots between 7 and 7:30 o'clock.

Mrs. Van Schaik was followed on the stand by her husband, Fred. Haskell requested his account, and he offered it:

> I was fixing fence in the south corner of my lot when I heard a shot. I turned toward the Cowan farm, and I saw Graham coming from the direction of the Cowan barn. He was carrying a gun. He was gone out of my sight for a few minutes. The next I saw of him he was on the steps of the rear porch of the Cowan house. He went down the steps and towards the barn and passed from my sight. Then, shortly, I heard a second shot.

"How much time would you say elapsed between the two shots?" asked Haskell.

"Somewhere between five and ten minutes," recalled the witness.

Attorney Lee then subjected Mr. Van Schaick to a sharp grilling, but he did not waiver in his story.

Fred Stone was a farmer living about a half mile from the Cowan farm. He testified next that he was passing the Cowan farm when he heard a shot ring out. He explained, "At that time I saw only three men working in the hay field at the Mace farm adjoining the Cowan farm." Haskell asked if any of the men looked like Graham, who had testified at the coroner's inquest that he had been helping with the haying at the Mace farm at the time of the shooting. Stone replied, "None of them looked like Graham."

Another witness, Miss Goldie Trim, ran a roadside stand on the Mace farm. She recounted,

> I heard a loud report, and fifteen minutes later I saw Graham coming down the road toward the Mace farm on a bicycle. He was pedaling fast and turned into the driveway at the Mace farm. He left his bicycle and headed for the hay lot.

Miss Trim, too, was examined closely during the cross-examination. The Defense asked if she recalled seeing a Mr. Gibbs' truck broken down near the Mace farm on the day in question. She responded she had seen the truck but was not sure of the day.

Miss Trim's parents were called next. Mrs. Trim corroborated her daughter's testimony about Graham coming to the Mace farm on his bicycle. She placed the time she saw him at about 7:15 p.m.

Other witnesses were called during the morning session: the man who brought Reale to Cortland in his automobile and the night superintendent at the Cortland hospital. Blood-stained undergarments and shirt were exhibited, and the hospital employee identified them as those she had removed from Reale when he was admitted at the hospital. Mrs. Reale, wearing widow's weeds and heavily veiled, took the stand, too, and through an interpreter identified the garments as belonging to her husband. Finally, Irving Bacon, who lived on the farm owned by Graham, testified he had passed the Cowan farm shortly after 7:15 o'clock and saw three men working on the Mace farm. He knew them and identified them as Burt Crain, Ernest Crain, and Henry Sherman. Haskell asked him, "Did you see Graham there?" "No" was the reply.

William Jones, the prosecution's gun expert, was then called to rattle off figures related to trajectories, muzzle velocities, striking energy, and range of accuracy. He stated he had examined Graham's rifle on July 1 and was sure it had been fired "recently." After a short recess, Haskell called Dr. Frank Forshee and Dr. Charles J. Kelley to the stand. After the physicians concluded their testimonies and with several more witnesses expecting to be called, Haskell announced, "Your Honor, the People rest their case." This came as a stunning surprise to everyone present.

Eyes turned to the Defense table. After a moment's hesitation, Attorney Lee stood to open the case for the defendant. According to the press, the veteran attorney made "a brilliant plea." His intent was to show that Graham was not at the Cowan farm at the time of the shooting.

As if Haskell's announcement had not been shocking enough, Lee's next announcement added further drama to the courtroom scene. Concluding his impressive opening statement, Lee approached the accused man and quietly stated to the court, "The defense will call for its first witness the accused, Mr.

Eugene Graham." A deep silence descended upon the courtroom. A pale and haggard-looking Graham stood up and walked quietly to the witness stand at 5:10 p.m. His estranged wife of twenty years was in the courtroom, and during the recess she had come forward quickly and spoke with the accused for a few brief moments.

During the examination, the court had difficulty hearing Graham. His voice was scarcely audible. He cleared his throat frequently and complained of a bad cold. After having the witness state his name, age and occupation, Lee continued questioning and Graham responded.

"How long have you been a farmer?"

"Nearly all my life."

"Have you been in the sand and gravel business?"

"For more than twenty-five years."

Graham then testified he was married at the age of 19 and became a widower at the age of 21. He later married again.

"Where is your farm?" he was asked.

"About one-half mile from the Cowan farm on the East Homer Road."

"Did you on June 28 manage the Cowan farm?"

"Yes."

"How long had you managed it?"

"About twenty years."

Lee then elicited from Graham that in the afternoon of June 28 he had gone to Cortland and returned by 4 o'clock. Between 4 and 5 o'clock he tended to the stock and went by bicycle down the highway to offer help to a truck that had broken down. At 5:45 he had supper with Mrs. Cowan and a laborer on the farm, Patrick Kane. After supper, he went and sat in a chair. Looking out the window, he observed the Crane brothers on the Mace farm getting in their hay.

"It looked stormy," stated Graham, "so I thought I would help them out."

"And did you?"

"Yes, I took my pitchfork and rode by bicycle to the Mace farm and helped them get in a load of hay."

In response to his attorney, Graham entered a formal denial of murdering Reale. He maintained he did not know the deceased and had never seen him in his life.

Next, Graham was cross-examined by DA Haskell.

"Do you recall making a visit to the county clerk's office a few days prior to June 28th?"

Graham admitted he had, and Haskell continued.

"Did you then look at the title of the Lehigh Valley railroad to land at the Cowan farm?"

Graham replied, "No, I didn't. She did."

"And who is 'she'?"

"Mrs. Cowan."

Haskell then inquired as to the number of drinks the defendant had taken on the afternoon of June 28. Graham said he took one drink before going to the Mace farm to help with the haying. At this point the gavel came down as Justice Hill adjourned the case until the next morning.

Friday, November 21 saw Graham spending an uncomfortable hour and a half on the witness stand as Haskell subjected him to a grueling cross-examination. The defendant shifted uneasily and reluctantly admitted to being present between the two Cowan barns where he allegedly fired the shot that killed Reale.

Haskell probed further and asked, "Mr. Graham, did you look down the lane toward the potato patch where Mr. Reale was then working?" Graham noticeably gulped and stammered. After attempting to evade giving an answer, Graham had a Bible placed in his hands by Haskell, who asked him the question again. Graham refused to answer one way or another.

Haskell then handed the defendant a copy of the testimony he had given at the coroner's inquest. Graham was asked to read it aloud, but he managed to read only a part of it. Haskell then read aloud the entire statement which conflicted sharply with testimony made by Graham thus far in the trial. The defendant was further discredited when Haskell handed him a number of papers for him to identify. These were records of convictions against him. One was for carrying a loaded revolver without a permit. Another was for disorderly conduct and reckless driving. Thirteen were for public intoxication. Graham appeared to be taken aback.

While the Prosecution scored points during the cross-examination of Graham, the Defense scored a point with the testimony of the next witness. Ernest Crane of Cortland took the stand and swore Graham was pitching hay in a barn on the Mace farm at the time the evening train came by on the night of the murder.

The afternoon session began with a big crowd pouring into the courtroom. Rumor had circulated that Mrs. Cowan was being brought into the trial from her jail cell. An audible murmur arose at 2:20 p.m. as the sheriff entered with Mrs. Cowan and seated her next to Attorney Metcalf. She was then summoned to the stand. She testified for the Defense that on the evening of June 28 she had seen three men in a field, and one of them had drawn up a gun and fired toward the railroad tracks. She testified she heard, in all, three shots fired.

"I saw two men in a potato patch, and the one with a blue shirt on threw his hoe in the air. I saw the dirt fly."

Before this, she swore Graham had helped her round up the chickens. She stated he had, at one point, thrown an old iron kettle at them and it broke noisily on the cement. Later, he whacked an old fishing pole so hard against the side of the barn that it broke. After he took a drink of buttermilk, she said he put on his straw hat and pedaled his bicycle down to the Mace farm to help pitch hay.

Attorney Lee asked her, "Were you there when Mr. Reale and Mr. Colasurdo came up the lane?"

"Yes, I stopped a car for them," said Mrs. Cowan.

She, also, maintained that Graham had carried a cultivator handle that day to and from the house which could from a distance be mistaken for a gun.

DA Haskell then took up the cross-examination. The newspaper reported that he treated Mrs. Cowan in "a most gentlemanly manner." He pointed out contradictions in her testimonies. She repeated that Graham had broken the fishing pole against the side of the barn, but Graham said he broke the pole against the corn crib. She said she did not know where Patrick Kane was that evening, but at the inquest she had testified he had gone to Cortland. She claimed she stopped the car for the wounded Reale, but Colasurdo testified Mrs. Cowan refused to be of help and he had stopped the car. The driver confirmed Colasurdo had stopped him. Mrs. Cowan tried unsuccessfully to evade answering the question "Did you and Mr. Graham go to the county clerk's office to look up the deed of the railroad property where the potato patch is located?"

Reluctantly, she admitted she had done so because "I had some property I was anxious to sell."

"You did call the County Clerk that day, did you not?" probed Haskell.

"Yes," admitted Cowan, but she denied Graham was in the room with her at the time.

Cowan then stepped down, and Patrick Kane, her employee, took the stand.

Haskell asked him, "How much pay do you receive?"

At this, Kane turned to the judge and said, "I object."

The justice and the entire courtroom broke into great laughter. Even Graham, who had remained perfectly immobile during his ordeal, tossed his head back, covered his mouth with his hand, and enjoyed a hearty laugh. Haskell pressed Kane again to answer the question. The doughty little farmer replied, "I don't know." This drew forth more laughter. There was a map in the courtroom that had been frequently referred to during the trial. Kane was asked to point out a certain site on it. He replied, "I don't know anything about your old map." With that the witness was dismissed.

Another witness called forward was a cousin of the accused, Fred Graham. He recalled fishing with another man named Burt Kane near the county house on the day in question when he heard two shots and a bullet whizz over his head. The press reported that Burt Kane could not be called to corroborate this testimony because "he is the man that hanged himself in county jail last summer."

Witness Fred Van Schaik was recalled by Haskell to take the stand next. The district attorney wanted to clarify some confusion caused by Attorney Lee's earlier cross-examination of Van Schaik. It had come across that Van Schaik had testified during the coroner's inquest that he could not tell if it was Eugene Graham he had seen. In fact, not all of Van Schaik's testimony from the inquest had been read before the jury by Attorney Lee. The record showed Van Schaik had been asked "Was Mr. Graham himself on the day in question?" and this was in reference to a possible state of intoxication. To this Van Schaik had answered, "I don't know. I wasn't close enough to see." After this disclosure, Mr. Lee chose not to question the witness further, and the court was then adjourned until 10 a.m. Monday. The jurors were instructed they could attend the Dairymen's League meeting on Saturday with an officer present (which they did), but they were to discuss the trial with no one. They were admonished to take care and not take cold or run the risk of getting sick at this crucial point in the trial.

The morning session on Monday, November 24, was devoted to the testimony of Albert H. Hamilton of Auburn, expert criminologist brought in to negate the testimony made earlier by the gun expert William A. Jones. Hamilton swore that a 25-caliber bullet from Graham's Winchester rifle could not have made the holes in John Reale's clothing. Under cross-examination, Hamilton was asked by Haskell if he was intimating that he, the sheriff, or Jones had tampered with the garments since June 28th. Hamilton said he had nothing to say other than he knew what Jones was capable of. Haskell, also, got the witness to admit he had earned his doctorate in pharmacy. Hamilton introduced seven photographs of the area around the murder site he had taken on July 11th. Because the area had changed several days after the murder, Haskell objected to the photos unless the jurors could see the area in person. Thereupon, Justice Hill ordered transportation be arranged by 2 p.m. to take the jurors, attorneys, sheriff, and officers to the Cowan farm. He said he would take the news reporters with him. Recess was then called at 12:30 p.m.

That afternoon, an hour and a half were spent viewing the Van Schaick residence across from the Cowan farm, the Cowan farm barnyard, and the area between the barn and corn crib when Mrs. Van Schaick heard the gunshot. The proceedings were interrupted by the unceasing squealing of pigs in a nearby pen. The judge ordered them to be fed to keep them quiet.

The trial resumed back at the courthouse by 4 p.m. Several final witnesses were called by both the prosecution and the defense before the Defense rested its case. Both sides were expected to make their summations the next day.

At 8 a.m. on Tuesday, November 25, standing room was at a premium in the packed courtroom. After seven days, the murder trial of Eugene Graham was coming to a close. The *Cortland Standard* reported later that day that

> Both Mr. Lee and Mr. Haskell outdid themselves in presenting the case to the jury. Mr. Lee not only lived up to his established reputation but even bettered it, but he was no whit better than the prosecuting attorney, Mr. Haskell, surprising even his more close friends by the thorough, conclusive, efficient, and effective manner in which he presented the evidence from the People's perspective.

Described as "impressive" and "eloquence itself," Mr. Lee reminded the jurors they "stand for justice." If they doubted the bullet killing John Reale came from Graham's gun and if they doubted Graham was at the Cowan farm at the time of the killing, then they must acquit the defendant.

Haskell began his summation by thanking the jurors for their attention to the evidence submitted by both sides. He stated he and they had a duty to perform:

> I have been chosen by the People of Cortland County to represent the People of the county and state. In this trial I have done only my sworn duty. I am not trying to crucify Eugene Graham, as has been said by the defense. I have endeavored to the best of my ability to do my sworn duty.
>
> There are two roads in this case—the straight road of truth and veracity and the crossroad of reasonable doubt. The People followed the straight road and pointed out milestones along the road.

He reminded the jury that no one was able to confirm Mrs. Cowan's testimony of seeing three men east of the rail tracks. But five men saw Graham at the time the People say Reale was shot, and four saw him with the gun, though two at the time did not know him as Eugene Graham. Haskell used the map in the courtroom to point out conditions at the time and as the jurors saw them at the Cowan farm the day before. He dismissed Hamilton with a few sentences and reminded all that Graham's alibi of working in the hayfield at the time of the shooting had been destroyed.

Haskell concluded his summation and recess was called at 12:40 p.m. Later, after receiving instructions from the judge, the fate of Eugene Graham was handed to the jury. After eight hours of deliberation, the jury said they had reached a verdict. All eyes, especially those of the accused, were anxiously focused on the jury as they filed in and returned to their seats. At 10:45 p.m. the court clerk called out, "Jurors, look upon the prisoner. What say you of your verdict — guilty or not guilty?" Roe Conrad of Harford, the first juror selected, replied for the jury, "Guilty. Guilty of murder in the second degree." A news reporter observed that "Mr. Graham received the verdict without a tremor," but "tears stood in the eyes of the district attorney" as he heard the verdict. No doubt, he realized another thing he would be thankful for in two days on Thanksgiving Day. Almost immediately, Justice Hill sentenced Graham to prison in Auburn, New York, for twenty years to life.

The next morning, Graham awoke in his cell at the county jail and greeted Sheriff Henry with the words, "My life is ended." He admitted to the sheriff that he regretted having not given up a habit of intoxication. He confessed he had been drinking on the night Reale was killed, but he still contended, "If I killed him I do not know it." By law, Graham had ten days to get his affairs in order. This he did under the sheriff's supervision on Thanksgiving Day when he visited his own farm and the Cowan farm and turned all his property and personal belongings over to his son Leon. His pet parrot was given to Mrs. Cowan. Returning to the county jail, close friends prepared and served a Thanksgiving turkey dinner with all the trimmings to him and Mrs. Cowan in his cell.

On December 3, 1924, the great gates of Auburn Prison clanged shut behind convicted murderer Eugene Graham. Graham fully anticipated his release would only come through his death. He wrote as much in pencil on prison stationery in a letter sent on April 26, 1926, to Albert Haskell Jr. He still maintained his innocence and did not blame Haskell for only doing his duty. He cited prison "long-timers" who had been "commuted or pardoned by Governor." He then made an appeal: "if there is any thing you can give me any chear for the future it will be a Comfort for me hear. I should like to see the outside again and atone for every wrong I have ever done. . . ."

As it turned out, Graham did get out from behind the prison bars. After serving thirteen and a half years, he earned parole by good conduct. *The Cortland Democrat* of May 27, 1938, reported "he is in rather feeble health and his eyesight is failing." Friends brought him to the nursing home of Mrs. Daisy Cooper at 9 Ellwood Avenue.

As for Haskell, winning the Graham case brought him well-deserved accolades and words of congratulation. Several such letters were pasted into his scrapbook. One was from a fellow Rotarian, William G. Crandall of Homer, who commended Haskell for "the high class gentlemanly way in which you personally handled the Graham case." Another letter arrived from Associate Justice Rowland L. Davis. He pronounced it to be "quite a daring thing, to go all alone with a trial of that importance . . . without the aid of older counsel." Yet another message, bearing the Cortland Board of Supervisors letterhead and dated December 3, 1924, came from Marathon's Supervisor, U. H. Boyden. In essence, he told Haskell it did not take a murder trial for him "to find all these good qualities" in Haskell, and he enclosed the following news clipping:

Sheriff Henry (left) delivers Eugene Graham to Auburn Prison. A clipping found in Haskell's scrapbook. Photographed by the author.

Cortland County is to be congratulated upon its possession of District Attorney Haskell, for he has staged one of the shortest murder trials in the history of the state, brought it to a logical and just determination with the least possible expense to the taxpayers. It takes great ability to determine to handle such a case unaided, and all agree in preparing conduct of and final presentation he excelled. We don't exactly like his politics, but we like his way of doing his duty.

Chapter 8

Haskell Takes on the Klan

Two years after Haskell staged, as a prank, the fake contention between Ku Klux Klansmen and the Cortland Rotary Club, he found himself in a real confrontation with local Klansmen. The story reads like an adaptation for a blockbuster silent movie of the era, complete with open touring cars filled with hooded K.K.K. men racing through the darkness and descending upon a rural village in Cortland County.

The place was the little village of Marathon, New York, southeast of the city of Cortland on the banks of the Tioughnioga River. The time was sometime after nine o'clock in the evening of Thursday, April 10, 1924, ten days before Easter. Five black automobiles pulled up in front of the Central Hotel owned by Thomas Walsh. Twenty men, dressed in sheets and white hoods, disembarked. Some took up positions in front of the establishment while the others rushed inside. Lyman Cronk, the hotel's night clerk, was confronted by the white-garbed band.

"Where's Tommy?" demanded the tall one who appeared to be in charge.

"He's out of town," responded the startled clerk.

"Then who's in charge?" shouted the leader.

"Well, I'm staying here tonight," replied Cronk, who decided to ask a pointed question of his own. "What authority do you have to come into this hotel like this?"

His question was met with a saber blow to his upper torso delivered by the ringleader. The blow was enough to make the clerk lose his footing, but neither his clothing nor his skin was cut. A couple other hooded men seized him, shouting "Where's your stuff?" "Stuff" meant bottles of alcohol prohibited by the Eighteenth Amendment. A struggling Cronk denied that there was any there. Then the leader began calling off numbers in his hoarse, husky voice. Different men responded to these coded orders of a premeditated plan by running through the rooms of the hotel, tipping over beds, and taking the night staff quite by surprise.

Out in the street, pedestrians and traffic were being halted and detained by hooded sentries as the ransacking occurred within from cellar to attic. A small crowd was forming.

Meanwhile, west of the bridge, members of the Osco Robinson Post of the American Legion were hosting a gathering attended by nine members of the legion posts of Cortland and Homer. The business portion of the meeting was conducted by Commander M. S. Birdlebough of the Marathon post. County Commander Harold M. Clements of Cortland spoke briefly of the importance of membership for all posts and of the responsibilities entrusted to veterans. Claude McKinney, commander of Cortland City Post, No. 489, urged members to support the work being done at a camp for disabled veterans near the Raybrook Sanitarium outside of Saranac Lake. Henry C. Walrad, a member of the Cortland City post, spoke highly of the treatment he had received as a patient of the sanitarium. He asked those present to "assist their buddies in times of peace as they did so faithfully in the days of 1917–1918." A social hour was to follow including a light repast of sandwiches.

When the time came to eat, a member of the Marathon post was sent out to go over the bridge to a lunchroom to fetch the coffee. A few minutes later, he returned without the coffee and breathlessly explained, "I was stopped from crossing the bridge. There's a masked man, and he wouldn't let me cross." Not to be deprived of their refreshments, the veterans responded by marching out of the clubrooms, as if they were again part of the American Expeditionary Force of 1917. They proceeded to the bridge led by county commander Clements.

At the bridge, one of two robed individuals ordered the group to halt and to advance no further. "Are you a sheriff?" questioned Clements. When informed to the negative, Clements countered, "Nobody but the sheriff can tell me to stop when I decide to go anywhere." One of the guards then thrust his hand menacingly into his pocket and gave the appearance of having a concealed weapon upon his person. Unfazed by this move and at Clements order, "Come on, fellows," the group continued their advance across the bridge.

They came upon bottles smashed at the curb in front of the hotel and a group of citizens standing spellbound as a party of hooded men boarded automobiles. One of the Legionnaires, A. N. Robinson, unable to dodge one of the exiting vehicles, found himself stepping up on the car's fender and hood and being carried several feet before he was able to jump off unhurt. The vehicles sped out of town, with cut-outs open, engines racing, and running boards loaded with ghostly figures brandishing sabers overhead. According to a news reporter, "It was a dramatic exit." However, it was not an exit made without the license plate numbers of two of the cars being noted by the Legionnaires. The next morning the numbers were turned over to Sheriff Frank W. Chrisman and the district attorney, Albert Haskell.

At the age of thirty-three, Haskell, of 30 Charles Street, Cortland, had run unopposed in the election for the District Attorney post in 1921. Now, he was about to be thrust into the public limelight by this nighttime raid in Marathon and the ensuing opposition from the Ku Klux Klan.

The Ku Klux Klan had been founded in Pulaski, Tennessee, in 1866, by ex-Confederate leaders who sought a return of white supremacy in the post-Civil War South. Initially, their goal was to don ghostly attire and scare superstitious freedmen from voting. When that approach failed over time to yield results, more physically violent methods, including murder, came into play to "keep the black man in his place." With the end of World War I, lynchings of blacks by Klansmen were not uncommon in America, and Klan membership grew exponentially. "The Invisible Empire" had spread out West and well above the Mason-Dixon Line.

The Klan's "hate list" had also grown. By 1920, not only blacks, but Jews, Catholics, immigrants, and foreigners were viewed as un-American and unacceptable elements by the Klan, and Klan members had infiltrated American politics. Even President Warren G. Harding was sworn in as a member of the Klan in the Green Room of the White House. To express his appreciation, Harding presented the five-man induction team with War Department license tags granting them the right to run red lights anywhere in America. As the Klan grew in political strength, it would feel emboldened to conduct a march down Pennsylvania Avenue in the nation's capital on August 8, 1925. Carrying American flags, 35,000 Klansmen displayed their brand of patriotism and bigotry as they paraded past the White House with their hoods removed. "The Invisible Empire" was brazenly visible.

The Klan was certainly no longer a mere right-wing Southern organization by 1924. As reported by *The Cortland Standard* published on the Thursday of the raid upon Marathon, twenty-five men, said to be Klansmen, were arrested and ordered to be held without bail in Ebensburg, Pennsylvania. The Klansmen of Pennsylvania were charged with murder and riot in connection with a confrontation that occurred the previous Saturday in Lilly between townspeople and visiting Klansmen. After hearing conflicting testimony about the riot and the ensuing three deaths and multiple injuries, Judge John A. Evans declared that in the opinion of the court "it was unlawful in Pennsylvania for a body of men to assemble when dressed in gowns and masks." "Such demonstrations," he said, "tend to put people in fear and it is unlawful in this state to stage any demonstrations having that effect." The judge defined the law pertaining to rioting and declared that "any person who participated was liable for actions by anyone in the crowd."

In the 1920s, the Klan was active in Cortland County. There was an active recruitment of new members. Prospective candidates were handed a three by five card which stated:

> Mr. ________ of __(address)________ Your friends say you are a native born, white, gentile American Citizen (100% AMERICAN).
>
> Therefore, as you believe in America First and white supremacy at all times, you will not fail to be in the town hall, Homer, Monday, Oct. 1, at 8 p.m. KNIGHTS OF THE KU KLUX KLAN will speak upon the most powerful, secret, non-political and thoroughly American organization in existence. If you hear the rumblings in the distance, you cannot afford to miss this opportunity. Don't judge this great law-abiding order by hearsay. Come and hear the truth. Attendance incurs no obligation.
>
> THIS CARD MUST BE PRESENTED AT THE DOOR as this is an executive session of carefully selected sterling men. Your personal friends urge you to fail not in attending, also to keep this communication absolutely confidential.
>
> Yours for AMERICA.

Klan activities in Cortland County, including cross burnings on the hill east of Homer, had gone unimpeded because they had remained within the law. There was no disposition to arrest them. If anything, such meetings as those held at the Homer Town Hall, were protected under the First Amendment of the Constitution. They had a right to peaceably assemble, and they had a guaranteed freedom of speech. But this event in Marathon seemed to the law enforcement officials to be particularly egregious and merited action.

Speaking to reporters the next morning, District Attorney Haskell bristled with indignation: "Heretofore the Klan in this section has been treated as any other fraternal organization. Last night's occurrence prompts action!" Officials pointed out that this raid, the first public demonstration or overt act by the Klan in Cortland County, was in violation of the law. An investigation was to be launched immediately, and the guilty, if any, prosecuted. Affidavits had been obtained from members of the American Legion party, and evidence would be collected in Marathon. Haskell vowed, "Any of the Klan members identified will be arrested and prosecuted."

That afternoon, Colonel Robert L. Rice of Cortland was arrested. D.A. Haskell informed the press that Rice was the "king kleagle" of the Ku Klux Klan in Cortland and that two charges were being preferred against him—inciting to riot, following the raid by Klansmen in Marathon the night before, and being at the scene in mask in violation of the penal law. In addition, Paul Allen and Marvin Kinney had been "detained on indication of having been members of the raiding party." To these charges, Rice responded by denying knowledge of or any participation in the raid. He maintained that he had not authorized the raid and that it was "without his sanction or consent."

This was Rice's stated position when he was arraigned in Marathon that evening before Justice A. Carley Adams. A big crowd gathered for this event, and the newspaper pointed out that one man in the assembly caused a stir "when he removed his rubber boots and stood attentively in his stocking feet." Rice pleaded not guilty to the charges and demanded an examination, which Adams set for the next Wednesday at two in the afternoon. Bail was set at $500 and was promptly supplied by George F. Dann and Arthur L. Stevens. Not being represented by counsel, Rice asked the court for an adjournment to obtain a lawyer.

Four others were also arraigned at the time: Marvin C. Kinney, Paul A. Allen (but the paper incorrectly used the last name of Stevens), Irving L. Strauf, and Hartsell O. Adams. They were charged with disorderly conduct and pleaded guilty. Each was fined ten dollars. Since some of the men did not have enough money with them to pay the fine, Rice paid their fines.

In connection with the raid, Haskell managed to secure affidavits, some of which were sworn to by some of the men arraigned on disorderly conduct charges. Irving L. Strauf admitted to being stationed on the bridge as one of the guards, and the affidavit sworn to by Marvin C. Kinney read as follows:

> At 7:30 I started from the office of the Ku Klux Klan in Samson block [corner of Groton Avenue and Main Street, Cortland], alone, with instructions from Rice to join a party of eighteen men. All the members of the party had hoods and masks when they started out, which they put on about one mile from Marathon. Robert L. Rice, Kleagle of the Cortland branch of the K. K. K., was in charge of the party. Rice was the organizer of the expedition to go to the Walsh hotel in Marathon to look for booze. We went to the Walsh hotel, and when we reached there had our hoods and masks on.
>
> The members of our party searched the Walsh hotel for liquor. I was stationed outside to stop pedestrians as they came along the street. I probably stopped twelve to fifteen pedestrians. Captain Rice stationed me in an open space just below the hotel. Captain Rice was the leader and instigator of this trip to the Walsh hotel, and was in mask and hood. (cited in *The Cortland Standard* of Saturday, April 12, 1924, 2)

On the afternoon of his arrest, Rice granted the newspaper an interview. He emphatically stated,

> The Knights of the Ku Klux Klan did not sanction the raid made in Marathon on Thursday evening. The conviction of the four men for disturbing the peace interests me because they are none of them members of the Klan. Further, we will gladly pay $50 in cash to anyone who can prove they are members of the Klan. Our organization is solely for the protection of the laws of the land, and not for breaking them. (Ibid.)

The particular law needing protection in Rice's view was most likely Prohibition, or the Eighteenth Amendment, which in his estimation was being flagrantly violated by that Irishman Tommy Walsh of Marathon. At the conclusion of the interview, Rice handed a letter to the reporter which he claimed to have received that morning. The letter was sent from Truxton by the Reverend Bernard DeGraw. The Protestant minister warned Rice that reliable sources had informed him that "enemies of the Klan are but waiting their chance to shoot you," and he felt obligated to forewarn Rice to be on his guard. Boldly, Rice proceeded to offer a thousand-dollar reward for anyone who could prove that he had led or was implicated in the raid on the Central Hotel. He called for a mass meeting of Klansmen in Marathon.

The meeting at the Marathon Town Hall on April 12th was said to be attended by one hundred, armed hooded Klansmen. Armed anti-Klan protestors showed up as well, and law enforcement agents were present to quell any friction. No disturbance materialized.

At this meeting, Rice, the King Kleagle, pushed the envelope even further. He called for the impeachment of District Attorney Albert Haskell. The crowd cheered. Rice went on: "The Klan is after the gumshoe politicians. . . . We'll tar and feather every one of them. We have one or two to get in Cortland County. In Cortland there are 103 bootleggers, 67 in the Italian section alone." Rice announced that Cortland's city officials were "heavily bribed" and "we are trying to find the bootleggers and then we are going to expose them." Then, his vitriol was directed back on Haskell. "He has failed to enforce the law!" "We declare war," he proclaimed, "on any officer who does not live up to his obligations." A large portion of his speech then became an attack on Catholics, Jews, and blacks, and the extolling of the virtues, aims, and objectives valued by the Klan: "There are no Catholics, Jews or Negroes in the Klan; they have their own organizations. We are the only Protestant, militant organization in the country and we have a right to organize!"

It was clear to any rational person in attendance that the Klan was using the most broken and unenforceable federal law in American history, the Prohibition law, as a pretext for going after Catholics in Cortland County. What did the booze-selling Irishman Tommy Walsh, the bootlegging Italian immigrants on the East Side of the city of Cortland, and the young district attorney of Cortland have in common? They were all Catholics—perceived as having allegiance to a Pope headquartered in a foreign land and participating in a liturgical ritual that involved the consumption of wine. To nativist Americans, Catholicism equaled an intolerable foreign practice and an affront to pure Americans. By their definition, "pure Americans" were W.A.S.P.—White, Anglo-Saxon (meaning English in origin), and Protestant. Though, with the passage of time and generations of marriages, it was increasingly doubtful that many under the white robes of intolerance could really claim to have 100 percent W.A.S.P. blood.

Not done yet with his rant, Rice then produced the letter from Truxton, which he claimed to be penned by a minister of that community, and read it to the hooded assembly:

> I have been informed from reliable sources that enemies of the Klan in Truxton [a reference to the Irish Catholic population known to reside there] are but waiting their chance to shoot you. I feel that it is my duty as a Protestant American and especially as a minister of the Gospel to inform you so that you may be on your guard. Yours for America, First, last and all the time. . . .

Then the Kleagle, the representative of bigoted threat and intimidation, concluded his diatribe by publicly challenging Haskell. He announced that he had been informed that very afternoon that a petition was being circulated by friends of the Klan in Cortland calling for the impeachment of Haskell if he persisted in pressing charges against the Klan leader. Rice's supporters in the assembly were enthralled and convinced that the battle lines were now drawn and that right was on the side of the vigilante enforcers of moral control.

By 2 p.m. on Wednesday, April 16, 1924, the Firemen's Hall in Marathon was packed to the doors with humanity, many from the city of Cortland. The crowd was said to number 300, including "a score of women." Even the stairs were filled by those eager to attend the examination of Robert L. Rice, kleagle of the Ku Klux Klan, on a charge of inciting to riot at Marathon on the night of Thursday, April 10th. Justice A. Carley Adams presided. The defendant was represented by Attorney Floyd W. Hoag of Syracuse. As Defendant Rice and then District Attorney Haskell, representing the People, entered the room, the place burst into raucous applause. Champions of each side in this legal contest were audibly present, but Justice Adams quickly squelched any further demonstrations in his courtroom. Press coverage indicated that there were two or three strangers in attendance who were alleged to be Klansmen and with whom the defendant's lawyer was observed conferring.

The Prosecution took the floor first. Haskell called as witnesses the four men who had made sworn affidavits—Marvin Kinney, Hartsell O. Adams, Paul Allen, and Irving Strauf—but when their names were called, there was no response. Their testimony was crucial to the prosecution of the case. Where were they? Why were they not there? A bit flummoxed, District Attorney Haskell explained to the court that the four witnesses called had not been subpoenaed since they had already made sworn statements but that he had expected Mr. Kinney to be present. Despite this setback, Haskell said he would like to proceed by calling three more witnesses. First to be sworn in to testify was Harold Clements, county commander of the American Legion. Clements told of how he and other Legionnaires had been ordered to stop on the bridge that night by two men in hoods and robes. He described how one of the men had stuck his finger out inside his pocket as though he had a gun. Finding that the men were without authority, he said that his group proceeded on.

Next to be called was Legionnaire A. N. Robinson. He told of bottles being broken at the curb.

The DA asked, "Could you smell what was spilled?"

"I could," answered Robinson.

"What did it smell like?" probed Haskell.

"Shoe blacking" was the response, and chuckles broke out in the room.

Haskell asked, "Do you know the smell of liquor?" More laughter emitted from the room.

"I think I do" was Robinson's reply.

"Was this liquor?"

"Not good liquor."

This was too much. Now everyone joined in the laughter. The judge, the lawyers, the defendant, everyone was unable to contain themselves and filled the hall with guffaws.

No humor was found in the rest of Robinson's testimony, as he described his harrowing experience of being struck by one of the cars as it left the scene. He said the car had come straight at him, forcing him to mount the hood and to be carried several feet before jumping off.

"Were you hurt?"

"No, I was not."

"Were you able to recognize the driver?"

"No, the driver wore a hood."

The last witness called was Claude McKinney. He affirmed that at least one of the cars had followed a zigzag course in leaving the scene. Like the two witnesses before him, McKinney told of noting two license numbers, of going to the court clerk's office to ascertain the names of those who had taken out these licenses, and then of complaints being lodged with the sheriff by Mr. Clements and Mr. Robinson.

All three witnesses were cross-examined by Attorney Hoag. He probed each one particularly about the actions of the men who had halted them. Robinson and McKinney were asked about their positions on the crosswalk when the car allegedly swerved toward them, as they had claimed in their testimonies. The Defense also questioned the two of them as to the width of the street and asked if there were ruts in the road. They said they had seen no ruts.

With the completion of the cross-examination, District Attorney Haskell stood and asked to address the court. He spoke firmly:

> I want to call attention to the spirit of fairness in which this case is being conducted. The prosecution is being conducted as any and all other cases arising

in the course of duty. Complaints were made to Sheriff Chrisman and to me. Affidavits were taken in the course of the administration of justice and a warrant was issued for the arrest of the defendant.

Haskell then moved for adjournment and asked the court, "without prejudicing the defendant," to issue subpoenas for the four witnesses who had failed to appear. Attorney Hoag said he had no objections, and all agreed to adjourn until Thursday afternoon, May 2nd, when court would resume at the same location.

With that, the gavel was brought down by Justice Adams. The subpoenas were served that evening. Again, the next day's *Cortland Standard* drew attention to the presence of two strangers in the court seated with Attorney Hoag: "He consulted with them from time to time, but their identity was not revealed." Other than this rather ominous observation, the paper reported that "Yesterday's proceedings were orderly, dignified, and devoid of excitement."

The case of the People vs Robert L. Rice resumed in Marathon on the afternoon of May 1st. The crowd of 300, mostly from Cortland, who had come "to see what they might see," expected the district attorney to call as witnesses the four men who had previously made affidavits implicating Rice. Instead, Haskell announced, "I am willing to stand on the affidavits of Hartsell O. Adams, Paul A. Allen, Irving Strauf, and Marvin C. Kinney, which have been put into the court record. I have no desire for a direct examination of these men, but they are in court for cross-examination if Attorney Hoag for the defense wishes to cross-examine."

Hoag replied, "If the District Attorney does not care for direct examination, I have no desire to cross examine."

The main witness of the afternoon was Lyman Cronk, whom the newspaper listed as a "rheumatic." As the caretaker of the hotel the night of the raid, Cronk was asked by Haskell to tell the court what he saw transpire.

"I saw hooded and blanketed intruders coming into the hotel."

"How did they enter?"

"Well, they filed into the room in nice shape."

"What happened when one of them asked who was in charge?"

"I said that I was staying here, and I asked him what authority he had to come into the place, and he hit me a blow with a saber. Right over the heart, too!" Cronk added.

"Was it a hard blow?"

"Well, I'd say it was. I was black and blue for two weeks."

"Were you scared?"

"Well, the saber had a sharp point, but I wasn't afraid the leader, the tall man, would stick it into me. I wasn't afraid at all; I knew they wouldn't hurt me."

"And what happened next?"

"The leader, the tall man, began calling off numbers, and as he did different men did his bidding."

"What did they do?"

"What did they do? They ransacked the place is what they did."

"Was any furniture destroyed?"

"No, no furniture was destroyed . . . but the beds were tipped over."

"Were any other weapons used?"

"Yes, one man had a revolver of blued steel."

Upon cross-examination, Cronk was asked, "Did you actually see any of the visitors tipping over the beds?"

"No, I can't say that I did."

"Did the man with the revolver make any attempt to use it?"

"No, sir, he did not."

"Did the visitors break anything at all?"

"Yes, they broke some bottles?"

"Bottles containing what?"

After a bit of a pause, Cronk gave an answer: "Embalming fluid, home cider, and colored water."

There had been frequent bursts of laughter during Cronk's examination, but this last testimony drew the biggest expression of amusement, to which the witness registered his personal pleasure.

Three other witnesses were questioned briefly, including G. M. Temple, the janitor at the hotel that night, but their testimonies added nothing of substance to the hearing. The next thing the much-entertained crowd knew the hearing was being adjourned. After a mere forty minutes, the crowd was visibly disappointed and let down.

The hearing was adjourned until May 17th, but as the press reported, it was essentially "without date," since the grand jury was to sit the next Monday and would report long before May 17th. The Rice case would obviously be one of those considered. At the close of the hearing, subpoenas for witnesses for the hearing in May were issued.

If any folks had anticipated a continuation of the battle between the vitriolic Klansman and the dedicated DA, they were in for a disappointment. A change of heart, perhaps prompted by sound legal counsel from the "two strangers" attending the hearings, brought the matter to an abrupt close. On the morning of May 15, 1924, Robert L. Rice, Klansman, pleaded guilty in Supreme Court to the charge of conspiring with Hartsell O. Adams, Marvin G. Kinney, Paul A. Allen, Irving Strauf, and some fourteen others not known to the Court in the Marathon raid of April 10th. The fine imposed was $400 or 400 days in jail. Rice produced a large roll of bills and proceeded to count out $400 in tens and twenties.

"In passing sentence," intoned Justice Rhodes from the bench, "I have proposed to be lenient as Mr. Rice has frankly admitted that he made a mistake and had no business being in Marathon under conditions and circumstances as charged and that he did not realize the seriousness of the offense. The Court is certain there will be no repetition and that the public will be protected should there be another offense." Then with a firm gaze fixed upon Rice, Justice Rhodes continued, "And should parties be brought before me for sentence, the penalty will be more severe." Duly chastised and $400 poorer, the defendant departed.

At noon, reporters asked District Attorney Haskell to comment on his recent nemesis. All Haskell would say, with a slight smile, was "I understand that Mr. Rice is leaving town." Later, the press would report that the Klansman "has not been heard from since." District Attorney Haskell was too modest about his role in driving the Klan out of the county. For the first time in the history of New York State, a Kleagle of the Ku Klux Klan was hauled into court, convicted, and forced to pay the penalty for Klan outrages.

Chapter 9

The Tragic Demise of Alton Howe

One of the cases DA Haskell did not include in his scrapbook involved the death of a child. The exact cause of death would forever remain a mystery.

It was Sunday, June 21, 1925. The schoolyear in nearby Homer, New York, had recently ended. Fourteen-year-old Alton Howe of 4 Maple Avenue had been promoted to the seventh grade at the Homer Academy. His parents, Mr. and Mrs. Worden G. Howe, rewarded him with a new bicycle. On that afternoon, after finishing his dinner, the boy changed his clothes. He slipped on a pair of overalls and a broad-brimmed hat. The hat was part of a new Boy Scout uniform he had just purchased with money he had saved up from his paper route for the *Syracuse Post-Standard*. Young Alton left his home and pedaled off on his new wheels. Around 4 p.m. the boy and his prized possession took in a performance of the Salvation Army Band on the Green in the village. Five hours later, he had not returned home. His parents were perplexed. The boy had never stayed out past 9 p.m. without calling home and letting them know his whereabouts. And it was getting late.

Alarmed by their son's disappearance, the Howes finally phoned the State Troopers and asked for help in locating the lad. Troopers Rann and Shaeffer searched all night and into Monday but without success. They looked for clues that might explain his whereabouts. His parents reported that he had left his money, watch, and keys on his bedroom dresser. This indicated the boy had not made any preparations to be away from home. Learning that the boy had been swimming much of late at Little York Lake, the two troopers trolled the lake waters. There was no sign of the boy. Boys who were his playmates claimed they had seen him and his bicycle at the band concert on the Green. After that they had seen nothing.

Monday night, the newspaper reported his disappearance. The paper reported that the boy's mother was "on the verge of a nervous breakdown over her son's continued disappearance." She had told the Troopers that "to her knowledge the boy had no quarrels, was in excellent health, [and] had passed his examinations successfully in school." She could offer "no reason why he should purposely remain away from home." The Troopers concluded that they could rule out the possibility that Alton had run off in search of adventure.

After two nights and a full day of fruitless searching, the Howe family, in their desperation, turned to a clairvoyant from Freeville, New York. The clairvoyant claimed the boy was in a dark place and that he had run into foul play "for refusing a pledge of secrecy to bootlegs [those making, transporting, and selling alcohol in violation of the Prohibition law]."

On Tuesday morning, June 23, Leon Witty, a Cortland electrician, reported to work. The worksite was the Homer Academy on the Green. Witty was to work on the wiring for part of a capital project on the high school portion of the Academy. Around 10 a.m. Witty was making his way back through the false work or timbering in the basement to locate the end of a pipe through which electrical wires were to pass. Upon reaching the corner, he looked up. In the semi-darkness, he spotted a body suspended above him. Unbelievably frightened, Witty made his way out and reported to his superior. The law enforcement and coroner were notified.

Alton's bicycle was found near a pile of bricks at the rear of the high school. As the *Cortland Standard* reported that afternoon, Alton's "lifeless body was found suspended by a rope from a rafter in the west side of the basement of the new Academy High school building now under construction." His feet were just a few inches from the ground. After Coroner Claude E. Chapin arrived on the scene, the body was taken down and delivered by Briggs' ambulance service to the boy's home. Later, an autopsy report showed that "death was due to strangulation and had occurred thirty-six to forty-eight hours prior to the discovery of the body." The only bleeding was from a skinned knee. That had been caused by a fall experienced days before the death. The boy had freshly bandaged the hurt "just before he left home Sunday afternoon. . . ." An inquest was ordered. The conclusion reached was that "death was brought about by suicide."

Such a conclusion was totally unacceptable to the grief-stricken parents. They claimed their son had given them no trouble, that he was a "good boy," and that he had gone off that afternoon in a happy frame of mind. They were not going along with the notion that "temporary insanity" was "the only explanation." There was another possible explanation—murder—and they demanded a fuller investigation.

Sheriff Frank Chrisman obliged. Investigators determined the rope used had been discarded by workmen at the worksite. The rope and the stick around which it was knotted were held as evidence and examined for any fingerprints other than the boy's. Occupied houses were within fifty feet of where the body had been found. No one had heard anything. Boys of Alton's age had helped in searching for the missing boy, and Chrisman quizzed several of them. A few reported that Alton had been "tormented by other juveniles with threats to 'get' him."

The village policeman, Legrande Fisher, explained to the investigators that two groups of village boys had been participating in a "sham feud." They had built shacks for their "headquarters," and conducted "raids" on each other. In this era, youngsters played outside a great deal and had play that was rich in fantasizing about "good guys" versus "bad guys" that today manifests itself in videogames played indoors about war or gangs.

This led the investigation to a cache of letters thought to have been written by the boys several weeks before the incident as part of their play life. There were references to "tying up" prisoners. The Syracuse *Herald* published the letters. This is one letter:

> Are you going to raid us tonight at 4 o'clock? We've got three men. We've got a prison and a lot of things. How many men have you got? We'll lick your men.

The letter was signed with initials. Another letter outlined the rules of engagement for the "sham feud":

> Let's have one club like this. If we get you and your men we can tie you up and take your clothes and tie you to a tree or something like that and you can do it to us. We can take you and tie you so long and then do something. We will raid you and you can raid us but have men that won't cry when we get them and have them brave. Don't try to be tied up. You must fight. Make handcuffs and stuff. Start it tomorrow. Get your men. Raid us first at 4 o'clock.

From this evidence, investigators constructed a possible scenario. Alton Howe had participated in this kind of roleplaying, was taken "prisoner" in a "raid," and was the victim of a mock hanging that went tragically wrong. The place where his body was found was at the end of a plank laid on trestles. It was reported that it was "almost an impossibility for anyone to have staged a hanging there against the boy's resistance." Perhaps the boy had willingly played the role of "captured victim" and an accidental strangulation ensued. But would the other boys have made no effort to free him or to get help or to step forward and report it? Would they just walk away without a troubled conscience? Were they so afraid as to keep the tragedy bottled up within and not confide what they knew to anyone? It seemed difficult to fathom that no youngster would step forward.

The suspicious circumstances and the parents' insistence that the boy was incapable of such an unaided act led Coroner Chapin to reopen the case. At this point, District Attorney Albert Haskell Jr., was called in to assist in the examination of the evidence at the Homer Town Hall. Seventeen subpoenas were issued for persons thought to have some knowledge to shed on the case. Apparently, District Attorney Haskell let the coroner's verdict stand. If so, then the case of Alton Howe remains a sad and tragic mystery—one of those unexplainable events that continue to cast "doubts in the minds of many."

The only remaining possible explanation was that after the concert on the Green, Alton Howe rode his bike around back of the academy and explored the construction site alone. He may have found the discarded length of rope, made a noose, and fashioned a hangman's gallows from the rope tied to a beam overhead. Climbing up on the plank supported by the trestle work, he unwisely placed the noose around his neck and lost his footing. The world of a kid's imagination may have ended in tragic reality. It was a mystery in Haskell's day, and it remains a mystery.

For Haskell, ironically, the sting of a sudden and untimely death of a much-loved son was what he was destined to experience himself in eight years.

Chapter 10

Tubercular Cattle Scandal

Mycobacterium bovis is a slow-growing aerobic bacterium and the causative agent of tuberculosis in cattle. It is related to Mycobacterium tuberculosis, the bacterium which causes tuberculosis in humans. It is highly contagious. The primary means of infection is through inhalation. M. bovis can jump the species barrier and cause tuberculosis-like infection in humans and other mammals and can lead to death. It was more prevalent in earlier times and an obvious concern to a state like New York with several counties involved in dairy production. One such county was Cortland County, where the economy was substantially based on dairy cattle. By 1925 one-third of the county's population was reported to be engaged in the dairy industry. Close to 35,000 head of cattle produced milk, the bulk of which was sent to New York City and vicinity.

To help control and eradicate the contagious disease, New York State passed regulations regarding the testing of cows and the identification of tubercular cattle with a "T" branded on their jaws and their removal from herds. Such a measure could seem draconian to dairy farmers who could not afford to have some or all of their cattle carted away and killed, but failure to comply could also have devastating consequences for a dairyman's herd and his bank account.

Reports in June of 1925 of trafficking in Cortland County of tubercular cattle in violation of the Farms and Markets Law of New York State made their way into the press and all the way to the capital in Albany. On the 25th of June, Governor Alfred E. Smith ordered a special grand jury presided over by James P. Hill, a Justice of the Supreme Court of the Sixth Judicial District, to investigate the violations and bring the perpetrators to justice.

As the county's district attorney, it fell to Albert Haskell Jr. to head up the investigation. His work took five months and involved assistance from state troopers, veterinarians, and investigators sent in by the federal and state government and representatives of the dairy industry. One hundred infected cows were discovered. Some had been sold by cattle dealers to unknowing farmers. Some cheaper cattle had been fraudulently designated as tubercular and removed from herds while more expensive but infected cattle were left untouched. During the investigation of the extent of the spread of the disease, dairy firms refused to buy milk shipped from Cortland County, and the dairy business was temporarily brought to a standstill. The press predicted there would be "startling disclosures" in the special grand jury's report.

The special grand jury began its sessions on Monday, July 20, 1925, and heard its last evidence eight days later. In that time, 125 witnesses testified, and the number of indictments expected grew from twenty to forty.

DA Haskell told the press, "No person has been promised immunity. Only two or three of the many people called as witnesses have been required to sign waivers of immunity." He added, "Immediately after the indictments have been handed to the court and filed, it is my intention to ask Justice Hill to order a panel of trial jurors. I am ready to go to trial in all the cases. I intend to push them all to a finish at this special term." When asked about rumors that some indicted persons might ask for delays or that some might ask for a change of venue, Haskell responded, "Barring any good reason for deferring trial, I plan to bring the entire matter to a speedy close."

The press reported that the investigation into the tubercular cattle scandal would likely lead to similar revelations in other counties, but Cortland County "is the first in which grand jury action has been taken" and the fact that "a grand jury has been able to go into such a mass of details and finish its task in less than two weeks is evidence of the thorough preparation made by District Attorney Haskell."

Those efforts came to light on July 31, 1925, when the grand jury returned thirty-nine indictments against eleven individuals, the majority of whom were prominent citizens of the county. Among them were two former sheriffs, one of whom was Frank Henry, who had concluded his term in December and had worked hand-in-hand with District Attorney Haskell on so many cases in the recent past. Another indicted was a former school commissioner. Besides several farmers, there was a local hardware merchant and his son, and a local garage proprietor. All were in court when the indictments were read, and each entered a plea of not guilty, with the privilege of changing to guilty on the next Monday. On that day, a special trial jury was to be drawn to try the cases beginning on August 11th. Bail was fixed between $1,000 and $5,000, depending on the number of indictments charged each man. All made bail except for Walter Totman, a cattle dealer, who had just been released from Onondaga County prison a week earlier for conviction for making false statements on an application for a license to operate a motor vehicle. His bail was set at $3,000.

Initially, when indicted and threatened with jail time, all eleven men pleaded not guilty. On the following Monday, having had time to reconsider, all eleven changed their pleas to guilty in the presence of a jampacked courtroom. Doing so meant no trials set for August 11 would be necessary, and the indicted could get the matter over with and avoid further trouble, inconvenience, and publicity. Before pronouncing sentence, Justice Hill heard attorneys and one judge speak in favor of the character of the eleven, and then Hill summed up the situation before him:

> There grew up in the county of Cortland . . . a conspiracy . . . by which the efforts of the people of the state and of the nation to prevent the spread of that disease was set at naught. The position which I hold this afternoon was not sought. Some of the men that I will have to pronounce judgement against were my friends and acquaintances. Others I know only by reputation. . . . I regarded it important that I investigate carefully to determine whether they knew what they were doing, or whether they acted without knowledge.

At this point, Hill pronounced sentence for each man, giving the relative guilt of each in the scandal as he saw it.

Daniel B. Grant as the head of the conspiracy to traffic in T-branded cows and with twelve indictments against him was sentenced to six months in jail and a fine of $1,500 and a sentence suspended until the spring term of 1926 on good conduct.

Another conspirator with a lesser role was Charles W. Ellis Jr. With three indictments, he was sentenced to six months in jail, a suspended sentence like Grant's, and a $200 fine.

The third participant in the conspiracy was Benjamin Kaplan, a butcher. Hill noted that while Kaplan should be credited with assistance given the district attorney in the investigation, he found Kaplan had not been completely frank on the witness stand. Therefore, Kaplan was to be confined to the county jail for three months.

Former sheriff Frank Henry claimed the infected cows did not originate in Cortland County but had been bought in Dutchess County. Hill did not find Henry to have been frank with the court but recognized the past contributions he had made to the county as its sheriff. Hill noted that Henry was "almost the first man that greeted me when I came into this county to go on the bench" and that he would prefer to reach the conclusion, if it were possible, that Henry had no guilty knowledge. The sentence meted out was two months in jail and a fine of $400.

Claude E. Dayton was labeled by Hill as "the tool of Mr. Grant," who had changed ear tags and substituted inferior cows for infected ones and branded them with the "T." Yet, he had helped some with the investigation. Accordingly, he was sentenced to thirty days in jail.

Another "tool of Mr. Grant" was Clarence Rood, a man with nine children to support, who did not profit from the situation and told the truth. He received a suspended sentence.

J. Allen Leach was fined $400—$200 each for sending two cows to one of his other farms in Texas Valley to escape testing for tuberculosis.

As for Walter Totman, Hill determined he was not part of the conspiracy but had "formed a conspiracy of his own" when he knowingly sold two branded cows. Two months in jail was his sentence.

Thomas Moore was fined $600 for three freshly branded cows. He was vice-president of the David Harum Canning Company in Homer and superintendent of the county farm.

Eber J. Bowdish was fined $100 for two tubercular cows.

Byron T. Grant, father of Daniel Grant, had only a slight interest in the conspiracy and was fined $100.

Jail sentences were to begin on the next afternoon. The press reported that one of the two men who drew the maximum six-month sentence visited Sheriff Chrisman to "pick out his cell" ahead of time on the second floor of the jailhouse where all would be together. He said he was ready to take what was coming to him, sought no favors, and was willing to join the prisoners who daily work on the courthouse grounds, mowing lawns and regrading Courthouse Park (formerly the Normal School campus). And, thus, the tubercular cattle scandal of Cortland County closed.

Justice Hill recommended the State come up with stiffer penalties going forward for such serious offenses. New York State Attorney General Albert Ottinger declared satisfaction that the cattle ring had been broken. He attributed success in gaining the indictments to the deputies of his department who assisted representatives of the Bureau of Farms and Markets in investigating conditions in Cortland and adjacent counties.

In a letter dated October 21, 1926, to the Honorable Albert Haskell, Joseph H. Wilson, Research Director of the New York State Board of Estimate and Control, commended Haskell's efforts in prosecuting the cattle ring. The letter revealed the politics at play at the time. Wilson more than implied that Attorney General Ottinger was trying to portray himself as "the great saviour (sic) of the State in the tubercular cattle situation." In fact, Wilson recalled that early on rumors had it that very little effort was going to be made to convict anyone in Cortland County, but that impression was dispelled when he arrived and had a conference with Haskell. "The night I had the conference with you and understood your position, I was glad to be able to report to the Governor that the investigation was safe in your hands, and that none of those guilty would be apt to escape." He continued, "It is my contention and belief that if the cases were not handled in the manner you handled them, there would have been no convictions in Cortland County." Wilson went on

Newspaper artist's depiction of seven cattle dealers changing their pleas. From a Syracuse, NY newspaper clipping in Haskell's scrapbook. Photographed by the author.

to fault the Farms and Markets Department for taking little interest in the case. He pointed out that "the Commissioner of Farms and Markets never came to Cortland County" and never consulted with its district attorney. A representative of the Department "objected at almost every step," and when photographs were taken of infected cattle, "the pictures were all seized by the Department of Farms and Markets and are still held by them." He concluded that political motivations explained why there would be an attempt made to give the credit for the successful prosecution to either the Department of Farms and Markets or the Attorney General.

To be fair, however, Commissioner Berne A. Pyrke of the Department of Farms and Markets had sent a letter to Haskell on August 7, 1925. "You had a very delicate situation to deal with and the result shows the competency with which you handled it." He added, "you have done a service not only to your own county but to the whole State, as well as to the other States of the Union in which tuberculosis control campaigns are in progress."

The best letter received by Haskell was from Justice James Hill. Dated October 26, 1925, the letter referred to the challenge the scandal had presented each of them:

> My judgment is that you and I came out of that situation with reasonably clear consciences, and your standing in your home community was not injured. The thing had dynamite in it, and we could easily have been blown out of the water. That means little to me, at my age, and the fact that my term of office runs for 12 years, but it has a meaning to you.

Once again, elected official Albert Haskell had a duty to perform in his community, unpleasant as it may have been, but nevertheless it was a duty from which he did not shrink. He had a job to get done, and he got it done. It served to enhance his reputation as an incorruptible, fair-minded man of the law.

Attorney George H. Metcalf committed to writing on November 21, 1925, that Haskell was "the fairest district attorney, as well as the best one, that this county ever had, barring not one." Metcalf went on to say he wished Haskell longevity so he might see his children "all grown up and leading useful lives." He pointed out that working for dollars does not give joy in life. Rather, "children furnish it."

As if to show future readers of his scrapbook that he concurred about the value of children in life, on the same page of his scrapbook as Metcalf's note Haskell affixed a note written in pencil by his seven-year-old son James. Dated December 5, 1925, only a couple weeks after Metcalf's note, the lad had written in his best cursive hand:

> Dear old Santie class i wish you wold bring me a 2 Wheel Bicell with a Brake on the Bicell my Father Said I cild Have 2 things For Christmas I wood like a Small Fire Engen With A Fire Stachen it Rings 9 times and Schutes out

Haskell seated with a candlestick telephone on his desk. From the collection of Dan and Linda Sweeney Quinlan. Used with permission.

> Dear old Santieclass I think you are a nice old feller and good I Will See you a Christmas night.
> From a good boy
> Mr. James Haskell

In his legal work, Haskell sought two personal things: to manifest integrity so his children could be proud of their father and to be a good provider of the wants and needs of offspring that gave him great joy.

Chapter 11

Another Murder Case and Retirement

The morning of Thursday, July 8, 1926, would be the last morning for Enrico "Harry" Graziani, a 38-year-old laborer with a wife and a four-year-old daughter. At 6:30 a.m. he stood in the doorway of his home at 102 Bartlett Avenue in the city of Cortland. A shotgun blast ripped through his right side. He died on the way to the hospital in a patrol car carrying the perpetrator to the halls of justice. Of course, this would be a case for District Attorney Haskell to handle before the day was out.

As Haskell learned, Mike Yuradi, known as Mike Reddy, was a 68-year-old employee on the farm south of the city owned by attorney O. U. Kellogg. He lived next door to Graziani and was arrested in the rear of his own residence a few moments after the fatal shooting. After Haskell obtained a signed confession, Reddy was arraigned before City Judge Louis R. Dowd on a charge of murder in the first degree, which meant the distinct possibility of a meeting with the electric chair in Auburn, New York. Reddy requested legal counsel, and the case was adjourned to the following Monday when the case would be taken up in a 10 a.m. hearing in the city court room.

According to his confession, the burly, six-foot tall Reddy was an Austrian immigrant from Hungary, had lived in Cortland for close to twenty-one years, and had not yet become a U.S. citizen. Hungarian was his native tongue, but he spoke Russian. He required an interpreter to communicate with Haskell and the authorities. He had married many years ago in Austria and had two children by his first wife. She died before he came to America. He now had no knowledge of either of his two children. He was living with Tutta, his second wife, in the extreme southwest corner of the predominantly Italian section of the city. The Reddy house faced north at 1 Commando Avenue and adjoined the Graziani residence which faced east at 102 Bartlett Avenue. Only thirty or forty feet separated the two houses.

According to statements by Reddy in his confession, by neighbors who witnessed the shooting, and by the police who investigated the case, after quarreling with Graziani, Reddy grabbed an old, rusty 21-gauge, single barrel shotgun. While standing in the hallway of his own home, he fired the fatal shot through the screen of his front door. Graziani was leaning against the casing of his open front door when he screamed "I'm shot" and fell back almost into the arms of his four-year-old daughter Mary. Investigators would find shot struck the front of the house and the front porches of adjoining houses on Bartlett Avenue.

Mrs. Graziani was the first to reach the side of her unconscious husband. She said she had heard the two men quarreling and threatening each other and was crossing the street to telephone the police when she heard the gunshot and returned to find her husband on the floor just inside their front door. Her screams attracted neighbors. Soon hundreds were at the scene. Dr. James Walsh was summoned to care for the hysterical woman.

Mrs. James Commando, living in the house adjoining the Reddy home, testified to sweeping her front porch and yelling for Reddy and Graziani to stop their quarreling. She said Reddy disappeared inside his house and within a few moments the fatal shot burst through the screen door. She then saw Graziani fall through his doorway. Others claimed to have witnessed the shooting. Seeing Tony Perfetti, Louis Corsi, and James Masterpola on their way to work, Mrs. Commando called out for their help. The three grabbed Reddy as he came out the rear door of his home. They held him until the police arrived.

According to the press, "the quick arrival of Officer George Dafoe in the patrol wagon probably saved Reddy's life, as a threatening mob had surrounded him and, spurred on by the hysterical screams of Mrs. Graziani, were threatening to take his life when the officer snapped a pair of handcuffs over the wrists and loaded him into the waiting patrol wagon."

Before arresting Reddy, Officer Dafoe, assisted by one of Graziani's neighbors, lifted the wounded man into the patrol wagon. No gun was found on Graziani nor in his home. With Albert Commando behind the wheel, Officer Dafoe and Tony Perfetti sped off to the hospital, only stopping at the police station to see Reddy duly taken into custody. Graziani was dead on arrival at the hospital, and Coroner Parsons arrived a few minutes later. The body was taken to the facilities of undertaker John McEvoy, where an autopsy was done. In all, 186 shots were probed from Graziani's body. His heart, lungs, and intestines had been punctured.

Meanwhile, District Attorney Haskell and Chief of Police Edgar Grinnell started an investigation. At Reddy's home, the shotgun and shells were found in a storeroom in the rear of the dirty and squalid house. One shell, empty, was discovered beneath a bag of grain and rags. In his confession, Reddy admitted to hiding it there when he tossed the gun into the storeroom. The screen door on the Reddy home showed a hole one inch square. The shredded pieces of wire frayed outwardly. The screen door was removed from its hinges and brought to the police station along with the gun and shells.

Within four hours of the fatal shooting Haskell brought Reddy and an interpreter into the sheriff's office at the courthouse. Undisturbed over the shooting, Reddy freely confessed to the murder. He even drew a diagram of the location of the houses and indicated where he and Graziani stood at the time the shot was fired. Haskell elicited a motive from Reddy, and Reddy explained:

> For more than a year the Italian fellow and I have had trouble. I speak a little Italian, and my neighbor, the Italian fellow, and I have little quarrels, nothing serious, for about a year. We had a fist fight about two months ago, and he knocked me to the ground. I have been afraid of him. He has threatened to shoot me at times. Tony Camillo, Joe Camillo, and Mrs. Camillo, they all heard him threaten my life on at least three occasions. I have trouble sleeping now.

"What has happened more recently between the two of you?" probed Haskell

> Last night, I was walking home from work at Mr. Kellogg's farm. As I was walking along the railroad tracks, I came upon him. He was lying in the tall grass along the tracks. He jumped up as I came near him. He called me a ________________ and said he was going to shoot me. (It was later determined that Graziani was not at this site on this date.)

"And how did you respond? What did you do next?"

> I hurried home to get away from him. After supper, I was working in my garden behind my home. The Italian fellow threatened to kill me again. To keep out of his way I hid out in my woodpile for two hours. I went to bed at 8 o'clock.

"At any time did you consume alcohol?"

"I had only a couple drinks of cider. I was sober," answered Reddy. "What time did you get up, and what happened next?"

> I got up at 5 o'clock this morning. I saw the Italian fellow standing on his front porch. We exchanged words and quarreled. I went back into the house and got my shotgun and aimed at his head.

Reddy was then shown the gun, shells, and screen door. He identified them as his. Then he signed the written confession.

At his arraignment, Reddy was calm and unfazed as the interpreter standing at his side repeated the judge's reading of the charge of murder in the first degree. In the back was Rosie Reddy, a small woman dressed all in black. She had been taken from her bench at the Wickwire Wire Mill factory following the shooting and temporarily housed at the county jail for her own protection. Now she sat calmly but appeared to be bewildered by what was going on.

As Reddy turned to leave the courtroom, he came face to face with his wife. He made a move as if to embrace her. As he did so, Mrs. Reddy let out a shrill scream and turned her back on him. She muttered something barely audible in Italian. Reddy simply shrugged his shoulders. Without saying a word, he proceeded out to the automobile waiting for him.

Earlier that morning, Mrs. Reddy had been interrogated to determine what she knew. In broken English she told of her futile struggle to prevent her husband from firing the shot. She showed bruises on her hands and arms where Reddy had hit her to break her grip on the shot gun while she had tried to wrest control of it.

"He hit me and knocked me through the door," she said. "So I went to work."

Other witnesses claimed she left later.

Graziani's funeral was held two days later at St. Anthony's Roman Catholic Church on the city's east side. At the Mass, he was remembered as "a most respectable and esteemed citizen," who had worked for a number of years at the Wickwire Wire Mills factory at the south end of the city. He was a communicant of the church and a member of the various societies of the church. Burial was at St. Mary's Cemetery on the west side of the city.

Feelings against Reddy were running high in the city, especially in the Italian neighborhoods. Things were bad enough that Sheriff Frank Chrisman thought it best to place a special guard of deputies around the jail.

Friday, July 9th was a busy day for Haskell. He wisely decided to have the alleged murderer examined as to sanity. He correctly figured the need to checkmate any attempt by Reddy's counsel to have the man declared insane. Thus, that morning he appointed three local physicians to examine Reddy and pass judgement on his mental health. The afternoon was spent gathering affidavits from all witnesses involved in the case. Before the day was out, the press was reporting that the trio of doctors had reported Reddy was found to be "insane." Haskell denied this information. He said it was rumors and that the examination done that day was only one of a series to be done over the next couple of days. Attorneys Kellogg and O'Connor were appointed to defend Reddy. It was understood they would argue Reddy should not be held accountable for the slaying as a result of the findings of a seven-person "commission in lunacy" appointed by the county and, therefore, Reddy should be spared a date with the electric chair.

During the four months Reddy spent in the county jail, his wife was a frequent visitor and brought him food and articles of clothing. Reddy became threatening and surly after her visits. The sheriff became suspicious. So, on one of her visits the sheriff had her searched by a matron. A bottle of liquor was found concealed in the bosom of her dress.

In the end, Reddy was committed to life in the Matteawan State Hospital for the Criminally Insane, the same asylum that had housed Irish American serial killer Lizzie Halliday who murdered one of the hospital's nurses in 1908 by stabbing her with scissors two hundred times. Haskell was commended for the unusual speed with which he was able to handle the second murder case of his career as district attorney.

One year after the close of the Reddy case, Haskell decided to end his six years in public office as district attorney. As of January 1, 1927, he would step down, and Attorney William Coon of Haskell's law office would become the next district attorney. In his last month in office, newspapers heaped on praise for his fine record. They noted how in five years of service he had prosecuted 225 cases in Supreme and County Courts. Of this number there were only seven acquittals and three jury disagreements. In addition, there were a large number of city court cases he was called to prosecute. The number of fines for all offenses turned over to the county treasurer totaled $13,857.30. The most notable cases cited were two for murder. Next to numerous liquor violations, there were 21 arrests for larceny, 15 for burglary, 11 for forgery, 11 for criminal assault, and one case of manslaughter.

One newspaper wrote of the case that drew state and national attention:

> With the exception of the murder indictments, the retiring official's most outstanding act was the successful prosecution of the eight prominent cattle dealers during the cattle scandal here two years ago. Fines turned over to the State totaled $3,300. In addition, four served jail sentences.

Another newspaper agreed that the tubercular cattle scandal was Haskell's most significant case and noted how it had revealed much about Haskell's character:

> Another piece of work Haskell accomplished was the punishment of men connected with the cattle scandal that rocked the entire state. This meant the sending of his own friends to jail. He had to choose between friendship and corruption and duty and justice for all. He chose the latter and six men, well known to the prosecuting attorney, served time in the county jail. These men, even after they have served the time and paid the penalty for their known misdeeds . . . are still friends of the attorney.

Yet another newspaper summed up the retiring public servant's career this way:

> Fairness and a strict sense of duty that was put to the test on several occasions and never found wanting has won for Attorney Haskell a foremost place in the history of prosecutors of Cortland County.
>
> The fact that throughout both terms he was indorsed for the office by Republicans and Democrats is proof of the esteem in which he was held by the people of the county.

After amassing a record like this, what could Haskell hope to accomplish next? Might he become a judge? A year before he announced his retirement, Haskell, at age 34, was elected president of the Cortland Trust Company, formerly known as the First National Bank. He resigned as secretary of the Civil Service Commission and as director and attorney of the Second National Bank, which he had been associated with for the past three years. He would continue the practice of law, of course, but a man of his reputation was certainly going to find many opportunities coming his way to exercise leadership and to get things of importance done for the community.

Haskell with four cartoons depicting his career path until 1927. A clipping found in Haskell's scrapbook. Photographed by the author.

Chapter 12

A Continued Career in the Law

From the end of his two terms as a district attorney until the end of his life, Albert Haskell Jr. continued to represent clients in matters of law. Many were fairly mundane. On some occasions, however, he was engaged in high profile cases. Such was the situation in 1928 when Haskell found himself in a case that would go through three courts before he could claim success for the client.

The client was the People's National Bank of Pulaski, Virginia. The bank brought suit against Lewis H. Hewitt of Cortland. The action of the bank against Mr. Hewitt arose out of the indorsement by Hewitt of two promissory notes made by a coal company located at Pulaski in the southwestern part of Virginia. Hewitt was a stockholder in the coal company at one time and its treasurer at another time. The original notes were given to the bank by the coal company in January of 1924 with Hewitt's indorsement on them. They were renewed from time to time until January 1926. The notes were for $25,000 originally, each being made for $12,500.

The People's National Bank refused to renew the notes in May 1926 when they came due and demanded payment of Hewitt. The coal company had arrived at a condition of insolvency, forcing the bank to look to the endorser for payment. Hewitt and the bank entered into negotiations during the few months that followed.

Adding some excitement to the matter was the arrival in Cortland in May 1926 of John S. Draper, an attorney from Pulaski, Virginia. Draper was brought in to assist the bank in possible litigation. Draper was a legendary attorney for his role in successfully prosecuting the infamous Allen Gang of the Blue Ridge Mountains years earlier. That sensational case commenced on March 13, 1912, when Allen Clan patriarch Floyd Allen stood before the bar at the Carroll County Courthouse to be sentenced to a year in the penitentiary for having taken a prisoner from a deputy sheriff. When the sentence was pronounced, members of the Allen Gang opened fire in the small court room, leaving a judge, prosecutor, sheriff, and two others dead. Draper was appointed a special prosecutor to bring the Allen Gang to justice. After a trial of 118 days, Floyd Allen was sentenced to die in the electric chair and other gang members received sentences of 10 to 25 years in Virginia prisons. The atmosphere was tense during the trial, and Draper's life was in constant jeopardy. During his time in Cortland, the celebrated attorney admitted to carrying a revolver in his hip pocket during the prosecution of the Allen Gang.

Draper's presence in Cortland had little effect on Hewitt, and the bank sued Hewitt. The bank was represented by attorneys Haskell and William C. Maher, during the brief existence of the partnership of Haskell, Maher, and [Paul] Kelly. Ironically, Hewitt retained the services of the Honorable Clayton R. Lusk. Lusk was the Cortland attorney a younger Haskell had interned under at the start of his career in the law. Lusk had also served for three months in 1922 as Temporary Lieutenant Governor of New York. Now Haskell and his seasoned mentor would be engaged in courtroom battle.

Meanwhile, Haskell's 74-year-old mother, with declining health, was engaged in a battle of her own. On January 29, 1928, Mary Gibbons Haskell died at the home of John Haskell on Prospect Street. Calling hours were held at the home of Albert Haskell on Charles Street. The funeral Mass was at St. Mary's Church on North Main Street, and burial was in St. Mary's Cemetery. There was little time to be consumed with grief; Haskell had only the month of February to prepare for the important upcoming trial.

The conclusion of the first trial in Cortland on March 9, 1928, found Lusk to be victorious, but Haskell appealed the verdict. The appeal was argued in Albany by Lusk and Haskell in May of 1929. This time, Haskell prevailed, and the verdict favored the bank. The case ended up next at the highest court in the state, the Court of Appeals. Haskell and Lusk faced each other there in January 1930.

This time, the court awarded final judgement to the Virginia bank against Mr. Hewitt in the amount of $24,075 with interest from May 2, 1926, together with legal costs. The total amount of $30,323.02 was believed to be the largest judgement ever made at the time against an individual in the history of Cortland County.

The next high-profile case involving former district attorney Haskell was a homicide. This time, the firm of Haskell and Maher represented the defendant. Haskell was able to get the charge reduced from murder in the second degree to manslaughter.

The incident began on Sunday, February 24, 1929, when John Clinch of 22 Railway Avenue (now South Avenue) in the city of Cortland was awakened around 3:15 a.m. by the sound of feeble cries for help. Throwing on clothes and hurrying downstairs, he quickly opened the door. There, on his porch, was a man on his back, arms outstretched, lying in a pool of blood. The man lifted his right hand. Each finger was so badly cut, they appeared to be more than half severed. The man asked Clinch to examine a deep wound in the pit of his stomach. Realizing the man was in a critical condition, Clinch summoned the police, who promptly took him to the hospital.

The man identified himself as Frank Antonuck of 4 Pine Street. He told the police he had been knifed by Fred Fadik after an argument over a game of poker hosted by David Deverick at his residence at 10 Railway Avenue. Officers were dispatched to Deverick's home and Fadik's home at 32 Railway Avenue. No card players were at Deverick's, and Fadik was not home.

At this point, all officers knew was Antonuck had been wounded severely at 10 Railway Avenue and had staggered out of the house into sub-zero temperature. He had walked unaided 300 yards to Clinch's porch, leaving a trail of blood in the snow. With the help of an interpreter, two officers went from house to house in the predominantly Russian neighborhood and finally picked up the trail of Fadik. It led to a home on the Virgil highway. Its resident had taken Fadik by car to Buffalo Street in Ithaca, not knowing the details of the trouble Fadik was in at the time. Later, Fadik was arrested in Ithaca and brought back to the county jail in Cortland.

Meanwhile, four men who had been at the card table with Antonuck and Fadik were rounded up and questioned. It was learned that the 40-year-old Fadik was from Russia. So, too, was the 32-year-old Antonuck, who had immigrated ten years ago, leaving behind his mother, three sisters, and a brother. Antonuck had been employed at the Wickwire factory but had been out of work for the past two months. Card games had been his means of gaining money. And, ironically, he and Fadik had been very close friends for three years. A verbal altercation over the card game became physical and led to the knifing of Antonuck, who was not expected to survive.

The fact that Antonuck was alive at the hospital later that morning was because of blood transfusions. Antonuck's aunt and uncle had been summoned to the hospital, but both refused to give a transfusion. Finally, John Guy of Texas Valley, a prisoner at the county jail, volunteered to give blood. However, shock, the loss of blood and peritonitis caused by a knifing were given as the cause of Antonuck's death that evening. He was buried in Cortland Rural Cemetery, and Fadik was charged with murder in the second degree.

When asked by City Judge Harry E. Kesler if he had counsel, Fadik pointed to Haskell, and Haskell asked for an examination for the prisoner. It was granted. As a result of the brief thirty-minute examination, Fadik was to be held for action by the grand jury. A jury was drawn but never had to make a decision in the case. Protesting that in his heart and mind he knew himself innocent of the death of his friend and fellow countryman, Fadik accepted the last-minute advice of his attorney and consented to a plea of guilty to manslaughter in the first degree. A sentence was immediately imposed of five to ten years in Auburn Prison.

Fadik had been the lone witness of the defense. He explained how he had a bad dream the night before the incident that warned him to keep out of card games and to avoid liquor. In cross-examination, Fadik admitted to reaching for and holding the knife during the physical tussle in a kitchen with Antonuck over the allegation made that marked cards had been used at the card game. Haskell declared he had believed Fadik innocent of any crime and that he still believed him guiltless of any criminal intention to stab his friend, but admission to having his hand on the knife indicates he "is technically guilty of manslaughter in the first degree." Even the coroner had determined the crime had been committed without intent or prior deliberation.

Haskell referred, as well, to the sordid character of the surroundings and circumstances and the type of eyewitnesses, some of them men with criminal records, who related the story, with some inconsistencies, of a fight among men more or less intoxicated. He said the trial had been fair. District Attorney Coon expressed his willingness to accept the plea. Judge Champlin explained that the maximum penalty was usually twenty years in prison, but because Fadik was a first offender the law permitted a lesser sentence. Thus, the sentence then meted out was five to ten years.

After three and a half years in Auburn Prison, Fadik was paroled in December of 1932. He returned to Cortland and immediately went to the hospital for an operation for appendicitis. He then took up residence in New York City, where he died in a hospital on May 8, 1937, at the age of 48.

Fred Fadik (on right) with his counsel Albert Haskell Jr. A clipping found in Haskell's scrapbook. Photographed by the author.

Going forward in private practice, not all of Attorney Haskell's activities were as high profile as the bank case and the stabbing by a man who allegedly failed to heed the warning of impending evil received in a bad dream. Haskell's legal expertise was sought by several entities in his community in the ensuing years. He had been the attorney, secretary, and director of the Cortland County Traction Company, and when electric trolley service ceased in the area, he became the attorney, director and secretary of Cortland County Bus Lines, Inc. He served as the attorney and director of the Edlund Machinery Company, the attorney and director of the Cortland Auto Supply Company, and a director of the Marine Midland Group, Inc. In addition to these activities, he represented most of the larger insurance companies in Cortland County in liability cases, including Aetna, Travelers, Standard Accident of Detroit, Maryland Casualty Co., and Fidelity and Deposit Co. of Maryland.

Near the end of his legal career in the firm of Haskell & Foley, in the 1950s and 1960s, Haskell was still going strong and receiving evidence of the close friendships he had garnered. Case in point, was the letter of February 19, 1953, he received with letterhead of the Cortland law firm of Lusk, Buck, Folmer & Ryan. It was from 81-year-old Clayton R. Lusk. It was addressed to the Hon. Albert Haskell Jr., 30 Charles Street, but it was signed with the man's nickname:

> You might be interested to know that on account of my numerous temporary disabilities this winter all of my Christmas cards have been laid aside and I have today just opened the one from Mildred [Haskell's second wife] and yourself.
>
> I often think of the very, very fine friendship which you and I formed early in our lives and which has continued unabated.
>
> Hoping that you both have a good year, and with affection to both of you, I remain, as ever,
>
> Sincerely yours,
> Clate

Another letter from Lusk was sent on December 30,1958. Expressing delight in receiving from Haskell a birthday letter of December 18, Lusk noted "our long and deep friendship. Nothing can break it." He closed with this clarification of his values: "I have reached an age where I care more for my friendships than I do for money or honors." He signed the typed missive by hand "Clate."

As Haskell did with his buddies during law school, as a lawyer in private practice he made a sincere effort to maintain a collegial relationship with his fellow lawyers through correspondence and practical measures. Two letters dated July 30, 1954, support this. One was from John T. Gardner, President of the Cortland County Bar Association. The other was from Homer attorney Henry D. Lucy. Both expressed appreciation for the annual invitation Haskell extended to the Bar Association to come to his Little York cottage, presumably for a dinner or a summer picnic.

Haskell's services were retained by at least three public schools in the county. The *Cortland Standard* of September 25, 1954, announced the New York State Board of Regents approved a $400,000 bond issue for an addition to the school in Marathon. Haskell posted the news clipping in a scrapbook because he was probably the school's attorney. In 1954, McGraw Central School of McGraw, New York erected an addition to its school. Haskell was the school's attorney, and as such he received a typed letter dated March 9, 1954, on school letterhead signed by Leroy A. Baer, Principal. The letter listed all who deserved thanks for efforts on constructing the addition, and the letter was going be enclosed in the cornerstone. Haskell was listed as the school's attorney. As late as 1963, he was still being appointed by the Board of Education as attorney for the McGraw School District. He was also the attorney for another small school in the county, Cincinnatus Central School. In March of 1959, the Cincinnatus School Board voted to secure the services of attorney Haskell as legal advisor for any facilities expansion that may occur. The January 5, 1962, issue of the *Cortland Standard* reported that of five proposals received by the Cincinnatus School District for the $380,000 bond issue for an addition, the First National Bank of Cortland came in as low bidder, offering an interest rate of 3.20 percent per annum with a premium of $271. Bonding arrangements were made through the Cortland law firm of Haskell and Foley in cooperation with Sykes, Galloway and Dikeman of New York City.

In the early 1950s, Haskell, in his 60s, found himself back in the courtroom again for a significant case. This time he was representing the County of Cortland in a lengthy case of negligence. Manning vs Cortland County was the case where Claude Manning, then of 168 Main Street, Cortland, sued the county for $200,000 in damages. Manning maintained that the county was negligent in its construction and maintenance of Locust Avenue hill where an accident occurred in the late wintry afternoon of November 26, 1951. The accident resulted in Manning having a portion of his right leg amputated and sustaining a double fracture of his left leg. Paul Tallman and Clarence Reeves were attempting, along with Manning, to get a ditched car back onto steep Locust Avenue when Manning was pinched between two cars and spent fourteen months in Cortland County Hospital.

Manning was represented by attorney Donald Mahwhinney and the county by Haskell with assistance from attorney Robert Sloan. The negligence case began early April of 1954 and, according to the press, "is running longer than any here in several years" and "is attracting the attention of lawyers throughout the area." Justice Joseph Molinari of Oneonta presided. The jury was comprised of eight men, four women, and two male alternates. The defense rested at 11:15 a.m. Thursday, April 15, in Supreme Court, with the statement that there was no negligence on the part of the county. Instead, Haskell charged there was contributory negligence on the part of Manning who was given a warning that a vehicle was approaching and failed to get out of the way.

The plaintiff had called nineteen witnesses and the defense twelve. The case was adjourned over Good Friday, Holy Saturday, and Easter Sunday, with attorney summations and the judge's charge to the jury taking up Monday. Defense witnesses included Carl Zamjohn, a civil engineer from Utica and Mrs. Susan West, supervisor from the fourth ward, who testified as to her observations of the driving conditions on the hill the afternoon of the accident. As "star witness for the defense," she said she and her son drove over Locust Ave Hill shortly before 4 p.m. and there was very little if any snow on the hill and the pavement was clear of packed snow. She testified that the return trip was made an hour later, and there was a considerable drop in temperature. Also, as witness was William Dwyer, Superintendent of County Highways. He told in detail what symbols and markings on cards in his office file meant as to snow removal and care of icy roads by the county.

Photographs of the hill taken by Richard Billings for the law firm of Lusk, Buck, Folmer and Ryan, who were then also representing Manning, were purchased later by Sloan after he first got permission for the sale from a member of the Lusk firm. It was noted in Mawhinney's summation that the owners of the two cars involved in the accident had made settlement offers to Manning: $9,000 from Lee Rogers of Cortland and $2,500 from Mrs. Dorothy Christopher of Freetown. Manning was trying to help Christopher get her car back onto the highway when the collision occurred. The settlement offers were accepted, so the county was the sole defendant.

On Monday, April 19th, at 9 p.m., after five and a half hours of deliberation, the jury found "no cause for action" against the county. Manning said he intended to seek a new trial or an appeal. In July, he brought a motion to set aside the verdict on grounds that a photograph of the Rogers car taken for the plaintiff had not been introduced into the trial as evidence but had been turned over to the jury during its deliberations. Haskell said this was the first the defense knew of such a photograph and if it got to the jury it was "wholly and solely through the mistake of Manning's attorneys." For all appearances, this was a strange way to invalidate a jury's decision. In September 1954, Justice Molinari denied the motion for a new trial on grounds that the photo was not prejudicial to the plaintiff's case. The county prevailed.

To mark the victory, Haskell inserted in one of his scrapbooks a typed letter from A. J. Twentyman, President of the F.H. Cobb Company (food wholesalers) congratulating Haskell on winning the case against the county. Cobb stated, "The people of this city and county should be very grateful. . . ."

The most complimentary letter regarding the Manning suit came with the date of March 8, 1955. The message from attorney Bob Sloan addressed to "Dear Albert" revealed much:

> The Manning case is definitely closed and the time for appeals elapsed. However, my sense of inadequacy to handle the case alone and my feeling of relief when you consented to accept the responsibility for possible defeat in the litigation remains clear and indelibly stamped on my memory.

Sometimes lawyers are prevailed upon to help expedite the adoption of children. The record shows Haskell took on such a project. Eva and Bob Baxter of Williston Park, New York, sent a letter on August 12, 1958, thanking Haskell for "efficient and generous service" in the matter of an adoption of "Melinda" that had just been officially approved "several days ago." A check for $3.70 was enclosed, along with the statement, "We can only say your generosity is exceeded only by your goodness."

Not only did clients recognize his expertise and good character, but Haskell was all too willing to recognize that in others. Thus, he agreed to be the main speaker for the testimonial dinner honoring retiring Judge Morse E. Ames, sponsored by the Cortland County Bar Association he helped to found thirty-seven years earlier. Held at the Cortland Country Club December 3, 1958, the grand affair was attended by judges and attorneys of the ten-county Sixth Judicial District. Haskell enthralled them by tracing Ames' career from the time he came to Cortland in 1918 through his present three posts: Judge of County Court, Surrogate Court, and Children's Court. Haskell called him "a legend in Cortland County."

A most unusual legal matter came upon Haskell next, and it was not one any lawyer would wish to have to confront. A head on car crash occurred on New Year's Day 1954 near Goodale Lake on Route 11 north of Homer. It claimed the lives of three and injured two. Among the dead was one of Haskell's sons, 29-year-old Charles Kelley Haskell, who was returning home from a New Year's party. He left behind his wife Rosemary and two children: Robert and Elizabeth. Damage claims were made against the State of New York. Only five years later did the Court of Claims in Syracuse award the estate of Charles K. Haskell $60,325 and interest from the date of death equal to $13,271.50. The Estate of John E. DeRock of Sidney won its claims, as well. The judge decreed that a hole in the surface of the icy pavement caused the accident and that neither driver was negligent. The attorney for the Haskell Estate was Charles' grieving father, Albert.

In June of 1962, Haskell experienced a heart attack. Being a practical man, Haskell deemed it time to take a promising young lawyer under his wing, as Clayton R. Lusk had once done for him. Thus, Richard J. Shay (1932–2016) joined the firm of Haskell & Foley at 69 Main Street. Like Haskell, Shay was a local man. He was a member of St. Mary's parochial school graduating Class of 1954 and a graduate of Le Moyne College in Syracuse. He had served as a First Lieutenant in the Marine Corp. He earned his law degree from St. John's University School of Law in 1961 and was admitted to State and Federal Bars in November of the same year. Like Haskell, he was a communicant of St. Mary's Church in Cortland. Officially, he became a partner in the law firm as of January 1, 1963, and Haskell proudly inserted a formal engraved announcement card in his scrapbook. In time, Shay became senior partner in the law firm of Haskell, Foley and Shay of Cortland.

Upon learning Haskell had taken ill, Justice Daniel J. McAvoy of Supreme Court Chambers in Binghamton penned a letter to Haskell on August 6, 1962. He wrote:

> The judges and the lawyers all respect you for the honesty and sincerity of your approach. So take good care of yourself and follow your doctors [sic] orders.
>
> Kindest personal regards,
> Dan

Lawyers frequently handle real estate deals, and in November 1962, the First National Bank of Main Street, Cortland announced the purchase of the adjoining Twentyman Building in anticipation of a need for expanded banking services for a solidly growing community. The Twentyman Building housed the Haskell & Foley law offices. Haskell handled the purchase as lawyer for the heirs of the Arthur J. Twentyman Estate.

A law firm, like any organization that is in demand, requires efficient secretarial help to handle a myriad of tasks. Mrs. Irene F. Jennings started work in September of 1922 as the secretary for Haskell's law office. As of April 1963, she had put in over forty years, and Haskell decided such dedication merited recognition. So, he arranged for her to be honored by the Cortland Chapter of the National Secretaries Association as "Secretary of Secretaries" for 1963. On the 22nd of April, she was feted at a dinner at the Shamrock restaurant on South Main Street, Cortland. In his letter to the N.S.A. Haskell explained how Mrs. Jennings was a "very capable and competent secretary. . . . By her dignity, diligence, and effort, she has brought great credit to herself and to members of the secretarial profession." At the dinner, Haskell commented on the tremendous help Mrs. Jennings had been to him throughout the years and graciously stated that he owed some measure of his success to her.

In all his years as a lawyer, Haskell had admittedly some unusual cases scattered among the more typical. One atypical case came near the end of his career, and it was argued by his protégé Richard Shay on behalf of the firm itself. Haskell, Foley & Shay sought the right to have their stairway over another person's premises. As the *Cortland Standard* of July 21, 1964 reported, "Unprecedented Court Decision Allows Law Office to Build Stairs Over Adjacent Premises."

The winter before this, plans were underway by three Cortland business organizations to put on a dinner honoring Haskell. Attorney Theodore Fenstermacher received a letter dated January 23, 1964, from William F. Fitzpatrick, President of the New York State Bar Association. Fitzpatrick indicated he would be unable to attend the dinner honoring Haskell on January 25th. He stated he was personally and professionally acquainted with Haskell over the past thirty years. Then, he added the ultimate compliment one attorney can give another: "In all my relationships with him, he has been fair, considerate and his integrity has been beyond question. My opinion of him, I feel, is entitled to unusual credit in view of the fact that in all our legal acquaintanceship, we were adversaries."

Chapter 13

The Political Arena

Anyone with political aspirations requires money or at least connections with "deep pockets," but an absolute essential is the possession of name recognition. By the end of 1929, at age 38, Albert Haskell Jr. had name recognition in spades. Eight years earlier he had shown political ambition when he ran for District Attorney of Cortland County with the endorsement of the Republican, Democratic, and Progressive Parties. Of course, it was an obvious advantage to essentially be able to run unopposed in his first try for public office. He garnered 7,894 votes, which was more votes than any other candidate seeking an office that year. This event launched him permanently into the public eye. Six years later, when he retired from the post, he could point to a most successful career record as a DA. Out of the 225 cases he prosecuted, he netted 215 convictions, and a few of them had been riveting newsmakers. He had been put to the test, especially with his potentially politically damaging prosecution of the county's tubercular cattle scandal, but he showed his mettle. He emerged with his good name intact and even enhanced.

Thus, a little over a month after the Stock Market crashed, a photo appeared in a newspaper on November 29, 1929, showing Haskell wearing round wire-rimmed glasses and a white fedora with a black band. Near the photo was this article with the heading "Former Cortland District Attorney May Succeed Wales":

> Albert Haskell Jr., former district attorney of Cortland county, president of the Cortland Trust company and prominent attorney is a receptive candidate for the office of state senator to fill the vacancy caused by the death of Senator B. Roger Wales of Binghamton. Altho the situation in regard to the choosing of a local Republican candidate is a little premature there appears to be a certainty even at present that if Cortland County is to be represented in the race for the senatorial office Mr. Haskell will be the selection. Party leaders of the county unhesitatingly admit the former district attorney measures up to every qualification.

Politics can be very messy, however, and circumstances can alter the plans of even the best of candidates. This is what Haskell and the Republican Party leaders of Cortland County soon experienced. The party leaders in the three-county district were undecided at the time as to the formal method to be employed in choosing candidates for the senatorial office. It was understood a primary election was to be held to determine the choices, but some felt the solution should come through a party convention.

Lieutenant Governor Herbert Henry Lehmann, a Democrat acting in the absence of Governor Franklin D. Roosevelt, indicated a special election was to be held on or about January 3, and the candidate chosen for the office would take up his new duties within a week after the legislature convened for the 1930 session. However, Cortland County represented by Senator Clayton Lusk and Broome County represented by the late Senator Wales had both had the senatorial office for three terms, and the impression prevailed in Chenango County that "according to custom and agreement [among Republican leaders]" Chenango County was now entitled to having its Republican candidate favored for the important office.

The party leaders of the three counties admitted that no formal written agreement ever existed between the counties in regard to the rotation of choices for the office. In Broome County the name being promoted for candidacy was the widow of the late Senator Wales. Three candidates were being prominently mentioned in Chenango County: District Attorney Ward N. Truesdell, James S. Flanagan and Assemblyman Bert Lord.

Nevertheless, Haskell was named by the Republican Party of Cortland County to run for the empty seat in the New York State Senate's Fortieth District. Some went so far as to predict he would win the special election. The shock came on December 4, 1929. Haskell withdrew from the contest. He provided the press this statement, making clear his position on the matter:

> When a vacancy occurred in this district, friends of mine, without consulting me, presented my name for the office. I was given assurance which led me to believe that I would have the support of this county if the position was to come here.
>
> I have not solicited support, fully realizing that Cortland county is a comparatively small part of the district and that any action taken here would be futile without the support of the other counties. While, as I understand it, there has never been any agreement for rotation of the office among the other counties yet I have been informed, there was an understanding at the time of Senator Wales' nomination that the leaders of Broome county would use their best efforts to have him succeeded by a man from Chenango county.
>
> I have a very kindly feeling for Mrs. Wales and a very high regard for the legislative ability of Assemblyman Lord who has sponsored many laws which have

> been of great benefit to this county. I shall be pleased to have the members of the senatorial committee from Cortland give their support to Assemblyman Lord.

Haskell was a savvy realist. He was aware that in a special election between candidates of two or three counties, Cortland County had the smallest population and there would not be enough votes to counter the votes from the other more populated counties. Besides, he had age on his side, and God willing, there would be other opportunities for him to seek higher office. And the diplomatic way he exited the race and supported Chenango County's claim that it was its turn to hold the Senate seat would be long remembered.

Coincident with Haskell's decision came news from Binghamton. Mrs. Alice C. Wales, widow of the late Senator Wales and most prominently mentioned as Broome County's candidate for the contested seat, announced that, while she had hoped to be able to carry on her husband's work in Albany, she was withdrawing from the field. She said she did not want to face a contest and was casting her support for New York Assemblyman Bert Lord from Chenango County. Thus, Bert Lord took Wales' seat and later served in the U.S. House of Representatives from 1935 until his death in 1939.

As the Depression deepened in America and a Democrat from New York State, Franklin Delano Roosevelt, won the presidential election in 1932, the Republican Party in New York State determined it was in its interest to bring in younger "new blood" if it hoped to win back its position of leadership. It was urgently sensed that the sooner new men gained responsibility the better, given the national change in leadership manifested at the polls in 1932.

Haskell agreed with the need for "new blood," and in May of 1933 he announced his candidacy for the Republican nomination for member of the New York State Assembly. The public and press rallied around him, but not everyone in his party. He was going up against Irving R. Rice, who had been the county's Assemblyman for fifteen years and had the support of Haskell's mentor and friend, the former state Senator Clayton R. Lusk. The *Binghamton Press* reported that this was a serious challenge to the seventeen-year-old "absolute political dictatorship" Lusk held in Cortland County. This was full of risks, but with risk comes opportunity. By all indications the public no longer wanted their interests decided by Old Guard politicians in a back room in Albany. The *Cortland Standard* endorsed Haskell and stated that he "has made good in each and every position he has been called upon to occupy" and that "it is in him to make good in the State Legislature. He should have his opportunity."

As his successful campaign neared the date of the primary election, tragedy struck the Haskell family. James Albert Haskell, a popular, sophomore football player in St. Mary's parochial high school in Cortland and the captain of the school's basketball team, came down ill. "Jimmie" was taken to the hospital on September 11. The next day, he died of what was diagnosed as the rapid onset of polio. The shocking, sudden loss of one so young from a prominent Cortland family was big news.

The school yearbook "Per Annos" was dedicated to the memory of James. His photo graced one of the front pages of the 50-page blue and gold annual. At the time of the commencement of St. Mary's Class of 1936, James' class, a prize was awarded in his honor. The James Haskell Memorial Prize of $25 was donated by Assemblyman Haskell and his wife and presented for the first time to salutatorian Leo Mayer. The recipient of the prize was to be "the student who had maintained a certain standard of moral courage, high principles, steadfastness to duties and to civil responsibilities [cited in *The Catholic Sun*, June 25, 1936, 2]."

In one of Haskell's scrapbooks is a photo of the 1932–1933 St. Mary's "Saints" basketball team. In the center, holding a basketball, is Captain Jimmie Haskell. The team won 12 of 19 games under Coach Harold "Deke" McEvoy. Interestingly, the photo was tucked away under a news article about the 1964 testimonial dinner for Haskell. It was as if he wanted to cherish his son's memory and not let go, but it had to be hidden away because it was simply too painful to recall. The boy's mother, Regina Haskell, died the year after the boy was to graduate. Jimmie's brother Joe said she died of a broken heart caused by Jimmie's untimely death. That may very well have appeared to be the case since she took to bed in her last years, mourning the loss of the boy, and never recovered. In actuality, she succumbed to cancer.

The death of Regina Haskell in 1937 led to some dramatic changes in the Haskell household. How was a busy politician like Albert Haskell Jr., then working in Albany, supposed to raise two boys and a girl on his own? He needed help. That assistance arrived in the form of a 30-year-old housekeeper and nanny named Mildred Cecelia Aungier from the Town of Tully, New York. At age 36, Mildred became Haskell's second wife. They married in Cortland on June 30, 1943. Before that, however, it was frowned upon for an unmarried man and an unmarried woman to reside together without another person present. To satisfy that social proscription, Elizabeth Donahue came to the Charles Street residence and lived in a room there for a good many years and was treated as family.

Mildred and Albert were a good match. She was a tall, big boned, stately looking woman. Later in life, with beautifully coiffed white hair, glasses, and a necklace of white pearls over a black dress, she had a very regal appearance. She was a diabetic, and the Haskell children would remember watching her give herself insulin shots.

The most challenging political tensions over alliances are those found in families. Son Joe never accepted Mildred as a replacement for his mother. He resented his father putting on an annual picnic at the lake for the Aungiers,

Jimmie Haskell holds the ball in photo of St. Mary's team 1932–1933. A clipping inserted loosely in Haskell's scrapbook. Photographed by the author.

Mildred's side of the family, but did not host one for the Haskells. It was a different matter with "Jean." She lost her mother at the tender age of ten. Her mother was so devastated by the death of a son that she was not there for her young daughter. Jean and Mildred bonded. To see them interact, one would never have imagined Mildred was not Jean's biological mother.

Summertime at the lake would find Mildred cooking Sunday dinners for the children and grandchildren. It was considered a big deal when Jean was finally able to coax her hardworking farmer husband Bob to come on an early Sunday afternoon to enjoy dinner and a swim at the lake before returning to the farm for his milking chores.

After Albert Haskell Jr. passed in 1964, it was a sad day for the Haskell and Sweeney families when financial circumstances forced Mildred to sell the cottage which had been in the Haskell family for so many years. It had been a place of retreat for Albert Haskell Jr., who would sometimes relax by sitting outside in a chair overlooking the lake listening to a ball game on the radio. Losing the beloved cottage was like losing one's identity as a Haskell.

A myocardial infarction related to diabetes caused Mildred's death on August 23, 1975. For Jean, it meant a further loss of identity. Years later, Jean was shown an old "home movie" taken by her father. In it, she saw her biological mother she had had trouble recalling. Flooded with emotion, Jean shed tears of joy.

Back on September 19, 1933, just one week after James Haskell's death, the all-important primary election was held to decide if Albert Haskell Jr. would be the Republican candidate running for the Assembly in the general election. Two amusing accounts appeared later in *The Homer Post* (September 22, 1933), which if to be believed, told of efforts made to get Homer votes for Haskell. One man "yanked a friend right out of the bath tub in his enthusiasm to glean a last-minute vote for Candidate Haskell." Another man was driving voters to the polls in his car. He overheard two passengers express support for Haskell's opponent, "so he took them for a ride around the block and sold them the Haskell program en route." Such efforts were not needed. Haskell carried 3105 votes to Rice's 1898. Haskell carried all polling places in Cortland County except Homer District 5, and he won the city of Cortland by a margin of almost 2 to 1. Immediately, Haskell called for a closing of party ranks. In the general election in November, he defeated Democrat Ralph Butler by a plurality of 4,678 votes, the largest in the county. On December 31, 1933, Haskell departed Cortland to assume his new duties as an Assemblyman in Albany. He was assigned to the Codes, Public Service, Internal Affairs and Revision Committee and served for the next three years.

When Haskell ran for another two-year term in 1935, he scored yet another resounding victory and returned to Albany. While Cortland County remained Republican, the Democrat state and national contenders were swept into office by huge pluralities, which raised the question: Did the county vote represent a repudiation of F.D.R.'s "New Dealism"? The record shows Assemblyman Haskell opposed the concept of Social Security in 1936. In an eight-page speech on a legal pad, he made clear his opposition of participation of the State with the federally proposed welfare system. The entire written speech was inserted in one of his scrapbooks.

Haskell, like President Hoover, believed that problems of poverty and unemployment were best left to voluntary and community service. He feared that federal welfare programs, as advocated by Franklin D. Roosevelt, would undermine individual character by making recipients dependent on the government. Hoover did not realize—and perhaps neither did Haskell—that the sheer size of America's economic problems of the 1930s had made the concept of "rugged individualism" meaningless. Nevertheless, Haskell continued to be an advocate for local support of organizations like Community Chest and later United Way.

It is notable, however, that Haskell was not opposed to a government owned park for all strata of society to enjoy. As a cottager neighboring Little York Park, he followed with interest the grassroots politics at play regarding the park's future use and inserted another clipping in his scrapbook. This one, from the November 9, 1938, *Cortland Standard,* reported the outcome of the vote on the proposition to purchase the park property on the lake for $7,500 for use as a county park. The county total was 4,188 votes in favor and 4,181 opposed. Seven votes carried the proposition to a narrow victory and determined the future of what is now known as Dwyer Memorial Park, which has been a recreational site enjoyed by many over the decades.

Another close and lasting professional and personal relationship Haskell developed was with fellow Republican Assemblyman Irving M. Ives, a young moderate from Norwich. Ives would serve in the New York State Assembly from 1930 to 1946. Ives was the Minority Leader in 1935, but he reached that post by forcing out powerful, 73-year-old Joseph A. McGinnies who had been in the Legislature for two decades. Haskell was the one who dared to introduce the resolution calling for a new minority leader to succeed McGinnies. Haskell was one of four assemblymen who presented McGinnies with a petition signed by 37 of the 73 Republicans in the Lower House asking McGinnies to withdraw from the race. McGinnies acquiesced. His name still went into nomination, but he was defeated, and Ives stepped in. Haskell, without a doubt, was instrumental in changing the political landscape in Albany.

Ives went on to be the Majority Leader from 1937 to 1946. Ives was the founding Dean of the School of Industrial and Labor Relations at Cornell University, where Ives Hall bears his name today. He was a U.S. Senator from New York from 1947 to 1959. In 1954, he ran unsuccessfully for Governor of New York. In New York state politics and in national Republican politics, Ives was known as a moderate member of his party and as a strong supporter of Thomas E. Dewey. Even after Haskell served three terms in the Assembly and lost the Republican primary in his bid for state senator, a strong bond of friendship continued between Haskell and Ives. After leaving the Assembly, Haskell was retained as attorney of the New York State Joint Legislative Committee on Industrial and Labor Conditions, the so-called Ives Committee, which was responsible for the introduction of far-reaching industrial and labor legislation.

In November of 1952, Haskell prepared and ran a full-page political ad in the *Cortland Standard* urging voters to support General Eisenhower for President, Richard Nixon for Vice-President, John Taber for Congress, and Irving Ives for the U.S. Senate. The ad claimed the ticket would address three "Main Issues": "Our Forgotten Boys" in the "Tragedy of Korea," "Softness toward Communism," and "Corruption in Government."

Assemblyman Haskell shakes hands with Speaker Joseph McGinnies as Assemblyman J. Austin Otto of Steuben County stands to the right on December 20, 1933. Photo by Acme News Pictures, Inc. From the author's collection.

During Ives run as the Republican candidate for governor, Haskell arranged for his friend to make a campaign stop in Cortland. A photo was taken on October 5, 1954, for the Syracuse *Post-Standard* of then U.S. Senator Ives standing with Haskell, Assemblyman Louis Folmer, and Mayor John B. Briggs of Homer at the American Legion Home in Cortland.

The next rally was in Watertown. There, Ives and his wife were splattered by tomatoes. Ives declared, "This is typical of Tammany Hall and is typical of the Democratic opposition which we are faced with at this time." Police later reported the tomatoes were tossed from a hotel roof by a gang of juveniles who quietly disappeared.

Ives was in a contentious political struggle with Democrat Averell Harriman. During his Cortland visit, Ives indicated he would not play favorites with the siting of the proposed north-south thruway [I-81]. It would be determined, he said, by the engineers on the basis of population and traffic density. Cortland and Haskell wanted it in the vicinity of Route 11 from Binghamton to Watertown by way of Syracuse. Ives, however, was from Norwich and the community wanted the highway to be routed through the

Chenango and Black River Valleys and nearer to Utica than Syracuse. Each community was aware that there were advantages to be accrued to them by a north-south expressway that would be similar to those accrued by the areas traversed by the east-west Thruway. The proposed expressway was a "hot potato," and Ives was aware that he could lose votes from whichever side of the issue he alienated.

In Watertown, Ives offered no apologizes for not supporting the construction of the nearby St. Lawrence Seaway and for supporting the federal administration's price support program for farmers which could mean dairy farmers being squeezed by support prices for feed grain. Meanwhile, on the same day, speaking to a crowd of some 5,000 to 6,000 workers in the New York City garment district, Harriman portrayed Ives as no friend to organized labor.

In Cortland, Haskell, the influential former Republican Assemblyman, fought for Ives using a matter of concern to residents of the county—the cost of education. Haskell ran an editorial in the *Cortland Standard* slamming Democrats for proposing a bill he said would raise school taxes. The problem of an inequitable state aid formula was also cited. The State, he maintained, needed to come up with more than the current $220 per elementary pupil and $274 per high school student locally. After that teaser, on October 27, 1954, a full-page political ad appeared on page 11 of the same newspaper:

> Republican, Independent and Democrat Voters
>
> Are You Interested in Education in Cortland County?
>
> STOP—LOOK—READ
>
> $35,000,000 in State Aid for Education is at Stake. In 1928 Governor Al Smith sought equal education for all children of the State and the Legislature passed and he signed a state aid law known as the Friedsam Equalization Formula which has worked satisfactorily since that time. The current Democrat Party is committed to a program of eliminating the equalization formula. An assistant to Democrat Mayor Robert Wagner of New York City has stated the equalization formula of 1928 should be scrapped in favor of a flat rate per pupil preferred by the Mayor.

The purported negative impact was then shown in a chart revealing what the tax rates would increase to by the effect of scrapping equalization in the payment of state aid to school districts in Cortland County. The ad went on to state that Mayor Wagner and Averell Harriman, the Democrat candidate for Governor, "are sponsored by Tammany Hall" and "You may be sure the Educational Program of New York City will be carried out at Albany if Harriman is elected Governor and Tammany controls the State." The ad closed with

> Keep Tammany Out of Our Educational System. Vote for Irving M. Ives, Republican Candidate for Governor Sponsored by Friends of Education in Cortland County

Ives appreciated the support he received from Haskell. In two letters—one in October of 1954 and one in November—he and his wife Marion expressed appreciation for the "glowing introductions" they received in Cortland and for a letter they received from Haskell that they felt had offered a "very sound philosophy" during the campaign. Ives lost and Averell Harriman narrowly won the governorship, in one of the closest Governor's races in state history.

Political traditions were changing. Women at this time were starting to become more active in politics. A Republican Women's luncheon was set for May 21, 1955, at the Cortland Country Club. Dr. Ralph Adams Brown of the social studies department of Cortland State University Teachers College and a Cortland Rotarian was to speak on "Youth and Politics." Mrs. Albert Haskell was chair of the luncheon and the one to call for reservations by dialing SK 6–7323. Haskell had a news article about this event his wife Mildred was chairing placed in his scrapbook on the same page where he placed a news photo showing her as the in-coming president of the Altar and Rosary Society of St. Mary's Church. In her own way, Mildred was a leader in local political and religious life.

On October 9, 1956, it was Haskell's turn to chair a Republican Party dinner and rally. He not only was the chairman of general arrangements but presided over the event. Held at the Skateland near the Homer-Cortland overpass, 800 people were said to have attended. Spiegle Wilcox and his orchestra entertained, but the big draw was the guest speaker, U.S. Senator Clifford P. Case of New Jersey, who would articulate why Dwight Eisenhower was better than Adlai Stevenson for President.

Case was an interesting and controversial figure in the Republican Party. As a member of the House of Representatives, Case earned a reputation as a liberal Republican, frequently receiving the endorsement of the Americans for Democratic Action, Congress of Industrial Organizations, and American Federation of Labor. A strong supporter of the Civil Rights Movement, he voted in favor of an anti-poll tax measure, a proposal to prevent segregation in the Women's Reserve of the Coast Guard, and the creation of a Fair Employment Practices Commission to prohibit discrimination in the workforce. He also opposed the establishment of a permanent House Un-American Activities Committee.

During his senatorial campaign, Case openly criticized Senator Joseph McCarthy, and pledged to vote against seating McCarthy on any committee with investigative functions. McCarthy's supporters called Case "a pro-Communist Republicrat" and "Stalin's choice for Senator." Case's sister

Adelaide was reported to be "an active member of several Communist front groups." It was later revealed, however, that the Adelaide Case in question was not the candidate's sister but a college professor who had died in 1948. A conservative faction within the Republican Party unsuccessfully attempted to force Case off the ballot, but he was endorsed by President Eisenhower and Vice President Richard M. Nixon.

On November 2, 1954, Case narrowly defeated fellow U.S. Representative Charles R. Howell by a margin of 3,369 votes. At the time, it was the closest Senate election in New Jersey's history, and a recount was held. Case won the recount by 3,507 votes. In the Senate, he was destined to compile one of the most liberal records of any Republican. He would be re-elected in 1960, 1966 and 1972. Case voted in favor of the Civil Rights Acts of 1957, 1960, 1964, and 1968, as well as the 24th Amendment to the U.S. Constitution, the Voting Rights Act of 1965, and the confirmation of Thurgood Marshall to the U.S. Supreme Court. Like Case or not for his stance on policies, Haskell was aware that Case was the Republican to enlist for a local party fundraiser. Case would draw a crowd.

Nelson A. Rockefeller, often referred to as "the last of the liberal Republicans," was New York's governor from 1959 to 1973. In his first run for governor, Haskell endorsed him. In late October of 1958, a typed letter came from L. Judson Morhouse, Campaign Manager at Republican Campaign Headquarters in New York City. The letter thanked Haskell for his campaign efforts locally for Rockefeller and Row A candidates and urged him to "redouble" his efforts "in the home stretch."

Right behind this letter came another typed letter. Marked "Personal & Unofficial" to "Dear Friend," the letter was from Louis J. Lefkowitz, the newly re-elected Attorney General of the State of New York. Dated November 25, 1958, Lefkowitz expressed to Haskell appreciation for "your hard work on my behalf in the recent campaign." He stressed he would "do everything possible to justify your faith and confidence in me" and would strive "to bring the Attorney General's office down to earth" and be accessible as "a true lawyer for all the people."

Lefkowitz was a moderate or even liberal Republican and part of the Thomas E. Dewey and Nelson A. Rockefeller faction of the New York Republican Party. He had been elected in 1957 by the New York State Legislature as New York Attorney General, to succeed Jacob K. Javits, who resigned after being elected to the U.S. Senate the previous year. Lefkowitz was re-elected in 1958 and would be re-elected four more times (1962, 1966, 1970, and 1974), holding the office for twenty-two years, the longest tenure since the office was established in 1777.

In February 1959, Haskell felt like it was the passing of an era. At age 86, former Republican State Senator Clayton R. Lusk and Haskell's early legal mentor and courtroom opponent died at his home at 38 West Court Street, Cortland. At the time, he was the senior member of the prominent law firm in Cortland of Lusk, Folmer, Ryan, Fenstermacher, and Yesawich. His obituary listed his credentials: Graduated Cortland Normal School in 1895; law degree from Cornell Law School in 1902; same year passed the Bar Exam; Cortland City Judge from 1904 to 1909; elected to State Legislature in 1918, serving 1919 to 1924 as state senator; Majority Leader in the Senate in 1921; Minority leader in 1923; Acting governor of the senate in 1922; and Chairman of the committee investigating seditious activity. Lusk's was certainly an enviable career in law and politics. If the ambitious Haskell had needed a role model, his longtime friend Lusk had provided one.

It was in April of 1959 that Governor Nelson Rockefeller's wife appeared via closed circuit educational television for forty-five minutes to one thousand pupils in the Cortland Public School System. She spoke of her role as wife to the governor. According to the *Cortland Standard* for April 14, a pupil from Ferdinand E. Smith Elementary School asked her opinion of a woman becoming president. She tactfully responded, "I wouldn't have anything to say about it, as long as she were properly qualified, and if she were it would be a wonderful thing for her." Haskell found this newsworthy and clipped out the article and photo of Mrs. Rockefeller for his scrapbook.

Another of Haskell's political acquaintances was the second Dean of the New York State School of Industrial and Labor Relations at Cornell University, Martin P. Catherwood. Haskell congratulated Catherwood on his appointment by Governor Rockefeller to the post of Industrial Commissioner. In response, Catherwood wrote a letter on December 27, 1958, to "Dear Al," recognizing Haskell's note of congratulations. He wrote that he was happy at the school and had no intention of giving up his "pleasant way of life in Ithaca" but "Mr. Rockefeller is very persuasive. . . ." He stated he intended to take a leave of absence from his professorship and to return to teaching instead of administration with no regrets. He noted, too, that he remembered Haskell's participation on the Joint Legislative Committee and of his stopping to chat with Haskell in Cortland just before he accepted the appointment as Dean of the School in 1947. He said he was interested to find in the past couple of weeks "that the School is better known and with more acceptance than I had recognized." Today, the most comprehensive resource in North America on labor and employment is the Martin P. Catherwood Library in Cornell University's I.L.R. School.

Haskell took an avid interest in politics at all levels: international, national, state, and especially grassroots. In regard to international politics, he was not reticent about expressing his opinions. At the end of a speech he gave during World War II as part of a St. Patrick's Day Banquet, he expressed his disdain for Ireland's neutrality during "a do or die time in the world."

At the local level, in the city of Cortland's mayoral contest of 1961, the sewer contract signed with the Smith-Corona Marchant (SCM) typewriter manufacturing plant south of the city was a political football for the Dems and the GOP to hurl at each other during the campaign. As a dyed-in-the-wool Republican, Haskell, of course, supported Morris Noss for mayor. Not one to shrink from the fray and willing to lend his name and influence to the cause, Haskell made a broadcast from the local radio station WKRT at 7:15 p.m. on November 2, 1961. His goal was to address "the irresponsible statements made in the current political campaign, which reflect on the Cortland County Development Company. . . ." As president of the Corporation and speaking at the request of the Board of Directors, he went public to clarify the development company's position in regard to the Port Watson-Tompkins Street Sewer.

The next day, the *Cortland Standard* ran a full-page reprint of his radio broadcast from the night before. A few days later, Haskell received a typed letter from the Cortland County District Superintendent of Schools, Chester A. Lacy, thanking Haskell for the article in the paper about S-CM and sewer extension. It read: "I sure hate to see someone trying to make the people think they were swindled, just for some votes. Thanks for giving the people the facts."

The facts reported on March 19, 1962, regarding Haskell's health were not good. He had suffered a heart attack that day and had been rushed to Cortland Memorial Hospital. The next day's press, however, posted "Haskell Better at the Hospital Today than Mon." Haskell's personal physician Dr. Edward Cummins confirmed in the article that "the attorney was in critical condition yesterday" but "has improved today." The septuagenarian appeared to have bounced back, but a heart attack is a warning that it is likely time to cut back on some activities.

This came at a time when Haskell could have had another crack at becoming a member of the New York State Senate. State Senator Janet Hill Gordon of Norwich was vacating her seat to seek Republican nomination for candidate for Congress. To fill the four-county 46th Senatorial District post, Haskell's name had come to the forefront. He was assured it was "a sure thing," but he deemed it best to decline.

The press explained, "The man who stepped aside in 1936 'to avoid controversy for the good of the Republican party' said today he will not consider being a candidate for any political office." Readers learned the "former Cortland County assemblyman announced that for personal reasons he should not be considered as a possible nominee for state senator" to fill Senator Gordon's seat. Haskell said he had consulted his family and physician before making the decision and planned to return to his law practice about June 4. Haskell was quoted as saying "Cortland has been good to me and whatever time I may have in the future for public or community service will be spend [sic] in my home county."

The article went on to provide some historical perspective on the matter:

> There has been a long-time informal understanding that the next time the post was open, Haskell was to be considered as a possible Republican nominee. Back in 1936, when Martin W. Deyo of Binghamton retired from his Senate post, Haskell was given the endorsement of Cortland and Chenango County GOP committees. However, Broome County had another entry, Roy M. Page, who defeated the Cortland lawyer by 150 votes out of more than 30,700. At first, Haskell was going to demand a recount, but later decided to stand by the results thus avoiding controversy 'and to do all that I can to further the interests of the Republican Party.' It has been 38 years since Cortland County has had a state senator. The late Clayton R. Lusk served in that post from 1919 to 1924. Prior to that Cortland had not had a senator since before the Civil War.

Following this announcement came the report that Assemblyman Louis H. Folmer of Homer had indicated he, too, was not interested in the vacant post "because he feels he can better represent the county in the assembly with his seniority positions."

"This has been a political week, if we have ever seen one," observed Rotarian Walter W. Grunfeld on May 17, 1962, in his column "Periscope" in his Marathon *Independent*. With Gordon stepping down to run for Congress, Grunfeld noted there had been new developments daily. He pointed out that "According to the gentleman's agreement upheld between leaders of the 46th Senatorial District, including the counties of Otsego, Chenango, Madison and Cortland counties, this is Cortland county's turn to offer a candidate to run on the Republican ticket." He reminded his readers that Haskell had been mentioned many times in the past. The reason was the man himself, ". . . a distinguished gentleman who has won the admiration of an army of admirers over a wide area, mainly because he is square, considerate, civic minded and possesses much experience in the field of civics and politics." He is "a former assemblyman from this county, has been around a long time and knows upstate life completely." Grunfeld stated Haskell "has since made complete recovery [from a heart attack] and the question now is how will this affect his chances of being nominated." He pointed out that other names considered have been former Cortland mayor Robert C. Kenney, Attorney Leland Taylor, and Assemblyman Folmer and that GOP leaders of four counties would assemble at the Colgate Inn in Hamilton, New York, to make the decision. With some confidence, Grunfeld concluded, "It is most likely that the next Senatorial candidate will come from Cortland county and the news within the next few weeks will be very interesting."

Indeed, the news was very interesting. On May 24, 1962, the area newspapers' headlines announced, "Hope GOP Choice for Senator After Haskell Declines Offer." "A complete newcomer to the political field," Leighton Hope of Cortland was nominated by the Cortland County Representative Committee. Hope was the president of Radio Station WKRT in Cortland, a director of The First National Bank, the president of the Cortland Rotary Club, and "a prominent citizen." Haskell was admittedly the first choice of the committee, but his recent illness "forced him to decline the nomination." This was the third time he had been offered the nomination from Cortland County, and this was the county's turn "under a rotation system between the four counties in the district. . . ."

Hope was not an unknown to Haskell. He knew him through Rotary. As the president of the Cortland County Development Corporation, Haskell had worked on many projects with Hope, the organization's secretary. Thus, a press photo on August 31, 1962, showed Haskell offering Hope congratulations and his full endorsement as the GOP candidate for nomination for State Senator. From 1963 to 1965, Hope would sit in the 174th and 175th New York State Legislatures. On January 8, 1966, he would be appointed as Secretary of the New York State Department of Conservation, and afterwards he was a Deputy New York State Park Commissioner. In Virgil, Cortland County, Hope Lake was named in his honor.

Haskell moved on, finding no shortage of political activities to keep him involved locally. For instance, in October 1963, more than 600 attended a gala Republican Committee dinner held at St. Mary's school cafeteria. It was an overflow crowd, and late arrivals were turned away at the door. Seventeen prominent Republicans shared the dais, including Haskell as a member of the New York State Republican Committee. There was Fred Young, State Republican Chairman; Senator Leighton Hope; Assemblyman Louis Folmer; and candidates then running for city and county offices. U. S. Senator Kenneth B. Keating from Rochester, New York was the guest speaker. Keating was introduced to the crowd as the one who alerted the country to the serious Soviet menace in Cuba. He spoke that night of his opinion that a bi-partisan foreign policy was needed in Washington. He complained, "We see confusion in South Vietnam. Our old friend Pakistan is angry at Washington. Our alliances are in disarray." He continued, "And at home we see persistent unemployment, failing to respond to outworn programs and confused economic thinking." He concluded, "We believe that our party is the best instrument for bringing reasonable people together in policies for the national good and in the national interest."

Other speakers stressed the importance of the off-year election at the local level. Fred Young stressed that "It is a time when the strength of the party must be shown. Make it an 'on' year." Once again, musical entertainment was provided by an old standby, Spiegle Willcox and his band.

As it turned out, it was hardly an "on" year election for Republicans. The November 6, 1963, issue of the *Cortland Standard* proclaimed, "Mayor Mack Wins All But One District." The Democrat professor of education at Cortland College was re-elected to another two-year term. In a predominantly Republican city, Mack ran six times stronger than he had two years earlier. The defeated candidate was Attorney Peter Brevett.

Three days later, on Saturday, November 9th, the Starlight Room of Cortland's Shamrock Inn was hosting a testimonial dinner in honor of Homer physician Dr. Robert Kerr. It was a Democrat Party affair. Kerr was a long-time Democrat and mayor of Cortland in the 1950s, and Haskell from the loyal opposition attended. In Haskell's time, stalwart members of the two political parties could fight tooth and nail politically but then gather as friends to toast each other.

Haskell filled his scrapbooks with news clippings about everything Republican. He continued to follow the Party's activities, such as appointments to State Supreme Court and nominations for County Judge and DA posts. Yet, there was one notable exception. The entire December 9, 1963, issue of *U. S. News and World Report* was kept by Haskell within one scrapbook. The issue was devoted to the assassination and funeral of President John Fitzgerald Kennedy, a Democrat and the nation's first Roman Catholic President. There were articles within the magazine on what JFK's passing meant for Washington and the business world. Keeping this one periodical reveals this was a significant and mournful event to Haskell as it was for all Americans but especially so for Roman Catholics like Haskell.

The Haskell political scrapbook contained another significant keepsake. It was a calling card with his image, stating the Republican Primary Election would be on Sept. 15, 1936. It informed that "Albert Haskell Jr., solicits your support as the Republican Candidate for State Senator from 40th Senatorial District (Broome, Chenango, and Cortland Counties)" and that he was "Running on his record as attorney, Cornell University grad, three-term NYS Assemblyman, DA two terms, and 20 years active experience in business, rural, and civic activities." Though he never attained this political office, he never gave up his interest in the political arena. Neither did he cease to use his name and political connections to influence perceptions and projects locally in matters of rural, civic, and religious life. This helped him to get things done for the "Crown City," the county, and Central New York. His voice carried weight; his opinion mattered. What one knows is important, but more so is who one knows.

Chapter 14

The Milk Strikes

For the most part, the economy of Cortland County in Albert Haskell Jr.'s time was based on one-third industry, one-third agriculture, and increasingly a service sector known as "the college up on the hill" in the city of Cortland. The earliest days of the county saw most of the population deriving their income from farming, and that was mainly from sheep and then dairy cattle. Land, crops, and cows continued to be economically significant in a predominantly rural environment, and an attorney like Haskell, who grew up in Cortland, needed to be familiar with issues that mattered most to farmers. And when you are an Assemblyman representing a large number of constituents in counties involved in the dairy industry it behooves you to take a strong interest.

Thus, it comes as no surprise that Haskell was well versed in farming issues and was known as a friend of the farmer and a supporter of dairying. Appropriately, even his only daughter, Jean, married Robert "Bob" Sweeney June 15, 1949. The young couple took up residence on the Sweeney Road in the Town of Cortlandville, and for the rest of their days were engaged in dairy farming and raising a large family "up on the hill." All told, there would be eleven children, and they were just down the road a piece from the farm of Jeremiah ("Jerry") and Martha Sweeney, Bob's parents. Bob had two brothers. Donald, the oldest, remained on the farm with his parents and never married. Albert, the youngest, had no interest in farming, left the homestead, went down into the valley to live and work, and married in 1945. When dairy farms in the county began to deliver raw milk to milk plants in the area via bulk milk trucks, ironically, Albert Sweeney would be one of the earliest bulk milk truck drivers. He and his wife Dorothy, from a large farm family on the Scott Road, had two sons, Martin and Paul. The former is the author of this biography.

The trouble with farming is that it is a gamble. Farmers are always at the mercy of things they cannot control—like the weather and the markets. Plants that require photosynthesis, like hay and corn, can be adversely affected by either too much or too little of sun and rain. One cannot predict if Mother Nature will cause drought or flooding or disease and insects. Prices for equipment and seed can fluctuate. More importantly, according to the economic law of supply and demand, if the market for dairy products declines, the farmer's income declines as well. In times of economic depression, the dairy farmer can find himself hoping he makes enough each month to keep the wolf from having a litter of pups at his barn door. Such was the situation for New York State dairy farmers in the Great Depression of the 1930s, when Albert Haskell Jr. was a New York State assemblyman.

Disruptions and civil disobedience were typically associated with organized labor during the Depression, but it should be noted that farm strikes (or "holidays" as they were sometimes called) also played a significant part in shaping New Deal politics and the creation of the dairy price support system. There were "milk wars" in St. Louis and central Illinois in 1931, and "holidays" in the Houston, Sioux Falls, Atlanta, Chicago, and Indiana milk markets in 1932.

The Sioux City Milk War of 1932 was the largest milk strike in the Midwest. The problem sparking this conflict was the "spread" between retail and farm milk prices in Sioux City, Iowa. The dairy farmers received just two cents per quart from local processors, while consumers paid eight cents per quart in Sioux City. The Sioux City Milk Producer's Association called the strike. Only after violence and mass arrests was it settled. At one point three thousand farmers marched on the jail at Council Bluffs, Iowa, forcing the local sheriff to release their fellow strikers.

Equally hard hit in the Depression were dairy farmers in New York State. Like their counterparts in the Midwest, they reeled under the effects of a decreased demand for milk and low farm milk prices. Both farmers and milk dealers felt the negative impact of a wave of retail price cutting sweeping through the New York City milk market in the early 1930s. As a result of this cutthroat competition, market relations nearly collapsed. According to the New York State Milk Control Board:

> Prices paid for milk had fallen to such a low level that dairymen could not possibly meet their most pressing obligations. Even the bare necessities of life could not be secured by many farm families, and many dairymen were threatened with the loss of the farms and homes in which their meager lifetime savings were invested.

In April 1933, a large group of dairy farmers in western and central New York organized a four-day strike in order to force the state legislature to implement price controls. As a result, the State's Milk Control Board was created. By August, farmers' opinion of the Milk Control Board had soured.

They charged that the Board's price fixing had favored corporations and their associated co-ops at the expense of farmers. The farmers then organized a larger and more confrontational strike in protest against the State's Milk Control Board. A *New York Times* reporter concluded the 1933 strikes "possibly . . . brought New York State closer to martial law than at any time since the Revolutionary War."

"Cortland Farmers Facing Riot Charges Waive Examination" was the title of a front-page article in *The New Cortlander* of September 1, 1933. Examinations were waived by fifteen Cortland County farmers charged with riot during a milk strike when they appeared before County Judge George H. Champlin. Their case was to be considered by the Grand Jury. H.K. Angell, attorney for the defense, said he would attempt to prove the strikers were not the first to start the riot. According to the defendants, "a truckload of [farmers], anticipating trouble, tried to get through the pickets and deliver their milk [at a milk plant]. The band of striking farmers peacefully attempted to persuade the men on the truck to go along with them in the strike for more money per hundred for milk. . . ." Then ". . . the men on the truck threw some bricks into the midst of the pickets. The bricks were returned, and state troopers arrived upon the scene." No charges were made of unlawful assembly, which is a misdemeanor. Riot is a felony. Three of the defendants were also charged with riot in Madison County.

Assemblyman Haskell entered the controversy by March 25, 1934. He called for a public meeting in the Cortland courthouse auditorium which was attended by 150 Cortland dairymen. The topic for discussion was the proposed milk control bill which was before the State Legislature. The farmers voted unanimously in favor of the bill but with fear that the federal government might exert control.

Later that year, Assemblyman Haskell introduced his "Four Square Plan" for stabilizing milk prices. It was designed to give a "square deal" to each of the four groups involved: farmers, distributors and dealers, pasteurizers and bottlers, and consumers. He introduced two bills in the legislature to support this plan. One bill was concerned with out-of-state competition which figured into the milk strikes. He was aware of legal precedents concerning out-of-state milk regulation and concurred with a piece in a farm journal which maintained ". . . legislation can and should be constitutionally enacted by the New York Legislature which will require that out-of-state milk and cream be produced under the same hygienic conditions as are imposed on milk and cream produced in the State."

A Syracuse paper reported "One of the outstanding plans to be discussed at the milk control [board] conference [called by Commissioner Charles Baldwin]at Albany Tuesday will be the 'four-square plan' of Assemblyman Albert Haskell Jr. of Cortland." The newspaper called it "a final attempt to settle the long, drawn-out controversy in the milk industry of the state between the producers, distributors, and the state milk control board." It was pointed out that Haskell's plan urged "cooperation of the pasteurizers and bottlers in an effort to eliminate cut-price milk from areas other than the New York milk shed." Haskell was aware that milk used in the New York metropolitan area came not just from New York but from four other states: Massachusetts, Vermont, Pennsylvania, and New Jersey, or a total of 75,000 farmers. Most belonged to Dairymen's League, Sheffield Producers, or small cooperatives that had sprung up in the past few years. An ocean of milk was being channeled into the metro area where the milk was pasteurized and bottled.

Haskell said this is the point where regulation is practical and possible. Here there should be a refusal to pasteurize and bottle milk for dealers who do not live up to the fair prices fixed by the milk control board for resale in the metro area. He complained that some bottlers were, in fact, subsidiary companies of the present distributors, and the most destructive practice depriving farmers of a fair price was price evasion by the distributors. His second bill called for making evasion of milk control prices a penal offense, punishable by fine and imprisonment. Despite the attempt, the matter seemed to be too complex for the state to remediate, and the controversy persisted for more years.

To make sense of the farmer's plight, John J. Dillon published an article in the January 2, 1937, issue of a bi-weekly journal, *The Rural New-Yorker*. Dillon wrote: "With the exception of a short period in 1883, and another from 1916 up to and during the war, dealers have fixed the price of milk for both producers and consumers. This custom is destructive of all economic order. It must and will be stopped." He complained that the law had vested control to the dealers, thereby rendering them a monopoly, and that financial figures had been kept secret within the Department of Agriculture. "An arbitrary price fixed by others is no solution to the milk problem," he stated. "We should ask the Legislature to restore to farmers the power collectively to determine the price and terms for the sale of their own milk, and to put the control of their milk business back in their own hands." To clarify further, Dillon explained that in a six-month period, the dealers reduced the price to farmers 27 cents and increased the price to consumers 47 cents, while the dealer gained 74 cents. This represented an increase of 74 cents per cubic weight in the spread between producer and consumer. This Dillon concluded was what the State's Rogers-Allen law had promised to reduce.

It was, also, in 1937 that matters became more complicated. A new group called the Dairy Farmers Union (DFU) organized yet another strike after farm milk prices hit their lowest level in fifteen years. The leader of the DFU was Archie Wright, a former organizer for the Industrial Workers of the World (IWW). Wright drew upon the language and tactics of organized labor and the farmers' penchant for direct action to gain greater political and economic power. The key for Wright was to effectively harness the energy of farmers' discontent and channel it into a more effective political force.

In July 1937, the DFU organized a regional strike against milk dealers in Northern New York, which was later expanded statewide. The goal was to halt the flow of all milk into New York City, the nation's largest milk market. Although many farmers saw no price increase after the strike, they learned one important lesson. Given sufficient organization and planning, milk strikes could be an effective weapon.

Haskell monitored the situation. In fact, Haskell compiled a 51-page scrapbook devoted to just the milk strike in New York State from October 28, 1937, to February 27, 1939. He, also, read and inserted a copy of a *Bulletin* put out by the New York State Bar Association on "The Constitutional Significance of the New York Milk Case" by Hon. Henry Epstein, Solicitor General of the State of New York.

The strike of 1937 saw 135,000 dairy farmers in New York State participating, according to state estimates. The *Syracuse Herald* of Thursday evening, October 28, 1937, ran this headline: MILK IS DUMPED AS STRIKE STARTS. It was reported that "Milk was destroyed or dumped and other violence broke out at widely separated upstate points Thursday as the Dairy Farmers' Union opened its statewide strike against New York City dealers." At Pulaski in Oswego County more than 500 pounds of milk from the dairy of a member of the Dairymen's League were dumped. At Richmondville in Schoharie County, milk of a Sheffield farmer was destroyed when kerosene was poured into his milk cans. At Herkimer, a group of men halted a farmer's truck and warned him "we'll burn your barn if you try to deliver milk tomorrow." At Eben in St. Lawrence County, union pickets complained to the Sheriff "that they were beaten about the head and hands by non-strikers after a party of pickets tossed an egg barrage at a truck loaded with milk." In Massena, Deputy Sheriffs were called for help at a dairy plant but were unable to prevent the forcible removal of 2,000 pounds of milk by picketers.

Archie Wright, chairman of the strike committee, announced from his office in Utica that plants in eighteen counties had cordons of pickets set up around them to prevent the shipment of milk to New York City. At the time, it was announced that three dealers had capitulated to the demands, which included an agreement to a basic price of $2.50 per 100 pounds for 3 percent milk (butter fat content) and the recognition of the DFU as a bargaining unit for milk farmers.

In Albany, the state's Commissioner of Agriculture, Holton V. Noyes, had expressed his hope that dairymen could satisfy their price demands without resorting to a strike, but he declined further comment. Governor Herbert H.

Lehman said he was keeping a close watch on the strike progress but had adopted a "hands off" policy.

Fred H. Sexauer, president of the Dairymen's League, appealed to that organization's members to oppose the strike and to make their deliveries of milk to the plants as usual. He claimed the majority of the state's farmers preferred the Rogers-Allen Law enacted by the last Legislature and signed by Governor Lehman on May 19. The Rogers-Allen Law superseded the state milk price fixing law enacted in 1933 after the violent North Country milk strike. The law enabled farm cooperatives to form bargaining agencies and milk dealers to form distributor bargaining agencies. Wright broadcast an appeal from Syracuse urging participation in the strike. Soon after, Homer S. Rolfe, president of the Metropolitan Bargaining Agency, urged members of that agency not to strike.

Wright hailed the first day of the strike a success, claiming it cut into the normal supply of fluid milk to New York City, which was normally 100,000 cans or 4 million quarts. However, the Metro Agency claimed only a 10 percent dent was made. Headquartered in Onondaga Hotel in Syracuse, the agency consisted of 90 co-operatives, including the largest in the state, Dairymen's League and Sheffield, which had milk plants in Cortland County. Their membership was approximately 45,000 individual farmers.

The first appeal for farmers of Cortland County to join the milk strike was made Thursday, October 28, 1937, at a meeting sponsored by the DFU held at Cincinnatus Central School. Charles Dumont of Franklin County and Fred Goodsell of St. Lawrence County urged sixty dairy farmers to join the union and aid the farmers in their strike. Goodsell declared, "It's about time farmers themselves had something to say about fixing the price of milk." He noted 15,000 farmers from eighteen counties were in the strike. He said, "You will have to strike if you are ever going to stabilize the market." Dumont charged the Metro Agency with being "controlled completely by Sheffield." He said, "This is a farmers' fight. You are morally bound to strike whether you think it is right or not." He said, "The farmer's only enemy is the milk monopoly."

Both speakers came to Cincinnatus in Cortland County directly from an earlier meeting in Center Lisle, Broome County. There, the county's members of the DFU voted 35 to 22 in favor of withholding milk from the Sheffield Farms plant at Center Lisle. Officials of the plant requested Sheriff Arlington B. Thatcher to post law enforcement agents at the plant in case of trouble. At the meeting in Cincinnatus, only 2 of the 75 dairymen in attendance voted for participation in the strike.

Wright urged strikers to not exercise any "unnecessary violence." He said: "Don't hurt anybody. Don't destroy any property. Strikes are won by using your heads and with hard work, tact and persuasion. Strikes are not won by dumping [others'] milk and breaking heads."

The second day of the strike saw a tightening of the fluid milk supply in the eighteen-county area. Wright claimed, “the strike is unquestionably gaining momentum.” The Metropolitan Agency announced on October 29: “The city will feel the shortage beginning tomorrow,” since milk ordinarily used in cream production will be diverted to fluid milk purposes.

The day was marked by violence. At a Hegeman Farms Creamery in Delaware County a fist fight broke out for a few minutes between strikers and non-strikers. The creamery reported its supply had been cut by 50 percent. In Chenango County 30 cans of milk were dumped after a truck was stopped. Only 32 out of 91 farmers made deliveries to the Sheffield plant in Lisle, Broome County. In Plattsburg, 100 pickets surrounded a milk plant preventing any milk from being delivered. The plant owner said, “pickets had full control of the situation on Friday.” A non-striking farmer was a victim of vandalism. A five-ton haystack on the farm of Frank Follette, four miles northeast of Norwich, was burned to the ground. In Canton, state troopers carrying clubs escorted a farmer into the milk plant to deliver five cans via horse-pulled wagon. The farmer had arrived wielding a sickle-like corn cutter that he brandished toward pickets. Overripe tomatoes flew at Potsdam when Dairymen’s League truck drivers passed through picket lines. In Clinton County, a highway was strewn with tacks.

The story was different in Cortland County. Only eight small dairy farmers withheld their milk at the Hegeman Farms plant in East Homer. Managers of Borden’s, Sheffield, and Dairymen’s League plants in the county reported full supplies of milk.

Commissioner of Agriculture Noyes addressed the issue: “I don’t like strike methods. It leads to neighbors hating each other.” But he added,

> When the control of milk supplies is vested in dealers, it is in the wrong hands. As long as you give your milk to the dealer and say to him to take it all and six weeks later to pay you what it is worth, you cannot improve your conditions. The thing to do is to name your price and sell the dealer as much as he wants, but make him pay the price for what he gets.

Noyes designated $2 per 100 pounds as the price farmers must receive as an average the year round. He said he believed that cooperation of the dairy farmers under the recent Rogers-Allen law, which the union opposed, would result in “domination of the milk industry by the farmers.” He said, “Such domination is what Governor Lehman and the Legislature thought they were giving the farmer when the bill was passed.” Nathan Sacks, a milk dealer, called the strike an annoyance and vowed New York City would get milk from other states “and this section of the country will be left holding the bag.”

By November 1, approximately a dozen small independent dealers acceded to compromise price demands made by the union. Wright said tentative agreements had been reached that were 40 cents per 100 pounds less than the original union demands, but the focus of the strike was now against three of the country's biggest dealers: Sheffield, Dairymen's League, and Borden's.

The fifth day of the strike saw the first injuries reported that required hospitalization. Striker James Foley was taken to a Malone hospital for treatment of broken ribs caused by a battle with farmers trying to deliver milk. Stones joined eggs and tomatoes as missiles hurled by pickets. Sheffield Farms Co. reported that the barns of R. H. Van Husen of Schoharie County, a trucker for Sheffield, had been burned. In St. Lawrence County, a group of deputies escorted a truck to eight farms to pick up 35 cans of milk for the Dairymen's League plant in Madrid. Pickets stopped the truck near Madrid and started to dump the milk. The driver gunned the truck but pickets on the back continued to empty cans as the truck sped along. Several arrests were made for disorderly conduct. In one incident, rifle shots were fired at a truck driven by Leo Pete. The shots, apparently aimed at the gas tank, were imbedded in the back of the seat in the cab, and a man was arrested.

November 2, Election Day, caused a lull in the protests as hundreds of pickets left their posts to vote. The Metro Agency denied that the strike was having any effect and that there was no basis in fact to the claim that smaller dealers had signed any pacts with the union.

The next night, negotiators in Syracuse reported a 28-cent increase per hundredweight was agreed to by directors of the New York Milk Distributors Bargaining Agency and the Metropolitan Bargaining Agency. Yet violence persisted. A farmer at Little Falls was clubbed into insensibility. The new schedule of prices was to be as follows:

Class 1 milk, used for fluid consumption, $2.63 a hundred.
Class 2 milk, used for fluid cream, $2.23 a hundred.
Milk sold on a flat price basis, $2.48 a hundred.

Prices quoted were for milk testing 3.3% butter fat. The DFU demand was for $2.10 for 3% milk. Wright claimed, "We are going to keep the dealers on the run until they have signed up with the union, and then the farmers are going to have a square deal for the first time in a good many years." Confidence in a DFU victory in the 19-county strike was expressed by state senator Rhoda Fox Graves of St. Lawrence County, a farmer and a member of the union.

On Friday, November 5, the boycott moved into the ninth day. Wright said that the agreement of Metro Agency to increased prices for farmers "will not bring a strike settlement." Wright called the latest price agreement "an insult to the intelligence of the farmers," but he predicted the strike would be over in ten days. The next day, a new outbreak of violence at Heuvelton, near Ogdensburg, occurred. There 250 picketers gathered around the milk plant and bombarded milk trucks attempting to break the line with buckets of kerosene. A dead skunk was tossed into one milk truck.

Saturday, November 7, the tenth day of the strike, included fist fights, a couple of injuries, and the firing of shots. The union called for a mass meeting at the Starbuck Arena in Watertown Monday night. Following Saturday's violence, non-striking farmers formed their own picket line around the Sheffield plant in Boonville, and men armed with clubs rode each truck safely into the station. This marked the first time in the 11-day strike that non-strikers organized for their own protection. At Heuvelton, pickets arrived on Sunday to find a host of state police and deputy sheriffs ready for action. State troopers had been brought in from Long Island as reinforcements.

At Monday night's mass meeting, an audience of 2,500 to 3,000 cheered speakers for the union, including the Rev. Thomas R. Hazzard, Episcopal cleric from Dutchess County, who urged all dairymen of the state to join the movement, as the only means to address the farmers' plight. He told the audience "If they could add to their checks today what the Big 3 spent fighting them, farmers would have the best price they ever had." Ironically, from opposite corners of the boxing ring at Starbuck Arena, Senator Graves and William J. McKay of the Metro Agency debated or engaged in "duking it out" verbally. McKay was booed whenever he attempted to defend the Rogers-Allen law as a measure drawn up "in the best interests of the [farmers] of the state." He was met with shouts of "get out" and "shut up." Graves argued the law was a "dealers' bill" and that the dealers had established a powerful bloc in the Legislature, which adversely affected farmers. Also, on Monday, the first shortages of milk in New York City were reported.

On the same Monday, a meeting of officers of all locals in the Dairymen's League Co-Operative association of Cortland County was held in the afternoon in the auditorium of the County Courthouse. A resolution was approved denouncing strikes and aligning themselves with the Metro Agency. The committee signing the resolution was D. E. Bennie, Fred Crampton, and Rena Stiles. All agitation and illegal demonstrations were denounced as not contributing to a long-term solution to milk marketing problems. They felt the agitations were destroying the effectiveness of the bargaining agency.

As the strike entered the fourteenth day on Wednesday, November 10, Wright reiterated the demand that the DFU be recognized as the sole bargaining agency for the dairy farmers. In New York City, fifty consumer organizations planned a mass meeting to campaign for resistance to higher consumer milk prices.

From Buffalo, the division head of the Dairymen's League announced that farmers in seven western counties of the state would ask higher prices effective November 15th. The present price of $2.45 per 100 pounds for fluid milk of 3.5% butter fat content would increase to $3.

On November 11, the strike entered its third week with union leaders vowing to fight to a finish. At the Onondaga Hotel in Syracuse, Agriculture and Markets Commissioner Noyes gave a speech before the New York State Farm Bureau Federation. He blamed the farmers for the strife. He said they failed to cooperate and to bargain collectively under the Rogers-Allen Law. Also, he said farmers should diversify and not rely solely upon milk production.

Then, a few days later, Archie Wright sent telegrams to each of the county organizations urging the strike to cease. The message stated "This strike has been won as far as price increases are concerned. We believe it is impossible to enforce general recognition of the union by all milk companies at this time." Yet, on November 16, the *Syracuse Journal* reported that farmers in eleven counties, with Madison being the closest to Cortland, voted to continue the strike in spite of Wright's recommendation. In Clinton County, police were seeking a group of masked men who set up a log blockade on a highway to prevent a load of milk from passing. The farmer had been beaten ten days earlier and had been taking his milk under police escort.

Upon learning of the farmers' vote, Wright responded with vows to resume the picketing of milk plants and "to fight this thing out if it takes forever." Union representatives were sent to confer with representatives of New York City's Milk Consumers' Protective Committee. They intended to explain how much milk costs to produce, how much the farmer receives, and where the spread between the retail and farm price comes in. The Union appealed to the governor to call off the police protection provided the "monopolistic milk forces," i.e., the "Big Three" of Sheffield, Borden's, and the Dairymen's League.

The Rural New-Yorker ran an editorial calling the strike a "rebellion against the avarice and tyranny of a milk monopoly by Borden's, Sheffield Farms, and Dairymen's League corporations." It stated the monopoly had existed for 65 years and was now sanctioned by state law. The editorial said the sole dispute was this: Shall farmers control cooperatives and set their own prices on their milk or shall a group of self-appointed officials control and turn the power to fix prices over to the monopoly? The paper said that if the Rogers-Allen Law should be found to be constitutional, it should still be repealed.

It was reported on November 18 that "More than 1,000 mothers, mostly from New York's East Side, will stage a 'baby carriage' parade at the New York City Hall, Saturday, as a protest against higher milk prices."

On December 1, 1937, the New York State Department of Agriculture announced it was placing official support behind a movement to form a consumers' cooperative to purchase milk. Commissioner Noyes said he had no authority to set prices but felt it unreasonable for farmers to receive only about six cents per quart while distributors got fourteen cents.

Efforts were made to obtain help from the federal government to regulate the handling of milk within the state and milk brought into the state from other states. These efforts went on for nearly a year, with conferences held for the farmers, distributors, consumers, and representatives of the state and federal government to air their opinions. Out of this emerged a Federal-State program with uniform rules, which four out of five farmers approved in a referendum. On May 3, 1938, Commissioner Noyes had addressed several dairy groups at the Drumlin Country Club in Syracuse, giving his support to this secret ballot referendum for farmers to decide on the method of price determination. He said current law allowed the officers and directors of cooperative associations to cast votes on behalf of the whole membership. "I would feel," he made clear, "that any vote registered upon this proposition by officers and directors alone did not represent the true sentiment of the dairymen of this State."

Under the Federal-State Marketing Order, its administrator, E. M. Harmon, fixed prices of nine classes of milk, according to their use. He then equalized the prices into a basic "blended" or "pool" price, subject to butterfat and freight differentials. Dealers were also required to pay into a farmers' settlement fund sums in proportion to the amount of milk they handled and to make monthly reports on the amount of milk handled.

On October 18, 1938, the Central New York Cooperative Association, Inc. was organized without a dissenting vote. Meeting at the courthouse auditorium in Cortland, the new organization voted unanimously to join the Metropolitan Cooperative Milk Producers. 221 producers from Cortland, Onondaga, and Madison counties, who sent milk to Hegeman Farms plants in Cortland County, voted to affiliate with the agency.

But strife was far from over. Four cases were merged that dealt with the constitutionality of the Federal Marketing Act. A three-judge board would decide, and an appeal from their ruling would go immediately to the Supreme Court. One of the litigants was the Central New York Cooperative Association of Cortland, against whom the Government was bringing action for a refusal to make pool payments required under the marketing act.

On November 26, 1938, the Central New York Cooperative Association of Cortland, the Jetter Dairy Company of Oriskany Falls, the Rock Royal Cooperative of Delhi, and the Schuyler Junction, NY Milkshed Cooperative of Frankfort went to Federal Court to combat efforts of State and Federal Agricultural Departments to compel immediate payments into the farmers' settlement fund as required by the new milk marketing pact. The Cortland cooperative was said to owe $712.25 in pro-rata shares of administration expenses and $20,115.56 in its portion of the settlement fund. Legal counsel for the four was provided by attorney Willard Pratt of Utica. The next month Attorney Haskell was involved, too. In contesting the claim for $20,115.56, the Central New York Cooperative Association of Cortland was represented by Haskell. Judge Cooper upheld Haskell's contention and ruled the equalization clause was invalid.

January 17, 1939, was the date set for a conference of dairy farmers with the State's Executives and Legislators at Chancellor's Hall in the State Education Building in Albany from 2 to 6 p.m. The conference was being held under the auspices of the New York State Milk Committee. It was reported that the milk monopoly is "in a hysterical fury at the prospect of the State Executives and Legislators listening to anyone but themselves. They resent any attempt by dairy farmers to put the lie to the propaganda regularly handed out at Albany by their dealer-controlled lobby." "There will be a seat for every man and woman who milks a cow," vowed the Committee.

In 1939, the DFU organized the largest and most successful milk strike in state history. That year, the dairy industry was again thrown into turmoil following a federal court decision which declared unconstitutional New Deal regulatory controls enacted in New York. In August 1939, 15,000 DFU farmers from northern New York, the Mohawk and Hudson River Valleys, and Northern Pennsylvania and Western Vermont, voted to begin picketing and diverting milk.

By the strike's third day, the DFU had tightened its grip on the New York City milk supply with only scattered incidents of violence. The Union's ability to quickly accomplish this goal was due to two important factors. First, discontent ran so deep among the "rank and file" in 1939 that many farmers who were not DFU members joined the strike either by refusing to deliver their product or by arranging for DFU pickets to dump their milk. Second, sympathetic public opinion in the strike region and DFU allies such as organized labor proved important in completing the Union boycott of upstate milk plants. Union leaders such as the United Mine Workers' John L. Lewis sent telegrams of support, while the Transport Workers Union dispatched an organizer to help Archie Wright.

With the New York City milk supply cut by as much as sixty percent by the strike's third day, the DFU received assistance from New York City Mayor Fiorello LaGuardia. Hoping to avoid a milk shortage, the mayor called on the DFU and major co-ops and dealers to send representatives to a conference at the World's Fair Grounds in Queens, where he hoped to broker an end to the strike. On the strike's ninth day, Wright signed a strike settlement in which the large milk dealers agreed to increase farm milk prices and to recognize the DFU. Farmers, editors, and merchants hailed the DFU's triumph across upstate New York. The *Watertown Times* of August 22, 1939, pointed to "the overwhelming public support that the farmers received in their strike" as a significant factor in the Union victory.

The State passed a resolution calling for a report by a joint legislative committee of eight to the Governor and the Legislature on or before February 15, 1940. The committee would be authorized to "make a thorough and comprehensive study and investigation of the entire milk industry within the State and the persons, firms, corporations, and associations engaged therein, including all steps, operations and processes in the production and distribution of fluid milk, fluid cream and the manufacture and sale of dairy products, the cost of production, the price paid by the consumer, the return to the producers and dealers and the interrelationship of such costs and prices." Audits of dealers and cooperatives would be part of the thorough investigation.

In the months after the 1939 strike, the milk dealers and their allies red-baited Wright and attacked the DFU as un-American. Over the next few years, these attacks on Wright and the DFU eventually succeeded in splitting the Union and limiting its political and economic power. Technological changes in the dairy industry also made it more difficult for farmers to strike. Bulk tanks and farm pick-up meant that striking farmers could no longer block the local milk plants, which were consolidated and enlarged.

Haskell's experience with the tubercular cattle scandal, the milk strikes of the '30s, and his interaction with his son-in-law developed a real empathy in him for dairy farmers of New York State. His relationship with farmers of Cortland County continued. On January 4, 1954, at a meeting of the stockholders of the 115-year-old Cortland County Agricultural Society responsible for the annual Cortland County Fair, five directors were re-elected. In addition, Haskell was named to the unexpired term of the late Fred Crampton. Unfortunately, the 115-year-old County Fair was destined for extinction. Buildings on the fairgrounds were dismantled, and the Grand Union Company purchased a portion of land along Homer Avenue for $70,000 to build a supermarket. The Army expressed interest in purchasing a portion fronting Wheeler Avenue for an armory, and that building is there today.

Haskell saved a typed note of some historical interest from a Mrs. Lewis W. Hannum of Connecticut dated May 12, 1955. She stated she had received a check for $500 as partial distribution of the Cortland Agricultural Society stock she inherited from her uncle's estate. Her uncle was the late David Hannum of Homer, who was thought to be the inspiration for the main character in the hugely popular 1898 novel by Edward Noyes Westcott titled *David Harum: A Story of American Life*. Hannum was best known for his part in the great Cardiff Giant hoax of 1869.

Haskell was, also, the attorney for the county's Preble Milk Cooperative Association, which started on December 6, 1940, and by December 1957 had sold over 366,000,000 pounds of milk worth $17,500,000. When they held their 17th annual meeting in December 1957 at the Preble Fire Station, with over 200 farmers and wives present, Haskell gave a report on the co-op's progress during the past year. Deacon Doubleday from WSYR TV in Syracuse was the guest speaker. He spoke on the changing times facing the farmer. Haskell eulogized George E. McEvoy, one of the original promoters of the co-op, who had passed away.

Always in demand as a toastmaster for organizations' dinners, Haskell frequently placed programs for such events in his scrapbooks. One program was for the annual Cortland County Holstein Club Banquet held on April 24, 1958, at the American Legion Hall in Homer, NY. President Kermit Riehlman, Vice-President Dale Stoker, and Secretary William Underwood welcomed the 200 members and guests. The assembly heard Jack Nisbett of Columbus, Ohio, tell of the need for farmers to do better at marketing their product. William G. Crandall, prominent farm and cattle auctioneer from Homer, was presented a certificate for being a member of the club for thirty-seven years. In the program, Haskell penned in a note to himself about Crandall being one of the three oldest members of the Holstein- Friesian Association in New York State.

On November 15, 1961, the Homer American Legion was the site of another banquet. This time Toastmaster Haskell helped the Preble Co-Op mark its 21 years of operation.

Inside a scrapbook, Haskell placed a special certificate. On January 30, 1962, the longtime friend of farmers was presented a Membership Award by the New York Holstein-Friesian Association in recognition of "fifteen years of membership and faithful service." While he was proud of his relationship with dairy farmers, especially during the challenging milk strikes, he was equally proud of his many other political and civic engagements in the Cortland area.

Chapter 15

Civic Engagement

Throughout his life, Albert Haskell Jr. made many significant contributions to industrial promotion, business development, and the civic affairs of the Cortland area. Through his membership in the Elks and Rotary, he participated in local service projects. Other projects he took on had long lasting beneficial effects for communities in the county and further afield.

During the Second World War, Americans were encouraged to sacrifice in support of the war against the Axis Powers—Italy, Germany, and Japan—by buying war bonds. Mrs. Leon Starr, vice-chairperson of the Cortland War Finance Committee, arranged a series of large war bond rallies throughout the county with the goal of raising in excess of $2,850,000. Each school in the county was to host a rally. The Virgil Central School was the first to host a rally. Its quota was $10,000. Principal Raymond Hagadorn was confident they would reach it. A barbershop quartet sang, and there were movies, refreshments, and dancing, and Haskell gave a stirring speech to encourage the purchase of bonds.

In 1944, Haskell gave an Armistice Day speech at the Cortland American Legion:

> Never in the history of civilization has there been so much strength and power organized, directed and prepared for the one purpose of causing destruction of property and human lives.
>
> If we are to continue to live in a free country we must now be willing to make every sacrifice and we must purchase war bonds to the full limit of our ability in order to keep faith with those who are keeping faith through the day and night by fighting on land, sea and air all over the world.
>
> A splendid beginning has been made at the Dumbarton Oaks conference. and we are not going to be caught this time without a careful plan, thus eliminating one of the failures of the last peace conference [at Versailles]. Russia is an

> active partner this time in world plans, so that another cause of failure has been eliminated.

Haskell's optimistic prognostication proved to be incorrect. With the end of the war, the world entered the Cold War, a period of geopolitical tension between the United States and the Soviet Union, and their respective allies, the Western bloc and the Eastern bloc. It was characterized not by direct military action but primarily through economic and political actions, acts of espionage or proxy wars waged by surrogates, the threat of atomic bombs, and propaganda.

An American propaganda campaign was in operation in the 1950s. Inaugurated by General Dwight D. Eisenhower, it was called the Crusade for Freedom. Its public goal was to raise funds for Radio Free Europe; it also served to conceal the Central Intelligence Agency's substantial funding of Radio Free Europe and to generate domestic support for American Cold War policies. "Crusaders" across the country organized rallies, parades, and contests to raise funds from ordinary Americans in the struggle to thwart Communism.

Haskell was a willing and enthusiastic Crusader. In 1950 he was the general chairman of a county-wide Crusade for Freedom Campaign and solicited the participation of the superintendents of Marathon, Cincinnatus, and Cortland City schools. A speech on four cards was found in his scrapbook. It most likely was part of a Crusade for Freedom rally. It concludes with this admonition: "God help the people of this world if they turn their backs on His divine teaching and put their trust in the atomic bomb."

Public health was another area of interest to Haskell. In 1948, the American Heart Association transformed from a scientific society studying the number one cause of deaths, heart disease, to a voluntary health organization composed of volunteers and supported by professional staff. Support for the Association's mission started to become much more visible, with fundraising activities taking hold in communities and businesses. To address the issue of support for heart disease research, the New York Heart Assembly was organized. In 1952, Haskell was elected to serve as a member-at-large in the Assembly. He was, also, a member of the Heart Fund Committee charged with exploring ways for local heart chapters to improve their fundraising campaigns. On March 20, 1953, Haskell participated in a panel discussion in Syracuse as part of the Second New York Heart Assembly of the American Heart Association. He spoke on "The Basic Appeal of Heart" as a member of the committee on fund raising.

Ten years later, Haskell sent a letter to fellow Rotarian Walter W. Grunfeld of Marathon, New York, who was always writing positive things about his friend in the *Marathon Independent.* To the letter Haskell attached a copy of his speech in 1953 to the Heart Assembly at Hotel Syracuse. Haskell wrote, "As long as you have become my official biographer, I am taking the liberty of sending you a talk I made. . . . Little did I realize at that time that within a few short years I would have a heart condition of my own to contend with. . . ." He indicated that he thought Grunfeld might find some ideas useful for a future heart campaign in Marathon.

Besides heart disease, cancer has been a prominent cause for concern in the public health community. Haskell's first wife, Regina, had died from cancer. In 1952, there were 64 deaths from cancer in Cortland and 35 new cases reported, and unsurprisingly Haskell was listed as a director of the Cortland chapter of the American Cancer Society as of April 1953. The chapter established a local diagnostic tumor clinic at the Cortland County Hospital. They, also, established the Friendly Red Door, a project in the basement of Phillips Free Library in Homer where women prepared free bandages for local doctors to use in treating local cancer patients. By April 1953, Haskell was serving on the Board of Trustees of the Cortland County Hospital when the hospital opened new staff and consultation rooms in memory of the highly respected Dr. Charles J. Kelley.

Community Chest was the forerunner of today's United Way, an organization collecting a pool of funds from a community for the purpose of charitable giving in the community. The first Community Chest organization was in Cleveland, Ohio, in 1913. By 1948, the number of Community Chests across the United States surpassed 1,000. Cortland had a Community Chest organization. In 1954, the Advance Gifts Division of the 1955 Community Chest campaign met October 11 at the Cortland Y.W.C.A. to launch a drive to collect the first $62,500 of the $124,450 goal. The intent was to fund eight local service agencies and the county's share of the United Defense Fund (USO). A motivational speaker was needed to rally those who would be going forth to solicit funds. Haskell was selected, and he obliged by speaking about the importance of the drive to the community.

On March 26, 1957, the Community Chest was renamed the United Fund. A steering committee for the new organization named a sub-committee of five to nominate a tentative board of directors for the organization. Haskell was one of the five. Eight months later, a kick-off dinner meeting of the officers and chairmen of the County North Division of the United Fund was held at the Cortlandville Grange Hall at the intersection of Groton Avenue and Route 281 [a car wash is there now]. Haskell addressed the attendees with an inspirational message. He reminded the County North workers of the pride people of Cortland County rightly take in their fine schools and churches. He declared, "We must be equally proud of our welfare giving," and he called for the United Fund drive's ultimate success. General campaign chairman Randolph V. Miller of Homer announced that all welfare agencies in the county had been invited to join the United Fund. It was Miller who took the time on January 8, 1958, to send a letter on The Homer National Bank letterhead thanking Haskell for "the wonderful work you did during the United Fund campaign." Miller accurately summed up Haskell's valuable role this way: ". . . your speeches were a real inspiration to all of us and your willingness to come and deliver them at any time was a great sacrifice on your part." This first United Fund campaign exceeded its goal of $165,000—50 percent more than raised by its predecessor, the Community Chest, in the previous year.

The 1959 United Fund General Campaign Kick-off event was hosted at the Cortland Country Club on November 18, 1958, with a record attendance of 230. Of course, the guest speaker was Haskell. He noted that the first United Fund Campaign conducted the previous year was a success and took place during the county's biggest year of expansion in industry, in schools and colleges, and in home building. He emphasized that while material growth is a worthy pursuit, they must not lose focus on the "youth building agencies of the United Fund" that need support. The public, he said, "will meet you more than halfway" and Thanksgiving will be a happier one if your work is done "carefully, thoroughly, and sincerely." The goal to be attained was $169,800. Two nights later, Haskell was back at it again on behalf of the United Fund. This time he delivered the same motivational speech for the meeting of the County South Division of the 1959 United Fund Campaign held at the Marathon Grange Hall.

By the end of 1959, the United Fund was having some difficulty. All the worthy agencies had not decided to go along with the Fund drive. At a September 30, 1959, kick-off dinner for seventy campaign workers for the United Fund's Advanced Gifts Committee, a concerned Haskell told the group it was "a tragedy in our community." He said, "When you break up this package some agencies are going to be hurt and hurt bad—don't have any doubt about that." He voiced his opposition to "a free for all competition for the charity money in Cortland." He said when one charity gets more than its share of charitable dollars, it is only obtained at the expense of some other worthy charity, and the community suffers. The goal for advanced gifts was $100,000, and the total campaign goal for 1960 was $171,800. If not attained, it was not for lack of effort by Haskell.

At the next month's general kick-off dinner at St. Mary's school cafeteria, he put it to the attendees directly when he stated, "success rests on the people in this room tonight." Only fourteen agencies had agreed to share in the funds to be raised. He asked, "Which one of the agencies would you drop? Which one could we lose and still have the kind of community we want to live in?" He appealed to their sense of altruism and for Providential intervention: "You and I are fortunate to be able to be here, fortunate that some force motivates us to want to do something for someone else." He closed by saying, ". . . with God's help, this campaign will be a success."

In the 1950s, there seems to have been few organizations in Cortland County that did not have Haskell as an engaging toastmaster or main speaker for their events. The April 1955 Chamber of Commerce newsletter, "Cortland Compass," was sent out indicating Haskell, "a perennial favorite," would be "our toastmaster for our annual banquet." The *Cortland Standard* covered the event. Fred J. Bragan of General Electric in Syracuse spoke of the "lousy job" American businessmen had done of defending the American way of life, including the free enterprise system "in the face of critics who would have us change toward Socialism or Communism." That night, Haskell paid tribute to the Chamber's retired executive secretary Carl Cooper, whom Haskell called "a true ambassador in his community for the Chamber of Commerce, Cortland County, and the DL&W . . ." Cooper was ticket agent in Cortland for forty-four years for the Delaware, Lackawanna, and Western Railroad. On May 17, Cooper sent Haskell a typed letter thanking him for the kind words at the banquet and the reprints of the *Cortland Standard* pictures sent by Haskell.

The Preble Rod and Gun Club held a banquet-smoker for members and guests on May 17, 1955. As a club member and the toastmaster, Haskell introduced guests from the Conservation Department and Hal Craig, noted night club and TV artist. Sam Forcucci's eight-piece band entertained, and a special highlight was Don Steger of Cold Brook Game Farm, who exhibited his eight-month-old German Pointer and talked about the fine hunting dog and its care. Ten days later, Haskell was again a toastmaster. This time for the annual banquet of the Cortland Chamber of Commerce at the Hotel Cortland.

In March 1957, Cortland's Veterans of Foreign Wars sponsored an essay contest. Three judges picked the winners, and Haskell was a judge. Sometimes, his civic engagements required some humor like he showed in his earlier days in Rotary. Such was the case in 1958 when the County of Cortland celebrated the sesquicentennial of its founding, and males were urged to grow facial hair. Failure to become one of the "Brothers of the Brush" could cost one a fine of a couple dollars. It was a fun way to raise funds if one chose not to be hirsute. At a Kangaroo Kourt held on February 15, 1958, beardless "distinguished citizens" of Cortland were fined. Two light-hearted photos appeared in the press, showing Haskell fined $5 for bribing the "hanging judge," attorney "Pete" Dorset.

The Sesquicentennial of the county culminated with a weeklong celebration in July 1958. Since the Town of Homer existed before the County of Cortland was created in 1808, the special week commenced with a huge parade through Homer on Monday, July 21, 1958. The author remembers this parade; he and his father participated by driving a sulky pulled by Bandit, a hackney pony, from the Homer Drive-In south on Route 11 to A.B. Brown's [where the Central New York Living History Center is located now]. The County Chamber of Commerce and the Cortland Development Corporation, both of which had Haskell as an active member, had a beautiful float titled "Key to Success"—a white, flower-covered trellis with three pretty girls in white formal gowns. The grand finale of the week was on Friday, July 25. 30,000 people watched a giant Sesquicentennial parade through Cortland. The parade was a two-hour spectacle with 200 units traveling from the fairgrounds on Homer Avenue to Randall Field. Prizes were given out for winners of the "Brothers of the Brush Contest": best beards, moustaches, sideburns, and mutton chops. Appropriately, grand prize winners received electric razors. It was announced that "For the information of wives and other interested persons, the beards and other produce may disappear at midnight, as far as the Sesquicentennial office is concerned."

It is most likely Haskell concurred with the Y. M. C. A.'s motto: "Building Boys is Better than Mending Men." For that reason, he accepted the Cortland Y's invitation from President Gerald Barry to join their Industrial Club Study Group on Thursday evening, February 19, 1959. According to a Y brochure, "Our instructors lecture for about one hour and we then spend about the same amount of time on questions, answers and discussion." Haskell must have found the experience of working with young men to be rewarding.

The United Fund had its annual board meeting on January 15, 1964, at the Y.W.C.A. Robert F. Fanning was elected president. Haskell was scheduled to be the guest speaker for the meeting, but declining health prevented it. Morris Noss took his place and read the remarks Haskell had prepared. Haskell likened the United Fund to a business which has its good years and its bad years. The combined agencies under the United Fund umbrella, he stated, could certainly be termed "big business," and "We cannot have these agencies live and prosper without money." Haskell's prepared speech concluded with these words: "We should be eager to help those less fortunate than ourselves. They might be collecting for you and me." The admonition was based on the Golden Rule, the principle of treating others as one would want to be treated. In retrospect, Haskell was a humanitarian, and one can see that he embodied a statement once made by Harvard University's political scientist, Robert D. Putnam: "What really matters from the point of view of social capital and civic engagement is not merely nominal membership, but active and involved membership."

Chapter 16

Promotion of Economic Expansion in the 1950s

While involved in multiple civic engagements, Haskell, as a member of the Cortland Chamber of Commerce and the Cortland County Development Corporation, also played a pivotal role in promoting existing businesses and in developing new businesses in Cortland and its environs.

First, came the letter of December 4, 1953, from Carl C. Cooper, Executive Secretary of the Cortland County Chamber of Commerce, Inc., informing Haskell of his election to the Board of Directors for three years as of January 1, 1954. Cooper stated Haskell was to join the Board in their efforts "to make our City and County a better and more prosperous community in which to live." The challenge was eagerly accepted by Haskell.

An active Chamber of Commerce created committees in early March of 1955 to accomplish seventeen different tasks. These tasks included the creation of better road signs directing motorists "to Cortland," bringing nationally known speakers to Cortland, and forming a manufacturers division of the Chamber. Given his previous years in the New York State Assembly, Haskell took on the chair of the committee of legislative affairs. As such, he considered state and federal legislation and made certain recommendations to the Board of Directors.

In that position, Haskell was aware that the year before President Eisenhower had appointed General Lucius D. Clay to head a committee charged with proposing an interstate highway system. Summing up motivations for the construction of such a system, Clay stated,

> It was evident we needed better highways. We needed them for safety, to accommodate more automobiles. We needed them for defense purposes, if that should ever be necessary. And we needed them for the economy. Not just as a public works measure, but for future growth.

Haskell was aware, too, that initial plans called for a new four-lane highway connecting Pennsylvania and Canada. If such a north-south "expressway" was built, there was a strong possibility it could run through the center of the state parallel to the existing Route 11 and have benefits to the local economy. Taking a pro-active position, in mid-March of 1955 the Cortland County Chamber of Commerce, by unanimous action of its directors, requested the New York State Department of Public Works to take note of its opposition to the gravel pits developing along Route 11 north of the Village of Homer. Abandoned pits, they pointed out, are a hazard and detrimental to hopes of a north-south thruway through that area.

In the summer and fall of 1956, the Chamber of Commerce, realizing its limitations, laid the groundwork for the formation of a Cortland County Development Corporation (CCDC), Incorporated, secured investments from five hundred stockholders, and proceeded to bring in new industries. Not since 1916 had the City and County of Cortland seen any new industry. Forty years later, the CCDC was bringing in three new industries and 2,000 new jobs. Haskell had the honor of serving as the first president of the new not-for-profit CCDC in 1956 when shares in the Corporation were publicly selling for $50.00 per share to raise $200,000 for the construction of a new manufacturing plant.

The goal was to attract new industry to Cortland and help to expand present industries. Other business leaders in the Cortland community were on board with Haskell. Prominent names included George Wiltsie Jr., Harold Burgess, Leighton Hope, Charles H. Churchill, Harold P. Peck, Porter Bennett, and Morris Noss. Noss was Chamber of Commerce President at the time. Work had actually commenced in the Spring of 1956, when influential officials paid a visit. Commissioner of the New York State Department of Commerce, Edward T. Dickinson, and Charles J. O'Connor, an industrial development representative from the same Department, became familiar with what Cortland had to offer prospective new businesses. By the summer of 1956, both men had introduced George Feeley of the Trinity Equipment Corporation of Roselle Park, New Jersey, to the Cortland community "as a most desirable place for the new, expanding industrial firm to consider as a new home." (See *Cortland Standard* October 10, 1961.)

1958 was the year of the county's sesquicentennial celebration. It was a good time to be looking back on the past and looking ahead to what the future might bring. On May 7th, the 33rd annual Cortland County Chamber of Commerce banquet was held at the Hotel Cortland with attorney Theodore Fenstermacher as toastmaster. Haskell spoke on behalf of the "Development Corporation." One of his scrapbooks contains his typed notes for the speech with points to be made before 250 persons. He gave his interpretation of how the CCDC came to be. He spoke of how during the summer and fall of 1956,

"Boldly we set forth on this" [and he penned in by hand "Experience, without map or compass."]

"Our basic industries had served us well for many years—Industry, our Farmers and the State Teachers College."

"We were not in distress—times were good."

"The inspiration and groundwork and our main support came from the Chamber of Commerce—Its officers, directors and members."

"Tonight as a result of community effort—four new and expanded industries—Trinity—Cary—Badger-Northland—Smith-Corona."

"Road has been long—plenty of hard work—things that stand out in addition to the support of the Chamber":

1. Unity of our Board of Directors of the Development Corp., and willingness to give of their time, talents, and money to serve this community—every action has been by unanimous consent.
2. Cooperation between Town of Cortlandville and City. Our Mayor and Common Council and City Attorney and City Departments [and he added in pen: "especially Water & Public Works."] *This is interesting since the Cortland newspaper indicated that the Board of Public Works voted unanimously to recommend advancement of the city's sewer lines for use by the college and Smith Corona's proposed new plant on Route 13, "but with reservations." The majority of the four-hour Common Council session was devoted to this topic. The paper said the resolutions "passed almost grudgingly." So, this was not without some venting of concerns. And . . . according to the press, on May 20th, 1958, the Common Council would again enter into "a long and heated meeting" marked by contentiousness on the brink of losing the Smith Corona deal.*
3. Confidence and support from our whole county—banks, industry, labor, farmers, and professional people.

The last point Haskell made that night revealed his religiosity: "Lastly, with all our problems, we have had the feeling that there was a silent partner, who through His mercy and goodness has guided this community effort. It seems fitting and proper that on this happy occasion we should give thanks to God and humbly ask His continued help and guidance." Clearly, it was a time of less reticence to express faith publicly without fear of offending anyone.

Also of interest was the guest speaker at the banquet, the president of Hamilton College, Dr. Robert W. McEwen. He spoke of Cortland's development as being slow moving but productive under our democratic system. He spoke, too, of the effect of Sputnik, the first Russian-built satellite to orbit Earth, upon the American educational system. He said it would cause a national review of the effectiveness of our schools. He contrasted the centralized, controlled educational system of the Soviet Union with America's willingness to send too many to college and not be selective as were the Russians. He did say, and the *Syracuse Herald* of May 8, 1958, quoted him, that "The American public has made our educational system a 'scapegoat' for this country's failure to launch a satellite ahead of the Russians." He suggested that "the better students must be separated from the less skilled ones if they are to reach their potential." (*Compare that policy with the current goal of making all students "college and career ready" by graduation from high school.*)

Big, much anticipated news arrived on March 28, 1957. The *Cortland Standard* announced, "Trinity Equip. Co. Set to Come to Cortland." On the next day, the paper announced that Governor Harriman was scheduled to visit the site of the Trinity plant and to speak at the 32nd annual Chamber of Commerce Banquet on May 14 at the Skateland located on the Cortland-Homer Road. 1000 guests were anticipated to share in the expression of gratitude to the New York State Department of Commerce for its help in convincing Trinity to move its base of operations from New Jersey to Cortland.

The Friday March 29, 1957, issue of the *Cortland Democrat* reported more details. On the previous Tuesday, at the Hotel Cortland, the contract was signed which was to bring Trinity Equipment Corp. to Cortland. The company manufactured thermowells (cylindrical fittings used to protect temperature sensors installed in processes used in the chemical and oil industry) and a dehumidifier principally used in the communications and power generating fields. The deal included land purchase in Town of Cortlandville by Trinity and the advance of $200,000 by the CCDC for the construction of a plant of 40,000 square feet. The initial workforce was to be 200, with all but key personnel to be recruited and trained locally. George Feeley signed the contract as the president of Trinity, and Haskell signed as president of the CCDC. The event was part of a special CCDC Board of Directors meeting.

A cornerstone laying ceremony for the Trinity Corporation of Cortland was on May 15, 1957, and Governor Harriman was on hand. Haskell welcomed the Governor and posed for photos of the two shaking hands. Feeley explained that through the efforts of the CCDC presided over by Haskell the factory brought from New Jersey represented a sales volume of "a little over $2,000,000" and a work force representing "30 to 40 families."

The day included more events for the governor to attend while in Cortland. An avid skier, Harriman made a visit to see the progress being made on the new Greek Peak ski area in nearby Virgil. The itinerary included a visit to Cortland State Teachers College for President Donnal V. Smith to show the expansion afoot. Students must have been pleased that classes were

Governor W. Averell Harriman (left) greeted by Haskell in May of 1957 at the cornerstone laying ceremony for Trinity Corp. of Cortland, NY. A clipping found in Haskell's scrapbook. Photographed by the author.

suspended for the day during the governor's inspection. The Governor used his scheduled press conference time to announce his intent to call a special session of the State Legislature in June to block a $55,400,000 a year rate increase sought by the New York Telephone Company. The day concluded with an evening banquet at the Skateland hosted by the CCDC and a speech by its president.

1957 had been designated by the CCDC as a time for economic expansion, and the year finished up on a high note. On the day after Christmas, Smith-Corona, Inc. of nearby Groton, New York, signed a contract to buy the 600-acre Claude and Agnes Rorapaugh Farm on Route 13. This would give Smith-Corona room to expand to meet a growing market for their electric portable typewriters. At a luncheon following the signing at Hotel Cortland, Haskell, as CCDC president, asked the guests to rise and in his typical manner said, "men do not bring these things to pass entirely by their own efforts. I would like to ask a blessing and thank God for bringing a miracle."

And there was more to celebrate. Other strides had been made in 1957 besides the Trinity and Smith-Corona deals. Cary & Company had applied aluminum siding to a $175,000 garment manufacturing plant on an 18-acre site north of the McClean Road, west of Route 281. Up to 150 persons were expected to be employed there. With Haskell's assistance, the former Beaudry Wallpaper plant at 46 Elm Street in Cortland had been purchased December 6, and its 150,000 square foot facility was to be renovated as part of a major expansion of Durkee Domestic Bakery of Homer. Last, but not least, excavation had begun at the site of a much-needed future gymnasium-auditorium for St. Mary's School.

In January of 1958, another promising business venture was ready to go into operation. The Greek Peak Ski Center in Virgil planned formal opening ceremonies for January 11th. Governor Averell Harriman was invited back to Cortland, along with "other state officials," "prominent persons in the ski world," and Albert Haskell. The night before the dedication event, Greek Peak hosted a Stockholders' Dinner-Dance at the Cortland Country Club. The emcee was Haskell, who lauded President Robert Thompson and the developers of Greek Peak for their "courage, initiative, and tremendous amount of work."

At a press luncheon the next day at the Hotel Cortland, Governor Harriman recalled his visit to Cortland the past spring to see the economic expansion occurring in Cortland. Now Greek Peak would be added to the mix. He noted his personal interest in skiing came when he visited Austria in the 1930s. He observed that the ski center six miles south of Cortland, would be "a first-class development and make a real contribution to the skiing in our state." Forty ski centers would be operating across the state and accessible because of the state's expanding development of highways. Garment manufacturing was the number one element in the state's economy, and tourism was second. With ski trails of varied terrains and slopes, Greek Peak would add to the state's tourism and continue to develop into a top-notch resort.

Then, the Governor stepped outside into the brisk wintry air. Wearing a double-breasted winter coat, he stood in an open convertible parked on Main Street in front of the Hotel Cortland and greeted the crowd and the parade that marched past, including a couple hundred skiers. The parade ended at the Crescent Corporation building on South Main Street, where busses transported people as part of the motorcade out to the Peak.

There, 2,500 braved the elements as 16-year-old Snow Queen Deborah Bennett, the Governor and the architect, Robert Tallman, placed a plaque on the exterior of the ski lodge, indicating it was opened by the Governor in January of 1958. Then, the Governor asked the Snow Queen to snip the blue ribbon to officially open the 3000-foot T-bar lift. Slipping off his overcoat and donning a pair of skis, the Governor took the lift up to the top with Robert Thompson.

Merv Knobloch reported on the dedication in the January 13, 1958, issue of the *Cortland Standard.* Titled "Governor Reaches New Olympian Heights at Greek Peak Saturday," Knobloch gave a light-hearted description of the ease with which the Governor ascended 3,000 feet to the mountaintop. Then, given the region's plethora of towns with names from Greek Antiquity, he wrote:

> At the top of Greek Peak, not a politician or poet was around. Even if he wanted to rise above politics (maybe he did) and soar in verse, how often can a governor get a drop on the likes of Homer, town or poet, and Solon, twin or senator, in one fell swoop? It must have been a truly delightful moment for his governorship.

During his descent down the slopes, the Governor managed to remain upright, and at the end he said it was his "first chance to ski this season." "Very fine!" the governor declared when asked what he thought of the slopes. Then, he expressed his regrets at not being able to stay longer and headed off to the Broome County Airport and a flight home. Original plans called for his use of the Cortland Airport, but a heavy snowfall the night before called for a change in plans. Page Green Road was slippery for those returning to Cortland from the party and an impressive torchlight ski procession for ski instructors that night. One car was seen on its side in a ditch. The next day, Sunday, 1,000 skiers were said to be on the slopes of the newly dedicated Greek Peak Ski Center.

Of course, the success of a ski resort like Greek Peak depends heavily on Mother Nature to supply an adequate amount of snow. The only way around it is to use technology: a snow-making machine. And here is where Robert Thompson and Albert Haskell entered into an exchange of tongue-in-cheek letters about snowmaking. Thompson's letter has the incorrect year (force of habit from writing 1957 for a whole year), and Haskell attached it to his scrapbook.

Haskell's more serious response to Thompson was as follows:

> Of course, you and I know that the "One" we really have to thank for the snow, the cold weather and the wonderful success you and your Associates have had in the promotion and dedication of Greek Peak is the Good Lord who guides and directs our every act and deed.
>
> Perhaps "He" will not mind our injecting a little humor into the situation which looked a little desperate during the Christmas holidays, when dust was taking the place of the much-needed snow.
>
> This community is grateful to you and your associates for the splendid results you have achieved. The success of the venture up to this point gives promise of a bright future for Greek Peak.

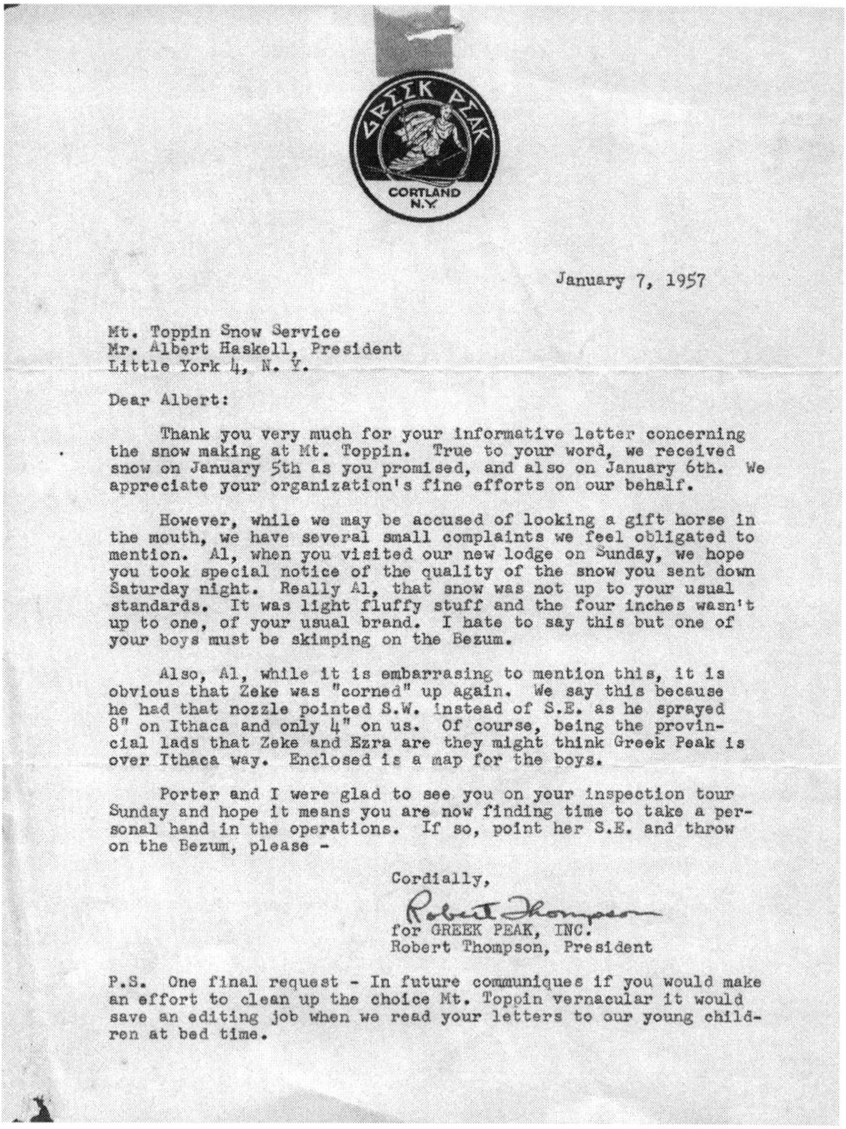

GREEK PEAK
CORTLAND N.Y.

January 7, 1957

Mt. Toppin Snow Service
Mr. Albert Haskell, President
Little York 4, N. Y.

Dear Albert:

Thank you very much for your informative letter concerning the snow making at Mt. Toppin. True to your word, we received snow on January 5th as you promised, and also on January 6th. We appreciate your organization's fine efforts on our behalf.

However, while we may be accused of looking a gift horse in the mouth, we have several small complaints we feel obligated to mention. Al, when you visited our new lodge on Sunday, we hope you took special notice of the quality of the snow you sent down Saturday night. Really Al, that snow was not up to your usual standards. It was light fluffy stuff and the four inches wasn't up to one, of your usual brand. I hate to say this but one of your boys must be skimping on the Bezum.

Also, Al, while it is embarrasing to mention this, it is obvious that Zeke was "corned" up again. We say this because he had that nozzle pointed S.W. instead of S.E. as he sprayed 8" on Ithaca and only 4" on us. Of course, being the provincial lads that Zeke and Ezra are they might think Greek Peak is over Ithaca way. Enclosed is a map for the boys.

Porter and I were glad to see you on your inspection tour Sunday and hope it means you are now finding time to take a personal hand in the operations. If so, point her S.E. and throw on the Bezum, please -

Cordially,

Robert Thompson
for GREEK PEAK, INC.
Robert Thompson, President

P.S. One final request - In future communiques if you would make an effort to clean up the choice Mt. Toppin vernacular it would save an editing job when we read your letters to our young children at bed time.

Thompson's letter with Greek Peak letterhead. A clipping found in Haskell's scrapbook. Photographed by the author.

May God continue to give his blessing and guidance and may you and your associates have continued health and courage to carry on this great community enterprise.

After "Cordially yours," Haskell signed his name and added "Snow Manufacturer."

Of course, the ribbing of Haskell about snowfall did not stop there. Fellow Rotarians had to get in on the act, too. The *Cortland Clatter*, the Cortland Rotary Club's newsletter, ran this piece in its February 8, 1958, issue:

> Beezum Don't you think your job is now complete, Al? We were all rooting for you when you helped out the Greek Peak boys, but enough is enough, and we now think you should call a halt [to the snowmaking]. We Rotarians over 60 were all for the snow, but when it gets up to where it gets in our ears, we frankly have to object. We now suggest that you save the rest of your Beezum until next winter. Bill Dwyer says you can store any surplus in the County Garage.

Joking about the mythical Beezum (with apparently more than one spelling) continued into the next winter. A limerick was delivered on February 24, 1959, during a Cortland Rotary Club meeting:

> The Greek Peak Boys called upon Haskell.
> They accused him of being a rascal.
> He continued to tease 'em,
> But delivered the beezum.
> What more, pray tell us, can they ask Al?

Chapter 17

"Elder Statesman" of Cortland's Industrial Growth

With all the success Cortland was having at economic expansion by 1958, Haskell was garnering a justifiable reputation locally and across the state for his leadership in business promotion. A letter of March 26, 1958, from Herbert C. Howe of the Rome, New York Chamber of Commerce, thanking the 67-year-old Haskell for meeting with the Rome Chamber of Commerce the day before, referred to him as "the 'elder statesman' of Cortland's industrial growth." Though advancing in age, he still kept up his interest and active participation in Chamber of Commerce and Cortland County Development Corporation activities.

In April of 1958, Haskell applauded the Cortlandville Town Board for rezoning three significant parcels of land from agricultural to industrial use. This was the 210 acres belonging to Mrs. Agnes S. Rorapaugh on both sides of Route 13 south of the city of Cortland. Rezoning would allow for the future growth of Smith-Corona. Haskell, also, applauded the forming of a Chamber of Commerce in Homer. The business organization held its first annual banquet on April 10, 1958, at the Homer American Legion Hall. Chamber of Commerce leaders from national, state, and neighboring levels attended. Edmund Karam, the president of the Homer Chamber of Commerce welcomed the distinguished guests, which included Haskell as the president of the Cortland County Development Corporation. A close rival to Haskell as a popular public speaker was Louis Wolner, supervising principal of the Homer Central School District, and "Lou" served as the evening's toastmaster. Wolner cited the efforts to "bring summer stock to Homer which would utilize the Town Hall theater building and bring economic good to the village."

Be it at the grassroots level or the national and international level, Haskell continued his interest in economic matters. For him, all economics was local. April saw him sharing the dais with Representative John Taber of Auburn, New York, the ranking Republican of the House Appropriations Committee.

This was at a luncheon meeting of the Cortland Chamber of Commerce at Hotel Cortland. Taber was the guest speaker. He spoke on the need for the nation to maintain industries. "One of the worst things that could happen," he stressed, "would be for America to depend on products manufactured abroad." Industry, like troops, he said, must be kept in the country's front line of defense. Taber continued, "If we do not keep those things in mind, I fear for the safety of the United States. For that reason, I just do not see how the United States can continue reciprocal trade agreements. They are not reciprocal!" He urged for judgement to be exercised when it came to the amount of importing of products. He also complained that the Social Security disbursements of 1957 exceeded receipts by $500 million and by $950 million in 1958. Unemployment disbursements exceeded receipts by $800 million in the present year and by $100 million the previous year. He said, "What we need to do to get out of this recession is to have those people out of work do something . . . making something that will bring prices down." He complained of the 10- to 14-month gap from the time of appropriation to the actual cash to be provided for federal works jobs.

It was also in April of 1958 that the Cortland Chamber of Commerce confronted a major concern. The organization was in the red. A breakfast was planned to launch a drive to recruit 100 additional members and to use the dues garnered to put the organization back in the black. Haskell expressed his opinion that not belonging to the Chamber was "a shameful thing." Dan McNeil, chairman of the membership drive committee, said that new members would be "buying a share in the community." They would be participating, too, in stimulating new industrial developments in the area, claimed Haskell.

Unemployment was a concern in 1957and 1958. A statewide conference of labor and business leaders was held on May 2, 1958. Democrat Governor Averell Harriman sent a report developed by the conference to Republican Albert Haskell. The report addressed four points agreed upon at the conference for "maintenance and strengthening of consumer and business confidence in the economic future." In a cover letter from the Executive Chamber in Albany, signed by the Governor as simply Averell Harriman, the State's Chief Executive Officer stated, "I sincerely hope you will join me in pressing for action on the four points. . . ."

This was not the only time the State prevailed upon Haskell for assistance. In a typed letter dated August 7, 1958, addressed to "My dear Al," Charles J. O'Connor of the Bureau of Industrial Development in the State's Department of Commerce, indicated he would be in Cortland on Wednesday, August 13, "in the late afternoon" and needed "a few moments of your time." He wished to give some information on a proposed New York State Association of Industrial Development Agencies, and there would be some papers to be signed. This was because Haskell was being asked by "Chuck" to "act as a director of the temporary board until an election of directors can be held on October 2 in Syracuse" for organizing "this new Association." Haskell consented, and at the organizational meeting in Syracuse he was elected a vice-president in this new Association.

As a leader and mentor, Haskell was appreciated by many. One who valued him was the Cortland Chamber of Commerce's first full-time executive secretary, a young man named Richard M. Day. After a farewell party for "Dick" in August 1958, the man sent Haskell a complimentary letter:

> I would like you to know that because of our close association, you have enriched my life manifold. As you so aptly expressed it the other evening, I have learned many things that will be invaluable to me later in life. I am aware that whatever success the community had in securing new industry, belonged in large part to you. I certainly hope that you will continue to have the vision to lead the younger men into building a prosperous Cortland.

Meanwhile, the vision of a typewriter factory in Cortland proceeded to become a reality. The foundations were being prepared. On September 16, 1958, thirteen bids were received from contractors wishing to erect the new factory requiring 665 tons of structural steel. The bids were opened, and the low bid of $574,000 went to Vincent J. Smith, Inc. of Johnson City, New York. Interestingly, this general contractor was the same one that built St. Anthony's Church, the San Rocco Lodge Hall, the Cary & Co. buildings on Route 281, and the additions to Parker and Pomeroy schools—all located in Cortland. Later in the month, construction of 14-inch water lines commenced so water would be available to the Smith-Corona plant by October 1st.

By October 7, 1958, Smith-Corona had become Smith-Corona Marchant (S-CM), and the *Cortland Standard* reported the groundbreaking ceremony for the S-CM plant took place under "a bright sun" indicating "a bright industrial future for the Cortland area." Haskell was the master of ceremonies. Earth movers and a bulldozer fell silent as the ceremony commenced. Elwyn Smith, president of S-CM, Inc. said "Smith-Corona Marchant is marching on, expanding—We are going places and glad you are going with us." He invited the Cortland community to grow along with the company. Haskell graciously introduced Smith as the man who "makes the dream come true," but everyone knew the Cortland Development Corporation and Haskell were instrumental in making it happen. Smith invited Haskell to share in turning over the first sod on the building site 400 feet west of Route 13. With a broad grin, he said to Haskell, "As I recall it, you do it like this," and he placed his foot on the gold-plated spade. Haskell did the same with his spade, and photos were taken of both men beaming along with other dignitaries. Formality was suspended as Smith asked, "Who has a lucky penny?" He then took a penny from his own pocket, tossed it into the broken sod, and covered it over for luck.

When the sun set, Haskell's day was not over yet. That night, he attended the Cortland County Republican Committee dinner meeting at the Skateland, where the guest speaker was Republican gubernatorial candidate Nelson A. Rockefeller, along with his wife and son Stephen. Eight hundred were in attendance. Rockefeller's major attack on the Harriman administration was for a vacuum of leadership in Albany in fighting organized crime. He posited that crime had continued unabated since a summit of gangsters took place in Apalachin, New York in 1957. "Gangsters find New York State a good place to do business," said Rockefeller. For this occasion, attorney Leland Taylor was dinner chairman and toastmaster, assisted by Assemblyman Louis H. Folmer. Haskell's day was already busy enough.

Only a few days later, Haskell was invited to speak at the first fall Tully Chamber of Commerce meeting held at the Maples in Pompey. There he shared his "prescription for community growth, cooperation, and prosperity." Folks wanted to know the secret to Cortland's success in attracting new industry, and he outlined a plan of action. First, it was paramount to have unity among all community leaders in the belief that expansion is wanted. "If there is division," he said, "you are wasting your valuable time." Then, create an industrial promotion committee where all matters are confidential until a firm decision is reached. A brochure must be crafted to tell the community's story because industrialists will want to know about the area's accessibility, topography, water and sewer supply, churches, schools, and labor supply. He suggested using the State Department of Commerce for assistance, and he reminded the audience that the industrialists' wives will play a part in any decision regarding moving to a new town. They will look the town over, and no decision gets made before wives are consulted. He said Tully faced increased potential because of the anticipated completion of the Penn-Can Expressway [future Interstate 81].

Haskell gave a similar talk on November 10th in Marathon. After its first year in existence, there was talk of disbanding their Chamber of Commerce. In addition, the prospects of the Penn-Can Expressway coming through Marathon had been met with overwhelming disapproval. Two hundred sixty people had signed a petition in opposition. So, the fledgling Chamber of Commerce put on a Booster Dinner at the Masonic Temple. Haskell's friend Walter Grunfeld introduced the guest speaker. He called Haskell "an inspiring man" filled with "vitality and sincerity" and "one of the outstanding leaders of Cortland county today . . . a 20th century civic leader who has surrounded himself with young men who are deeply concerned with the future welfare of the community."

Haskell met the task head on. Later, Grunfeld wrote that Haskell offered "forceful and straight-from-the-shoulder words." Haskell pointed out that he had not come to Marathon to tell half-truths but to offer observations from one interested in the future development of the area. He encouraged the Marathon Chamber of Commerce not to disband but, instead, to engage in an industrial expansion program, exactly because the Expressway was scheduled to be built right through Marathon. The highway presented incredible potential for their community. He warned Marathon "the old order changeth" and changes will take place "whether you like it or not, and you must be prepared to live in new conditions." The best approach would be for everyone to "be united for the common good." They could not hope for more business or more industry "if there is a divided opinion." "You must all work together. If you are not together, you might as well give up before you start." He went on to share the same recipe for success he shared with Tully. He even reminded the ladies present of the major role women play in the relocation of industry. Executives consult their wives before making major moves. Women look for a clean town, churches, schools, and the friendliness of community members. Haskell rhetorically asked, "What do you have to offer any new concern which might want to come to Marathon?" His answer: water, land, employable men and women, utilities, schools, and churches. He concluded by asking if Marathon was willing to accept the status quo or willing to work and work together for positive change? Afterwards, he received his answer; the Chamber membership voted 35 to 1 not to disband.

Grunfeld followed up with an editorial in his Marathon newspaper of November 20, 1958, extolling Haskell's address to the Chamber of Commerce. He said that Haskell "is a product of this area. As such, one would expect that his approach would reflect the traditional ultra-conservativism of so much of our leaders in the past. Yet, he does not have these characteristics at all, and Cortland County is better off for it!"

Actually, Haskell defied being neatly pigeonholed as progressive or conservative. On some matters, like Social Security, he was quite conservative, and preferred seeing local United Way funds and not tax dollars used to help welfare agencies in the community. On other issues, like construction of Interstate 81 through farmland, he was quite progressive. Basically, it came down to his taking stances based purely on what he thought was the right action to pursue for the future of the community.

Newspaper journalists hailed the progress made in Cortland and the prospects of a "bright future." Paul Peffers of the Syracuse *Herald American* wrote an article in the Sunday, October 12, 1958, issue claiming "Cortland is Bright Spot in Upstate's Economy." Peffers wrote, "Cortland is the live wire among Central New York communities." The reason cited was an active Chamber of Commerce and an industrial development committee and determined citizens seeking expansion. "Cortland has a bright future," he proclaimed because of all the new businesses, which he itemized, and access to the new Route 81 that would intersect with the New York State Thruway at Syracuse. He noted 55 percent of Cortland's goods were durable and 45 percent non-durable, a good balance for withstanding recessionary times. The older businesses would benefit as well. Cortland Line and Newton Line, he stressed, were responsible for half the fishlines made in the U.S. Other Cortland firms, like Wickwire, Brewer-Titchener, Thompson Boats, Grummon Boats, and Brockway Motors would realize benefits. And agriculture would grow, especially dairy, cabbage, and maple syrup. Of Cortland County's labor force, 6 percent was unemployed; so, it was not a distressed area.

On Monday, October 20, 1958, Haskell was again elected President of the CCDC at the annual meeting of its stockholders at the First National Bank. Working with him would be George H. Wiltsie Jr., as Vice-President, Harold P. Burgess as Treasurer, and Leighton A. Hope as Secretary. The next month, on the 12th, Haskell, through his membership in the Cortland Chamber of Commerce, was moving on to yet another project, stimulated by the Interstate highway that would bring more traffic Cortland's way. He and fourteen others had been appointed to a newly created hotel exploratory committee. They met at the First National Bank. After considerable discussion, the committee decided to invite a hotel expert to meet with the committee at an early date for the purpose of exploring the possibilities of constructing a new hotel-motel to serve the community and the traveling public.

At the Cortland Rotary Club noon luncheon meeting on January 20, 1959, at the YMCA, Haskell introduced George Feeley, president of Trinity Equipment Corporation. Feeley's topic was "High Hopes" for the future. He announced that just the day before the firm had received orders for dehumidifiers for nine Atlas missile sites. Military contracts are a lucrative part of the business, and the firm invests five percent of its sales in product research and development. The firm moved to Cortland from Roselle Park, New Jersey, on November 18, 1957. He said, "Everything we expected to find here, we have found. Everything committed to be so, is so."

Haskell said they had first met on September 28, 1956, and after a five-hour meeting, the community pledged to raise $200,000 and Trinity pledged to move to Cortland. The Development Company was instrumental in raising the money to bring Trinity to Cortland. Feeley described the history of the firm: started out as a part-time business in Orange, New Jersey in 1941. Incorporated in 1947, it went on a full-time basis. In 1948, they set up a plant in Roselle Park. In 1951, they expanded by buying out a Long Island firm. Most interesting to the Rotarians was the fact Trinity received about a thousand offers for possible locations throughout the nation. Feeley said the New York State Department of Public Works urged them to look over

Cortland. According to the Club's *Cortland Clatter* of January 17, 1959, the program provided Rotarians with "a better understanding of Cortland's newest and most modern industry," and a recognition that Haskell's "tremendous efforts were a vital factor in making Cortland a part of the Trinity story. . . ."

At 7:30 p.m. on January 14, 1959, the cafeteria of Cincinnatus Central School was buzzing. The Cincy Chamber of Commerce was holding its 14th Annual Banquet. One hundred thirteen members and guests enjoyed a ham dinner and a series of amusing pantomime sketches by the ever-entertaining Pat Mcgrady. The guest speaker was Albert Haskell, Cortland attorney.

Haskell was taking his motivational road show to the eastern part of the county. He continued the theme he emphasized at Tully and Marathon: a community can move ahead or back, but any attempt to move forward is doomed from the start without all the organizations in the community united behind the effort to attract industry. He said there must not be the attitude in the general public that "our town was good enough for our fathers and grandfathers, so it is good enough for us." He stressed that every small town should do everything it can to make itself attractive to others but especially to their own young people who otherwise would be inclined to leave and to establish residence elsewhere. He listed once again the four steps to be taken to get a small industry to move into a community like Cincinnatus. Of course, they should note in a brochure what makes the community a wonderful place in which to live and work, including ready access to the new Penn-Can Highway that will pass through the county. He must have been drawing from his own experience when he summed up by stating that one should not be just taking from one's community but giving of time and energy to make it a better place in which to live. He left the gathering with a rhetorical question: "What do I owe Cincinnatus, and what can I do to help repay this debt?"

It was at this time that the Hotel Exploratory Committee of the Cortland Chamber of Commerce pushed forward. Organized on November 12, 1958, the committee met on November 18 with Myron D. Hockenbury, President of the Hockenbury System, Inc. Hockenbury outlined a method of financing and building a hotel in Cortland. The Hockenbury System was contracted for $750 to survey Cortland for the feasibility of putting up a hotel. Said report was delayed until February, instead of January 1959, to give other hotel management groups a chance to weigh in. No other groups showed any interest in building a hotel for Cortland. So, Mr. Hockenbury gave his report on February 11th. Three recommendations of the Committee ensued. A new hotel in Cortland is a necessity. Any unnecessary delay would be unfortunate. The Hockenbury System recommended that the Chamber enter into a campaign with this view "when time and circumstances are appropriate," and the committee concurred.

Finally, the Committee diligently canvassed local opinion in the City and County of Cortland to get a true picture of the possibility of financing a new hotel at the time. While there was agreement that a new hotel was needed, public opinion did not feel it was the time for such a venture and that it was doubtful the needed financing could be provided within the next few months. In its report to the Chamber-at-large, the committee asked to be discharged since its specific task had been completed. The translation was likely that a campaign for a hotel was dead.

Hokenbury wrote a letter to Haskell accepting the notice of the Committee's recommendation to the Chamber but noting that the rise of motels in the Cortland area will mitigate against any campaign for a hotel. Hockenbury complained of his own bad experience when staying at "a room in the outskirts of the city." He wrote, "It was too cold to take a bath. All I had, in effect, was a bed and a bed light. I had my meals at the diner and used a telephone at the back of the diner. My headquarters was my automobile which most of the time was too cold to use." He added, "The old Cortland Hotel was a little better than this." The Hotel Cortland was, indeed, "old" and had filed for bankruptcy. As a landmark in the city, its days were numbered. Hockenbury recommended an 80-room inn-type hotel with a restaurant and facilities for handling 350 banqueters.

In early March 1959, Marine Midland Trust Company of Southern New York, with a branch office in Cortland and Haskell as an officer, announced it was spearheading a national campaign promoting the advantages for industrial growth in Cortland County where sixty-four industries already were prospering. "The Nation Looks at Cortland" was the theme of an advertising campaign sponsored nationally by the bank, touting the attractive features of the county. The ad appeared in *Business Week* on March 7, in *U.S. News & World Report* on March 23, and in the *Wall Street Journal* of March 26. The ad contained a photograph of the steel framework of Smith-Corona Marchant's new plant under construction in the Town of Cortlandville. In the foreground, standing in the snow and discussing site plans they hold, are Haskell, president of Cortland County Development Corp.; Elwyn L. Smith, president of Smith-Corona Marchant, Inc.; and Hugh H. Williams, senior vice-president of Marine Midland Trust Company of Southern New York.

By March 11, seven-ton half sections of pre-cast concrete wall were being hoisted into place by a crane as the new S-CM plant was expected to be closed in within a few weeks. On the evening of April 8, S-CM executives were the guest speakers at the second annual banquet of the Homer Chamber of Commerce. Wilbert L. Smith II, grandson of one of the company's founders and son of the present president said one of the reasons the company wanted to build a new plant for manufacturing typewriters was because "typing has now become the second most popular course in high school and

Marine Midland Trust Company advertisement touting Cortland. A clipping found in Haskell's scrapbook. Photographed by the author.

a typewriter is no longer a luxury since one out of every four families owns one." The company was anticipating an expanding market because of the post-war "baby boom." Homer School Superintendent Louis Wolner was the toastmaster for the event, and other honored guests included Haskell as president of the Cortland County Development Corporation.

Haskell continued to place news clippings in his scrapbooks. One, from the April 9, 1959, *Cortland Standard* indicated the State was planning a 4.4 mile-long, four-lane highway to link the City of Cortland to South Cortland. The reason was to accommodate the increase in employees traveling to work at the new S-CM plant on Route 13. This clipping was in stark contrast to another clipping on the same page of the scrapbook that must have caused a chuckle from Haskell when he cut it out. This one was from a daily section of the paper called "The Good Old Days." This included an article from April 1, 1909:

> There are a great many people who have come to believe that the horse must go and the carriage along with him, and that the automobile is the vehicle which is coming more and more and has come to stay. Albert E. Haskell of this city, who was for a time on the road for the Cortland Wagon Co., and has been with the Cortland Cart and Carriage Co. of Sydney, has stated that there is already a reaction in some parts of the country from the automobile craze and vehicles. The rage of the auto is on the wane, and people are going back to horses.

Only in his father's dreams. What would Haskell's father have thought of all the cars on expanding roadways in 1959 and of his son's aversion to keeping the status quo in matters of business development?

Not all of Haskell's efforts at business development panned out. How can one expect to win them all, given the tight competition among communities seeking businesses willing to relocate or expand? Plans called for Badger Northland of Kankauna, Wisconsin to open a branch office and warehouse at the southwest corner of Route 281 and the McLean Road. It never came to pass. Massey Ferguson bought them out in the mid-1970s. Still, Haskell's track record as a promoter of new businesses in Cortland was amazing.

It is difficult to have everything a potential new business may be looking for. For example, communities who wish to promote business and industry need up-to-date transportation service. So, on the night of December 3, 1958, eighty people gathered at the Commando Restaurant in Cortland for the first dinner meeting of the newly formed Cortland Aeronautical Association. Mr. C. B. Friday, Director of the Bureau of Aviation of the New York State Department of Commerce, addressed the gathering. He said a community without adequate air service in the near future would be like a community without a railroad or trucking fifty years ago. He said that one of the questions prospective businesses ask about a community is "How close is the nearest airport?" It makes a difference for business travel and for shipping of freight—both raw materials and finished products. Haskell, a busy fellow, could not attend due to a conflicting engagement, but he sent a letter which was read expressing the support of the CCDC. Friday maintained that only 21 percent of air travel was for pleasure. He pointed out that the National Safety Council reported that a man riding in a scheduled air carrier was four times safer than a man riding in an automobile. A Cortland Flying Club was started in 1928–1929, and the City of Cortland took over the airport west of the city in 1940. Friday said this was a good site capable of expansion and Cortland should take advantage of this. A color film was shown next: "The Flying Businessman." It showed the increasing reliance of business on aviation.

Over 100 directors, officers, and guests of the Marine Midland Trust Company of Southern New York had a dinner meeting at the Cortland Country Club on September 14, 1958. At the event, Haskell, officer of the bank and president of the CCDC, was presented a plaque for thirty-three years of continuous service with the Cortland bank.

In the last half of those years, the city of Cortland had seen a 21.7 percent increase in the number of its households. The national increase was 17.5 percent. The "Baby Boom" of post-World War II America meant an increasing demand for factory-made goods and services. Economic expansion was afoot, but the downside was the competition to be anticipated among retailers.

Cortland created a Junior Chamber of Commerce (Jaycees), a leadership training and civic organization for people between the ages 18 and 40. On April 23, 1959, the "elder statesman" of Cortland's industrial growth was part of a five-man panel hosted by the Cortland Jaycees at the San Rocco Lodge on Pomeroy Street in Cortland. The topic was "Where to Cortland?" Second Ward Alderman Morris Noss cautioned that local businesses had to prepare for competition from shopping centers outside the city. He predicted that in two or three years the proposed arterial highway [Interstate 81] would make Cortland a suburb of Syracuse and only "30 minutes from downtown Syracuse." He correctly prophesized, "It would be bad if downtown Cortland became a secondary shopping area to plazas outside of Cortland."

Speaking for the CCDC, Haskell noted, "Youth, the real life-blood of a community was not taken into consideration 25 years ago in the shape of the community." He said he lived in Cortland for 68 years and for 45 years he observed "a Chinese wall around the city." "People were satisfied with what they had and wanted no more. Four years ago, that wall was broken and through the efforts of the Chamber of Commerce we started out on a new industry program." He thanked the Jaycees for their aid in the project, congratulating them on having sold $30,000 worth of stock in the CCDC.

As for the future, Haskell said, "Gentlemen, the future of Cortland is what you make it."

Dr. Franklyn S. Barry, Superintendent of Schools, spoke of the importance of education in attracting business to a community. "You wouldn't move into the finest community," he said, "if it didn't have good schools." He cited the problem of attracting good teachers without attractive salaries and of getting across to parents and taxpayers "just why education costs so much."

Edward M. Feeley, sales manager for Trinity Equipment Corp., said, "The community did a superb job and wonderful selling job to us." Haskell must have derived some satisfaction from knowing he had been the kingpin of that sales pitch.

In the late '50s, following one of Haskell's ingredients in his recipe for economic success, the Cortland County Chamber of Commerce put out an impressive brochure titled "Live, Learn, Earn in Cortland County." The brochure enumerated the advantages the County offered as a place in which to "live, learn and earn." It boasted "A student in Cortland can go to school from kindergarten through a four-year college course without paying a cent of tuition." The State University Teacher's College at Cortland was expanding its dormitory accommodations. It stated, "The city school system is a model one," and that there was closed circuit TV for classrooms. It included a photo of the Homer Central High School as one of five centralized schools in the county offering "secondary education second to none for rural young people." Eighty-six different manufacturing plants was why the NYS Department of Commerce had stated "there is less unemployment per capita in Cortland County than in any county in the state." In the county, farming is an "Important Industry." Churches of all denominations can be found. Cortland manufactures drill presses, sheet metal, braided fishline, boats, lingerie, Brockway trucks, and typewriters. For amusement and recreation, there is golfing at the Cortland Country Club, fishing in Grout Brook, and swimming at Wickwire Municipal Pool. A photo of Governor Harriman on a ski lift at Greek Peak gave recognition to the area's prime ski center. Besides being the center of New York State, Cortland's water supply was touted as "second to none." To visualize the area as a "Good place to live," there was a photo of Assemblyman Folmer's Federalist-style house on South Main Street in Homer.

Perhaps in response to the publication of the brochure, Haskell's Rotarian buddies simply had to get in some humorous jabs when paying a compliment. Rotary's *Cortland Clatter* for Tuesday, May 19, 1959, printed "What a Fish (Bass) Story":

> We were simply amazed at the growth in usage and the marvelous results now being obtained by Al Haskell's "Beezum." Too much publicity should not be

> given, however, as without a hotel in our community, we could not possibly house the bass fishermen, the mosquito scientists, and the lovers of skiing. We do approve of the government getting into the picture, as they need all the assistance possible in their constant study of air space and missiles. We are certainly proud of our scientist!

The 34th Annual Banquet of the Cortland County Chamber of Commerce took place on May 19, 1959, at the Moose Lodge, 159 Main Street, Cortland., where Haskell also held a membership. That evening, Haskell was there not as the toastmaster but as the president of the CCDC, who was to introduce the guest speaker, Republican Lieutenant Governor Malcolm Wilson. Wilson told the 271 attendees "The State Department has been so impressed by the business climate created here by your development corporation that it has begun to emulate their ideas." If "Imitation is the sincerest form of flattery," then Haskell and the CCDC must have felt complimented to be told the quality of their work was deemed "worthy" enough to be copied.

On October 15, 1959, Haskell sent out a letter to stockholders of the CCDC announcing in its fifth year a dividend of 2 percent, the second such declaration. Also, he cited the erection of the S-CM typewriter factory as a milestone in the history of the development corporation.

An indication of just how much fame and respect Haskell had garnered at the state level came on October 29, 1959. An examination of the program for the Third Annual Statewide Industrial Development Workshop held in Rochester, New York under the auspices of the state's Department of Commerce reveals the 4 p.m. invited speaker was "Hon. Albert Haskell Jr., President of CCDC, Inc." His topic, not surprisingly, was "Keep New York Industry in New York."

It was not just industry that Haskell wanted in Cortland County. He wanted the new Interstate Highway to cut through Cortland County. Some in the state were lobbying for the route to link Binghamton and Utica. Members of a regional Penn-Can Committee of Cortland, Syracuse, and Binghamton met on December 28, 1959 "to discuss ways to expedite completion of the Tully-Binghamton link of Route 81." The meeting was arranged by the local Highway and Transportation Committee of the Chamber of Commerce chaired by Cortland real estate developer James Yaman. Held at Cortland's Shamrock Inn, the group heard firsthand from Assemblyman Louis Folmer the bill proposed for the preferred route, which would be submitted to the State Legislature in January. Those invited included Haskell, representing the CCDC.

The importance Haskell placed on the delivery of quality education in any community seeking to attract new industry was well appreciated in Cortland. He had a fine working relationship with the college in Cortland,

and frequently the institution prevailed upon him for financial support or, on some occasions, for the use of his name. Case in point, he was invited to serve on the Honorary Committee of both the Sixth and Seventh Annual SUNY Invitational Basketball Tournament (1962 and 1963). In 1962, Tournament Chairman Leo Meldrim and Program Chairman Ross L. Allen explained in the typed invitation "We wish to use your name to add prestige to this sports event which will bring eight colleges to Cortland to compete." The program for spectators at the tournaments listed 55 names of the Honorary Committee with Haskell as Chairman. The back cover listed financial contributors, and Haskell was included there, as well.

The matter of an airport to service the business community of Cortland raised its head again in 1962. On June 20, Haskell as president of the CCDC, along with Morris Noss and James Yaman, was present at a "meeting of industry, city and town governments . . . called by the Chamber of Commerce Highway and Transportation Committee [chaired by Yaman] to determine the advisability of maintaining the airport." At the time, the city owned the airport but stated it was unable to apportion additional funds for its maintenance. Mayor Joseph Mack said the city would be willing to turn the airport over to the county, but that decision would be up to the Board of Supervisors [forerunner of today's County Legislature]. Local captains of industry all spoke of a need for an airport. Local industries were owned by out-of-town companies, which required them to be in contact with headquarters. Cortland's Trinity had merged with Pall, a manufacturer of an array of filters for sundry processes, and it became Pall Trinity Micro. The merger, it was noted, was made feasible by the existence of the airstrip in Cortland.

According to the next day's *Cortland Standard*, "Albert Haskell, president of the Cortland County Development Corp., called for looking at the problem with vision, 'to forget politics' and the public loss of taxes for what is the 'best thing for the county of Cortland.'" He hinted at the possibility of another industry coming to Cortland with the creation of 200 to 250 new jobs, but the parent firm was so far away from New York State that an airport would be essential. He stressed the urgency involved: "Negotiations are not in the dream stage, but in the stage of actual drawing of options on at least one or two sites."

The only note of opposition at the meeting came from Glenn Alexander, Supervisor of the Town of Cortlandville, who said the town board had received expressions of objection to the airport. The "airport problem" had existed through the previous three city administrations—Keeney, Gabriel, and Mack—and was rising again. Essentially, the question came down to: Was the Cortland airport merely recreational in nature or a necessity for business to operate? Today the county owns the airport, which also goes by the name of Chase Field after Cortland-born Air Force Major General Levi R. Chase.

The industry that Haskell had hinted at during the meeting was in the midst of negotiations over real estate, and its name was even withheld from the press. The August 1, 1962, *Cortland Standard* was only able to report that the land in question was behind and adjacent to the Niagara-Mohawk substation on Route 11 across the Tioughnioga River from the Sewage Disposal Plant. The land was owned by farmer William Diescher. Haskell, Noss, and George Wiltsie of the CCDC had been working on this project for the past three months. The Town of Cortlandville was petitioned for the rezoning of the property from agricultural to industrial. In the same night's newspaper was a legal notice announcing a public hearing for August 13th.

On the day of the hearing, the *Cortland Standard* informed the public that the business being invited to Cortland was the Chris-Craft Corporation. The Thompson Boat Company, with its plant on Elm Street in Cortland, was a wholly owned subsidiary of Chris-Craft. The Elm Street plant would continue to manufacture wooden lap-strake boats, while the new plant would make fiberglass boats for distribution throughout the country. Advances in fiberglass had made small powerboats more affordable for the middle class and being much easier to transport and maneuver than wooden boats, they had great appeal. Haskell, Noss, and Robert Thompson of Thompson Boat Company jointly announced that if the rezoning were approved construction could be completed by next January so boats could be available for the next summer's market.

Citizens at the zoning hearing registered concerns about noises and odors which are often common to factory areas. Thompson assured them the nature of the manufacturing process would not generate such problems and that the attractive landscaping and architecture envisioned would, in fact, enhance the area. Several people at the public hearing praised the efforts made to bring the new industry here and cited the benefits to be gained by the community. It was noted that the 250 x 750-foot plant would be within a half mile of the planned Interstate Route 81 interchange at Polkville. That night, the Town Board unanimously OK'd the zoning change.

What few probably knew was exactly how instrumental Haskell was, in spite of recent infirmity, in pulling wires behind the scenes to pull off a complex real estate deal. In his scrapbook is a copy of a letter dated June 11, 1962, from him to Henry Gallien Jr., of the New York State Association of Industrial Development Agencies, Inc., of Albany. Haskell, who had had a heart attack only three months earlier, informed Gallien he would be "putting in half days at the office for the next month or six weeks . . . so I am going to be around to bother you for a little while longer." Haskell explained succinctly that "our immediate problem" is that the site for Chris-Craft is property owned by William Diescher, a farmer who also owns land to be appropriated for the construction of Interstate 81. "Now Diescher will not give us a figure on the site which Chris-Craft might be interested in until he makes a settlement with the State of New York," wrote Haskell. "What I want you to do in plain language is to get in touch with the Department of Public Works and see if anything can be done to expedite the settlement of the State of New York on the land they will take belonging to Diescher." The urgency was clearly noted: ". . . I don't have to tell you that we are in some pretty hot competition because Chris-Craft is primarily located in Florida, but . . . if we get a fair figure for the land, we would probably be favored with this expansion in Cortland County."

Gallien responded five days later. His typed message indicated he would "light a fire under the State authorities . . . and get back to Mr. Thompson as soon as possible." On the same letter, Haskell scribbled out a note by hand: "The key to making the Chris-Craft deal was to get Diescher—the owner of the land which Chris-Craft wanted—a fair settlement for other land appropriated by the state for highway purposes." Haskell seemed to want posterity to know about the pivotal role he played in clinching the complicated Chris-Craft deal with its multiple moving parts.

Seventy-five persons attended the groundbreaking ceremony for the Corsair Division of Chris-Craft on the morning of September 13, 1962. Thompson, Haskell, and Noss each used a separate gold shovel. Thompson, looking across the field to the hill above Route 11, said: "The new highway [81] to be built halfway up the hill over there will someday be loaded with boats from Cortland." Haskell praised Thompson's interest in the community and stated that without it "we wouldn't have this ground-breaking today." He also paid respect to the established industries of the county who made Chris-Craft feel welcomed. It was noted that the site puts fiberglass boats within a radius of "one-third of the concentrated wealth of the country." The Chris-Craft move was clearly viewed as a victory for Haskell and for Cortland.

At the same time Haskell was dealing with the complexities of the Chris-Craft deal, the challenging issue of maintaining the airport was still being debated. The editors of the *Cortland Standard* sided with Haskell. In an editorial of August 23, 1962, they cited his lawyerly and persuasive appeal: "The people represented around this table today, if they want an airport in A-1 condition and operated in the way it should be operated on a minimum basis, and if they set their hearts and minds to the task, will be able to accomplish it."

What the Cortland community had accomplished thus far had been considered impossible, and the Syracuse *Post-Standard* of August 26, 1962, saluted the Cortland Chamber of Commerce and the Cortland County Development Corporation for what they had done in the past five years. The paper stated it was a "most competitive business" to sell Cortland as an ideal place for industry to locate or relocate, but the CCDC had done it. They enumerated the five enterprises that had been attracted to the area since 1957: The Trinity Equipment Corp; Cary & Co.; Smith-Corona Marchant (S-CM); The New York State Conservation Department's new office building on Fisher Avenue in Cortland to serve an eight- county regional district; and the Chris-Craft Corp.

The editorial outlined the remarkable history that had been made. Six or seven years ago, they noted, the picture was not so rosy. Cortland had not attracted any new businesses in 40 years. One thousand five hundred residents commuted to jobs outside the county in Syracuse and Ithaca. Young people, finding few job opportunities, were leaving the area. The Chamber of Commerce decided to act. In 1956, they held a one-day membership drive. Two hundred twenty-five new members were signed up in just one day. A meeting was called. The members were asked what the community needed. Everyone agreed; it was new industry. Industry was seen as the life-blood of any mid-20th century community. Without it, the population would dwindle, and established businesses would suffer. So, the Chamber contacted the NYS Dept. of Commerce, asking for assistance. The Department sent a New Jersey corporation that was looking to relocate. A vacated factory in the city of Cortland was shown. The Trinity Equipment Corp deemed the site unacceptable but thought the Cortland area was an ideal location for their new home. Members of the Chamber met in New Jersey with the members of the Board of Directors of Trinity and found that if a good offer was made, they might be persuaded to come to Cortland. The problem was that the Chamber was not chartered for the next step that needed to be taken—the acquisition of real estate and the ability to make the necessary commitments. The solution was the chartering of the CCDC in 1957—done in only two days, thanks to the assistance of the State Commerce Department. The CCDC went right to work. Trinity was contacted and offered a factory to be built for them. A fund-raising drive commenced and managed to raise $200,000. It was truly a community effort. Five hundred fifty citizens purchased stock in CCDC at $50 a share. Albert Haskell was elected president of the corporation and encouraged all to pitch in: the city, the town of Cortlandville, and the utility companies. The town established a water district for the new Trinity plant and NYS Electric & Gas provided power facilities. The next project was to entice Cary & Co. to remain in Cortland. After 30 years, the firm was becoming discouraged, was receiving offers from all over the country, and planning to relocate to the south. The CCDC obtained land and influenced them to build a new factory. The biggest coup for the CCDC was S-CM, with three plants in the Cortland area employing 4,000. The CCDC acquired the land and, working with the city and town, provided utilities and a sewage system for the large South Cortland plant. The fifth project was to assist the State Conservation

Department in its plans to build a new regional office building. The overall development of business in Cortland was nothing short of stunning.

The NYS Department of Commerce joined in with saluting Cortland. In its September issue of "Business in New York State," Commissioner Keith S. McHugh stressed the work done by development corps, the only organizations eligible to receive loans for industrial expansion under the $100 million New York Job Development Authority program. Haskell and the CCDC were cited as an example of the state's "outstanding development corporations."

Even outstanding development corporations can have their setbacks. In the summer of 1958, the CCDC had expended $8,938.19 to extend a waterline from the water district in the Town of Cortlandville to the S-CM plant. It was thought at the time that the water district would be extended and that the money, less depreciation, would be repaid. As of the end of September 1962, that had not come to pass. This was one of three points Haskell made in his letter to stockholders of CCDC dated October 1, 1962. Secondly, Haskell thanked the stockholders for investing in the CCDC, which he said meant "you were investing in the future of Cortland County." In his concluding paragraph, he announced, "I am voluntarily retiring as President this year and I can only express my deep appreciation for the privilege which has been mine to serve your corporation and the community."

While he was stepping down from a leadership role, Haskell was not relinquishing participation in the CCDC. He would continue as a director of the CCDC. As outgoing president of the Cortland County Chamber of Commerce, Morris Noss was elected to succeed Haskell as CCDC president at the annual stockholders meeting on October 15. At this meeting, Haskell gave credit to Noss for the success of the Chris-Craft industrial promotion project. It was noted, too, that stockholders would receive the usual dividend of 2 percent per share, according to the annual statement.

Attracting new business to a community is one thing; getting them to remain is another matter, especially if demographics, the work ethic, or economies change. That became apparent in an editorial by *The Journal and Courier* of Groton, NY, published on October 5, 1962, in the *Cortland Standard.* The piece was drawing attention to a warning from S-CM executive John Wilson that the business was contending with a labor shortage. An inadequate labor force for the night shift had meant going as far as a 75-mile radius of Cortland, including Pennsylvania, to get enough workers for two plants in Cortland and one in Groton. A high rate of absenteeism—200 per day—was unreasonable. S-CM was cited as the largest employer in Central New York outside of Cornell University. One of every six families in Cortland County had a member or relative working for S-CM. The labor problem was a sign of things to come.

Once the personal computer replaced the typewriter as a "word processor" and cheaper labor could be found in Mexico, S-CM would depart, and Cortland would no longer be "the typewriter capital of the world." Once small dairy farms in the county began to decline in number and big "agri-business" firms emerged with huge herds of cows being milked around the clock, the number one employer in the county was destined to be "the college up on the hill."

Another issue that a community cannot afford to ignore is accessible parking near its shopping venues. The lack of parking was addressed by Haskell and fourteen business leaders in mid-February of 1963. Together they formed a new corporation to be known as Cortland Park and Shop, Inc. Its purpose was "to improve parking in downtown Cortland and thus increase shopping . . . downtown." Each of the fourteen business leaders made substantial purchases of stock to form an operation similar to those in other communities being counseled at the time by the National Parking Association. Haskell and others committed their own time and money to addressing areas where Cortland could be made better.

The wisdom of an "elder statesman" in industrial growth was often valued by Haskell's counterparts in other communities. Richard F. Torrey was the executive assistant to Syracuse Mayor Donald Mead. In 1958 Torrey began his career at Niagara Mohawk. Thirty years later, he retired as senior vice president. He served on numerous bank, college, insurance company and hospital boards, and economic development agencies. Philanthropy and fund-raising were hallmarks of Torrey's life. On February 28, 1963, Torrey sent Haskell a typed letter, thanking him for thoughtful comments made in writing about an award Torrey had recently received. "And you, Al," he wrote, "are among those whose friendship in the business world I have treasured. After each visit we have had, I always felt I had learned something from listening to you."

In late May 1963 Haskell received a second ring upon his gold ground-breaking shovel. The first one was for the S-CM plant; this one was for Chris-Craft's Corsair plant. He was presented the ring by the Board of Directors at the conclusion of a tour of the plant's layout—a preview of an open house planned for the public in June.

For Haskell, November 4, 1963, was a significant day. He and others gathered for the closing of the mortgage on the Trinity manufacturing building by the CCDC to the Cortland Savings Bank. It must have felt like "mission accomplished" for Haskell and the CCDC. Three days later, the accomplishment and Haskell's guidance as CCDC president were cited in a *Cortland Standard* editorial with an appropriate heading: "Did the Impossible."

In retrospect, there is no question the task facing Haskell and the CCDC in the last half of the 1950s was a daunting one. How do you go about selling your community to a large organization as a potential spot for building? You must convince them that you have a place in which they will prosper and where a good business climate exists. You must point out that Cortland is in the center of New York State and within easy access to the great industrial centers of the Northeast via good highways and a railway. Of prime importance is an abundant water supply. So, you point out that the water department is capable of supplying close to 15 million gallons per day, when its peak consumption does not presently exceed 3 million per day. You must convince them that there is an adequate labor pool in the area with a ready supply of skilled workers, without a large annual turnover. You must finally convince them that they are wanted by the community and that their employees will be welcomed and be happy. For sure, it was not an easy task, but obviously Haskell and his allies had the facts and the salesmanship skills needed to pull it off. They had faith in themselves and in each other.

Chapter 18

A Man of Faith

While Haskell clearly had faith in himself and in others, there was no doubt he had faith in his God which kept him centered in challenging times. He was a life-long communicant of St. Mary's Roman Catholic Church on North Main Street, Cortland, which was a short walk from his home on Charles Street. And while he did not "wear his religion on his sleeve," neither did he feel inclined to hide it.

As if it were not enough to be a member of Elks, Rotary, Moose, Eagles, Cortland Grange, Volunteer Firemen of Cortland County, Cortland County Federation of Sportsmen's Clubs, and the Preble Rod and Gun Club, Haskell found time to be the president of the Holy Name Society of St. Mary's Church and deputy grand knight of the Cortland Council 233 of the Knights of Columbus. Add in all the meetings of the Cortland County Bar Association, Cortland Chamber of Commerce, Cortland County Development Corporation, and the local Republican Party, among others, and one has to wonder if he ever took a meal at home with his family.

One of the earliest clubs Haskell joined was the Cortland Elks, and the menu for a Valentine's Day Dinner in 1918 consisted of olives, celery hearts, pickles; Roast Hoover Chicken and escalloped potatoes; buttered rolls and pepper sandwiches; shrimp salad; doughnuts and assorted nuts; fromage and diable; cigars and cigarettes. Entertainment included Dillon's Orchestra and Cole's Jazz Band songs for group singing, such as "Good-bye Broadway, Hello France" and "A Stein Song" with this lyric: "For it's always fair weather, when good fellows get together, With a stein on the table and a good song ringing clear."

But Haskell believed "man cannot live by bread alone," and that the soul needed nurturing, too. Thus, he regularly attended Mass and received Communion. He, also, believed that "faith without works is dead." Thus, during his lifetime, Haskell gave abundantly of his time, talent, treasure, and advice in support of the faith community in Cortland and in the Diocese of Syracuse, New York.

At Central High and in the early years of his professional career, he found he had a God-given talent at public speaking and was asked to be a toastmaster or the main speaker for a variety of organizations during his life. In 1940, he was toastmaster for the second annual banquet of The Holy Name Society of St. Mary's held at Hotel Cortland. Even into the 1950s, he was seen at head tables. At the St. Patrick's Day Banquet in 1953 sponsored by the Holy Name Society of St. Mary's Haskell was toastmaster.

The St. Patrick's Day Banquet of St. Mary's Church in 1955 was one for the history books. The event, with Haskell as toastmaster, was a sell-out. Four hundred attended at the San Rocco Lodge and were entertained by the noted harpist, dancer, and pantomimist Patrick Mcgrady of McGraw. Haskell introduced Father Herbert J. Clancy, chair of LeMoyne College's History and Political Science Department, who spoke on "St. Patrick and World Peace." "As the vigorous Christianity of St. Patrick conquered paganism in the 5th century," said the Jesuit, "so that same spirit must conquer atheistic Communism in our 20th century." The memorable evening saw Haskell calling upon Alonzo McAleer who was celebrating his own birthday as well as St. Patrick's. The septuagenarian remarked with a twinkle in his eye, "until this moment I've enjoyed a happy birthday." Then he proceeded to regal the crowd with a World War I song and a bit of harmonica music.

One of Haskell's last St. Patrick's Day toastmaster events was sponsored by the Holy Name Society of St. Mary's Church and held in the new school cafeteria. The next day's *Cortland Standard* reported that "Mr. Haskell reminisced about his feelings of Ireland and her people." He had observed that "The Irish are scattered all over the world. But wherever they might be, they get together on St. Paddy's Day to think about Ireland and the Irish people. When I think about Ireland, I think of the land of lakes and dells, the land of the fairies, and the humor, the poetry, the beauty of the Irish folk." But Haskell stressed that the greatest characteristic of the Irish people was their deep and abiding faith in God.

Besides taking on leadership roles in the greater Cortland community, Haskell accepted leadership of the Holy Name Society of his church. A Lenten Bulletin dated February 8, 1940, listed him as the Society's president and Father Paul Martineau as Spiritual Director. There were 405 members at the time, but only 150 had paid dues the year before. Paying dues was not required to be a member of this all-male organization that attended mass periodically as a group and followed up with a breakfast. The goal of the Society was to provide a forum for all men of the parish, young and old, to meet, to express love of Christ together, and to "better serve our God, our community and our Country." It was meant to provide good fellowship and mutual assistance to "make life's burden a little easier." Hallmarks of the group were prayers, moral support, and financial assistance. A member was expected to be an ambassador for his religion, by example, and to stand together with all members to show the world that religion is a vital and necessary part of daily existence. Haskell took this charge seriously.

Evidence of this is the early relationship he established with Le Moyne College, a private Jesuit college in Syracuse, New York. Founded by the Society of Jesus in 1946 and named after Jesuit missionary Simon Le Moyne, the four-year institution of higher learning was the first co-educational Jesuit college in the United States. The October 7, 1948, issue of *The Catholic Sun* was the Le Moyne College Dedication issue. Congratulations were extended by Diocesan clerics, Governor Thomas E. Dewey, Syracuse Mayor Frank J. Costello, Senator Robert F. Wagner, and businesses of Syracuse. One article listed the civic leaders of Syracuse and the area that served on Le Moyne's Board of Lay Regents, providing "assistance, counsel, and advice." Haskell was listed among the seventeen men (no women).

Sunday, June 10, 1951, was an historic day. Le Moyne College had its first commencement. Two hundred sixty-five students graduated, receiving degrees in the arts, science, social studies, industrial relations, and business administration, at the State Fair Coliseum. Four thousand were in attendance. The event was forced indoors by a day long rain. The next day's Syracuse *Herald-American* showed a photograph of Albert Haskell as part of the Jesuit college's Board of Regents seated in attendance at the graduation in academic regalia. By 1959, he would be the president of the 20-member Board of Advisory Regents at Le Moyne College.

Haskell gave of his largesse, as well, to Le Moyne College. He was listed as a patron in the program for the Le Moyne College Guild's annual building fundraising event. The event featured famed TV personality Ed Sullivan in person and his "Toast of the Town Revue" on Monday evening, November 16, 1953, in the Syracuse War Memorial Auditorium. The next year, in early July, Haskell received a typed letter signed by Mrs. H. Paul Nelligan on letterhead of Easy Washing Machine Corporation of Syracuse thanking him for his most generous gift to the Nelligan Hall Fund. Nelligan Hall was built in 1955 and is the oldest dormitory on the Le Moyne College campus today. It was remodeled in 2019.

Around the time Haskell emceed a 1952 Armistice Day Banquet at the American Legion Hall on Grant Street in Cortland, he was called upon to be one of several speakers at a surprise party at the Shamrock Inn restaurant in Cortland for Bob Martin. This was to honor Martin's 20th year of coaching St. Mary's football. The guest speaker was none other than James Harold "Sleepy Jim" Crowley, one-fourth of the University of Notre Dame's legendary "Four Horsemen" from 1922 to 1924.

Cortland's Knights of Columbus sent out notification cards that November 30, 1952, was the date set for a communion breakfast and memorial service for deceased members of Cortland Council 233. Speakers during the ritual service would be chaplain Rev. Joseph Delahunt and Attorney Albert Haskell.

An item Haskell placed in his scrapbook is interesting for its "tetch of gentle ribbing." It is a letter dated August 2, 1953, from Edward E. Blodgett of Ithaca, New York, who apparently had attended a gathering where Haskell gave the invocation, since the letter begins with "As a chaplain, you done fine! It makes me suspect that you somehow missed your calling. (Auld Fayther Haskell, we calls him. . . !)" A postscript at the end asks for "curb-stone advice." He asked if it is legal to commission two Cortland funeral directors to be "going cahoots on a single corpse?" He explained, "Out of sheer appreciation for yesterday, I somehow feel that I should make Earle [W. Wright] a down payment, and tell him to drift around and get me—come time. Heretofore, I'd had the thought blocked off for John McEvoy, on account of his sense of humor; it'll take one for the likes of me!" And Blodgett closed with a smiley face.

Another letter dated November 27, 1953, arrived from Rt. Rev. Msgr. Joseph B. Toomey, Director of Diocesan Charities and Welfare, Syracuse, New York. Toomey was advising Haskell that he was selected to be a member of the Board of Catholic Charities at a meeting held June 23, 1953. The motion was made by Bishop Foery and seconded by the Hon. Francis D. McCurn [prominent lawyer and judge] and unanimously adopted. When you have a reputation for being a kingpin in economic development, everyone calls upon you for service or funds.

In 1954, Haskell contributed fifty dollars to the development of the Jesuits' Christ the King Retreat House in Syracuse, but it was not only his religious denomination that benefitted from him. In June of that year, Martha R. Lawrence, secretary of the Board of Trustees of the First Baptist Church, Church Street, Cortland, sent Haskell a letter expressing "sincere thanks to you for all your work in the Williams case." Whatever service was rendered by Haskell, the letter indicated the Board felt "it was more than kind of you to do all this work without payment" and "it means so much to both Mr. Williams and the church to have this matter adjusted in correct legal form." In the same year, a letter came from the Cortland Assembly of God Board thanking Haskell for legal services provided and "for your generosity in giving of your time so freely to us."

Also, in June of 1954, when Haskell was four months away from launching a Community Chest Drive, he was the general chairman of St. Mary's Parish Development Fund, a campaign to raise $300,000 for the construction of a gymnasium-auditorium-social center annex to the school. The official launching of the campaign was at a kick-off dinner held in the church's parish hall at 1 p.m. on Sunday, June 6. Haskell announced that advanced gifts of around $25,500 had been donated to the Fund and that the general solicitation would begin immediately. The guest speaker was Monsignor Martin J. Watley, former assistant pastor of the parish and at the time Director of the Propagation of the Faith in the Diocese of Syracuse. Watley warned that the burden of the campaign rested on the 200 men participating in the parish canvas. Haskell concurred and noted, "We are marked men, but marked with a badge of distinction. We go out today to inaugurate the largest parish campaign ever undertaken in the city of Cortland, for the privilege of giving our children the very best we can provide." Plans called for a two-story addition that would have a regulation basketball court with folding bleachers seating 900 spectators, a stage, a meeting hall, and a kitchen. There would be a public entrance on Charles Street, the street where Haskell lived. In the basement level would be a shower, lockers, and sanitary facilities. At the time, 450 children attended the school, and 90 were of high school age.

The second Roman Catholic parish in the city of Cortland was and still is St. Anthony's Church. On Sunday, October 24, 1954, St. Anthony's Church Hall hosted a Holy Name Society Father and Son Communion Breakfast. A special treat was the presence of Carmen Basilio of Canastota, New York, the famous New York State welterweight boxing champion and number one contender for the world title. Basilio received communion at the 7:45 a.m. Mass and spoke during the breakfast that followed, along with Haskell, who was also presented a life membership in St. Anthony's Holy Name Society. The next day's newspaper had a photo showing Carmen Basilio signing autographs at the event for the young boys in attendance.

It is difficult to grasp how a man as busy as Haskell could find time to attend retreats at Christ the King in Syracuse. Yet, he received a certificate dated November 1, 1954, showing he had made ten retreats and was hereby proclaimed a Knight of Christ the King. He must have thrived on being active, for he was forever engaged in fund-raising activities, and the press covered them.

The *Cortland Standard* from December 3, 1954, announced Haskell was to head the Cortland County division of a seven-county Syracuse Diocese fund committee. $750,000 was the goal set for two construction projects: St. Pius X Hall, a home for aged and infirm priests, and a much-needed new chancery office building in Syracuse. Bishop Walter A. Foery made the announcement. Anthony A. Henninger, former Syracuse industrialist, was named the campaign chairman for Onondaga County. The chancery at the time had been built as the residence of Bishop Grimes and was never intended to serve as diocesan office space. As of late 1954, aged priests were at Loretto Rest, in private homes, and in hospitals. A new facility would be connecting with Loretto Rest and accommodating twenty priests. Bishop Foery sent Haskell two letters. One thanked him for accepting the campaign work, and the second was an invitation to a luncheon at Hotel Syracuse to discuss the progress of the campaign. By March 6, 1955, four of the seven counties of the Diocese of Syracuse had already reported success far in excess of their quotas for the construction of the two diocesan facilities: Oswego, Oneida, Madison, and, of course, Haskell's Cortland County.

If one is a life-long member of a Catholic parish, one is apt to be pastored by a succession of priests in that parish. Haskell had such an experience. He saw priests come and go at St. Mary's Church in Cortland, and, of course, a departing priest merited a send-off. That was the case on December 13, 1954. Two hundred fifty parishioners of St. Mary's braved bad winter driving conditions to bid farewell to Rev. Lawrence I. Horan, who had served them for fourteen years. Haskell, as the Master of Ceremonies, presented Fr. Horan a check in excess of $1,200 and spoke of the pastor's many accomplishments in the parish during World War II and the Korean War years. Horan's departure was part of a shuffling of priests. Fr. Stapleton from St. Margaret's in Homer was going to Fr. May's place in Oswego as he was transferring to St. Mary's, and Fr. Francis Walters from Oxford was being assigned to Homer. Three days later, St. Mary's new priest, Fr. George H. May, was the honored guest at a testimonial dinner on the occasion of his 29th anniversary of the ordination in the priesthood, along with Fr. John Quirk. The event was held at the Knights of Columbus Home in Cortland. Haskell saved the printed program. On the back, notes were jotted down for his comments that evening on "what a priest means to a Catholic man."

In mid-May of 1955, Haskell received a letter from Leonard P. Markert, Vice-President of Will & Baumer Candle Co., Inc. of Syracuse, acknowledging that Haskell had completed the balance of his pledged contribution for the construction of Le Moyne's Nelligan Hall. Markert made an accurate assessment of Haskell: "What you have done down through the years in helping causes is outstanding—it is outstanding not only because of the dollars represented, but of the great dedication behind all of your work."

Another recognition of Haskell's work on behalf of Le Moyne College came at the college's sixth commencement in June 1956. 145 graduated at the Syracuse War Memorial auditorium, and Haskell was one of four to receive an honorary doctorate degree—Doctor of Laws. Another recipient was the Most Rev. David F. Cunningham, Auxiliary Bishop of Syracuse. Haskell proudly placed in his scrapbook the citation read upon the conferral of his honorary degree and the official color photo portrait of him in academic regalia and the doctoral hood awarded by Le Moyne. He, also, included congratulatory messages from the Mayor of Cortland and his longtime Rotarian friend from Homer, Will Crandall.

In addition, there was a congratulatory note from Syracusan Raymond G. Castle, the regional manager for the New York State Department of Commerce and a Rotarian. Castle's note included this statement:

> I doubt if the people in Cortland will ever realize the tremendous amount of work and effort that you have been putting forth in recent months on behalf of the people of Cortland. However, I know that you are doing this because of your great love for Cortland and certainly not with the expectation of any reward.

Yet, one more typed congratulatory note came from Haskell's fellow lawyer and Rotarian Lee Taylor of the law firm of Fitzgerald & Taylor dated January 24, 1958. On behalf of the Cortland County Bar Association, Taylor wanted Haskell to know that the "service to the community [in the past two years] has brought a great deal of good will to the CCBA. You certainly exemplify the outstanding lawyer of our Bar."

In another scrapbook was inserted a letter of August 18, 1958, from Father O'Brien of St. Mary's, Cortland:

> Dear Mr. Haskell,
>
> You will be very pleased, I know, to hear that your friends at Cornell University donated quite a bit of football equipment to St. Mary's. This action was brought about through your gracious intervention on our behalf. I wish to extend the sincere thanks of everyone here at St. Mary's to you for your great kindness. If everyone were as kind, generous and hard working as you our work would be much easier. Although I am leaving St. Mary's . . . I shall always remember you & your kindness.

Once again, the Diocese of Syracuse entered upon a fundraising campaign. This time the appeal was for a new interior for the 116-year-old Cathedral of the Immaculate Conception in downtown Syracuse. And once again, Haskell was prevailed upon to lend his reputable services. A typed letter dated September 25, 1958, from the Most Reverend Walter A. Forey, D.D., Bishop of Syracuse, invited Haskell to lunch at the grand ballroom of Hotel Syracuse with him and "other Friends of Cathedral."

Schools and colleges are forever having to upgrade their physical plants. Thus, it was in 1960 that Haskell served on Le Moyne College's next building fund campaign. The press pictured him at a head table with four others: the Very Rev. Robert F. Grewen, president of the college; James D. Heffernan; Leonard P. Markert; and Msgr. Robert Dillon.

Le Moyne College was not the only post-secondary institution to receive Haskell's attention. The college in his own backyard, Cortland College, had Catholic students in attendance, and the Cortland Newman Foundation included Haskell. Catholic students attended Mass at St. Mary's, but it was decided that it would be more convenient if they had a place for worship and spiritual needs closer to the campus. Thus, in November of 1961, a Catholic Center near the college campus was planned by the Newman Foundation.

The Newman Center, as it was called, first came into existence at the building purchased in 1962 at 48 Clayton Avenue in Cortland. Later on, a new Newman Center would arise on Calvert Street near the campus, and in the 1960s its popular and intellectual chaplain was Fr. Edward J. O'Heron. Haskell and O'Heron enjoyed a close friendship. Haskell included in his scrapbook an undated, typed letter on Newman Foundation of Cortland letterhead from Father O'Heron. Addressed to "Dear Friend," the letter expressed gratitude for "the generous outpouring of time and talent and financial help" for bringing a Catholic center to fruition, for "bringing Christ to the campus," and for "providing the Catholic students with a spiritual home away from home." O'Heron added by hand at the bottom: "Many thanks for everything, Al. I must say that I've gotten quite a 'liberal education' in the last few months."

Haskell and his wife Mildred were known to invite the young priest to the Haskell cottage on Little York Lake for dinner and some summertime recreation and respite from the toils of the Newman Center. This was at a time when Haskell's grandchildren—Haskells and Sweeneys—were invited to enjoy some summer days at the cottage, too. One of the Haskell grandchildren, Joe Haskell Jr. expressed amazement at seeing Fr. O'Heron waterskiing and other priests normally clad in black garb wearing only trunks, swimming, and enjoying Manhattans and beer. Joe remembered another priest who was very tall and very heavy; the boat could not get this priest up out of the water to do water skiing. Indeed, young Joe discovered that priests "out of uniform" were human beings, too.

As noted, Haskell was quite ecumenical in the distribution of his time, talent, and treasure. Further evidence of this characteristic is his involvement with the establishment in 1964 of an Interfaith Center near the State University College at Cortland campus. Not affiliated with the state or the college, the Center was to be directed by representatives of the Jewish, Roman Catholic, and Protestant faiths. It was to house offices for the chaplains of the three faiths, a religious library, classrooms for teaching religious courses, social rooms, a secretary's office, a residence room for a caretaker, and a small chapel for worship and prayer. In February 1964, the Center received a gift of $14,000 from the McDonald Foundation of Hastings, Nebraska.

James McDonald was one of the founders of the J.C. Penny Company. Upon retirement, he made his home at 60 Tompkins Street, Cortland. Upon his death, the college inherited his home and $100,000. The building was used as an infirmary for a while. The goal for the Interfaith Center was $150,000. The McDonald Foundation pledged a total of $21,000. The remainder was to come from an appeals campaign directed at students, faculty, alumni, parents, and the townspeople. The latter appeal was made by nine local residents, and Haskell was one of them.

As with any organization, a church can be subject to financial difficulties and political nuance. St. Mary's Church was not immune. By 1964, its pastor, Fr. George May, decided to call a meeting of a committee to discuss church financing. In attendance on March 2 was James Yaman, William Pauldine, Mary Alice Bellardini, Vincent Moore, Dr. Joseph Mack, and Daniel McNeil. Mr. Robert Fanning was unable to attend, but he concurred with a summary submitted by the committee to Fr. May.

Before a successful parish financial campaign can be launched, reported the committee, an effort must be made to improve the overall parish morale and attitudes of the laity. The committee offered a plan, the formation of three committees: Finance, Church, and School. All three would work in cooperation with the pastor. The Finance Committee would be responsible for general fiscal management. The Church Committee would handle Sunday bulletins, general maintenance, ushering, and social functions. The School Committee was "to cooperate with the school administration to bring about the best possible program for the children of the Parish." To coordinate the three committees, there would be an Executive Board [or Parish Council] of six or eight members, among which would be the chairs of the three main committees and the church trustees. The summary noted that this endeavor was seen as a "general means whereby greater rapport can be established between Church and laity" and relieve some burdens of over-worked priests. This was the time, too, when the Second Vatican Council was meeting (autumns of 1962 through 1965) and consideration was starting to be given to increasing the role of the laity in the administration of parish churches. As a trustee of St. Mary's Church, Haskell received a carbon copy of the three-page letter sent to Fr. May which included the list of suggestions made by the group May had called to the Parish House on March 2 to discuss church financial problems.

Since the committee also called attention to a need for an "improvement of general parish morale and attitudes of the laity" and singled out the pastor for the cause of some of the malaise, Fr. May must have taken offense and threatened to take the matter to the bishops in Syracuse. Haskell tactfully and diplomatically reasoned with the pastor and urged him to reconsider and to not take it beyond the parish level. Haskell wrote that the committee's directness was "a little unusual" but pointed out that the members were "interested, sincere and are anxious to help you to work out any parish problems and after all, you did call them in, as you did the trustees. . . ." Haskell stated, "You have given eleven of the best years of your life to the people at St. Mary's. May God grant you many more years of health and strength to remain with the people at St. Mary's."

Then, being more direct, Haskell offered his assessment of the situation in the parish. Members of the younger generation have been "a little more critical of parish affairs than the old timers. This is probably a good sign."

Also, "You . . . have found out for the first time the criticism of some of the laity." Haskell admitted hearing some criticism about the school, and he noted being aware of "some criticism of long sermons and sometimes an intemperate remark creeps into the sermon which disturbs many parishioners." There were complaints calling for more formal ushering at communion time during Mass. Objections had been raised about the taking up of collection at the 12:10 p.m. daily Mass during Lent and the numerous envelopes sent out for financing the parish. "But none of these criticisms are catastrophic," Haskell quickly noted. "You are capable of handling this problem and I can't see any need or reason for it going outside the parish."

Haskell offered to have the committee's letters withdrawn, and he advised "the school problem" to wait until summer "when the new Mother comes to Cortland." Showing skill at crisis management, Haskell continued, "Let me humbly suggest that we have a cooling-off period until after Easter" when the pastor could set up an advisory financial committee to "attack this financial problem and solve it for once and all." Then, he closed with these words: "I am proud to be a Trustee of St. Mary's Church under your able leadership. . . . Should the time come when you want to put in a younger and more vigorous man, I shall be glad to honor your request for my resignation." What a carefully worded and insightful document. Haskell confronted the issue but suggested in true lawyerly fashion ways for resolution and indicated that if Father May was displeased with his unsolicited message, then he could feel free to fire the messenger.

As a man of faith who loved to go boating on his beloved Little York Lake, Haskell could probably agree with the philosophical advice once offered by the American journalist Hunter S. Thompson on how to handle life's adversities: "Call on God, but row away from the rocks."

Epilogue

On the morning of September 21, 1964, six days after his 72nd birthday, the earthly life of Albert Haskell Jr. came to an end. The *Cortland Standard* announced he had died at his home. That afternoon at 4:30 p.m. the Cortland Bar Association held a memorial service in the Courthouse for the "dean of the Bar."

Joe Haskell Jr., was 12 years old when his grandfather passed. He served as an altar boy at the requiem Mass at St. Mary's. As he recalled, this was no ordinary funeral service. Mass was offered by the bishop and attended by "every priest in the Diocese." Internment was at St. Mary's Cemetery.

At such an intensely sad time, memories surface. Joe Jr. thought back about the man he called "Grandpa." He could vividly recall the time he had used his grandfather's favorite fishing pole to catch a perch on Little York Lake. The pole broke. His father, Joe Sr, made him call his grandfather to report what he had done. Would his grandfather be angry? Tearfully, Joe Jr. phoned. His grandfather heard him out and responded, "Just tell me one thing. Did you catch the fish?" Recalled, too, was the story Joe had heard of the time when the Haskell boys—his father and his Uncle Charlie—broke the windows in the Little York Park pavilion. When Albert Haskell found out, he called the sheriff and had the two boys carted off to the jail for an overnight. Nowadays, it would be said that Haskell practiced "tough love" to teach his sons a lesson they would not soon forget. And, undoubtedly, they had to work to pay for the glass replacement. Neither was young Joe going to forget the time he and a cousin helped themselves to their grandfather's fine cigars. Grandfather caught them. He promptly made them sit down and to continue puffing on the Robert Burns panatelas until they were gone. The experience left the boys green around the gills and convinced they were not quite ready for cigar-smoking.

Children remember pets. Joe Jr. would later recall his grandfather had a playful black cat with a white spot named "Peener." And there was a dog, too, a beautiful English Spaniel called "Pudgie." Joe remembered how sad his grandfather was when "Pudgie" died and that his grandfather buried her on their property. The canine was very friendly but liked to stay close to its master. Is there anything one can discern of a man's character from his dog? According to W. Bruce Cameron, author of *A Dog's Journey,* "You can usually tell that a man is good if he has a dog who loves him."

What Haskell's grandchildren would remember most were the times they would be riding along in the backseat (no car seats then) of one of grandfather's luxurious Cadillacs with the window down and him smoking a cigar. He changed cars every year or two—always a black or white Cadillac purchased from Briggs Cadillac on Main Street in Homer. Those were carefree times. Life was good.

Of course, Haskell was eulogized in death, but the best "eulogies" were those made in his presence the year before at a Rotary meeting and, more significantly, just eight months before his passing at the timely grand testimonial dinner in his honor put on by three organizations: the Cortland Chamber of Commerce, its Retail Merchants Bureau, and the Homer Chamber of Commerce.

At the March 5, 1963, Rotary meeting Haskell heard his life summed up this way:

> Your full and colorful life has been one of excitement, adventure, strong community loyalty from the day you opened your practice of law. . . . You have on many occasions said that Cortland County has been good to you . . . and that you shall never be able to repay your community for what it has done for you. Let it also be noted here and now that you have given generously to [the] community, and that Cortland County, and its good people, shall remain forever grateful for all your outstanding contributions. Although you have enjoyed great success in many fields and in personal comforts, you have never forgotten the little man. You know the sting of tragedy, as well as the feeling of joy and satisfaction. All these experiences in your many fields of endeavor have made you an outstanding personality, . . . a fine and great gentleman.

This raises a question posed by biographers of great individuals: Is it the events that make the (wo)man or the (wo)man that makes the events? In Haskell's case, it appears very much to have been both. He had a personality that was driven to seize opportunities to make things happen for his community and region, and the things he made happen shaped and reinforced that strong personality that strived to accomplish even greater things. This was borne out by the three main speakers at the banquet in Haskell's honor on Saturday evening, January 25, 1964, in St. Mary's school cafeteria.

Theodore Fenstermacher spoke first of Haskell's career in law and politics. He quoted Oliver Wendell Holmes: "A man should live to serve the action and passion of his times." Fenstermacher pointed out that when Haskell graduated from law school and passed the bar exam in 1916, the times saw the rise of the corporation lawyer, "calling for a new, soulless kind of skill," but Haskell [chose to return to his small town] where he could "merge his 19th century humanitarian approach to the law with the disciplined skill of a modern solicitor."

Next on the program to speak was the President of Le Moyne College, the Very Reverend Nicholas J. Sullivan, S. J. He said, "I never meet Albert Haskell that I don't feel a little bit better. . . . All the good things he does are rooted in religious convictions." He commented that Haskell was about "humanizing society" and the strong role religion played in Haskell's life could not be separated from his other contributions to community life. Appropriately, the event was ecumenical: The invocation was given by a priest, the Rev. George May of St. Mary's; a minister, the Rev. Gordon W. Carver, president of the Cortland County Council of Churches was called to speak; and a rabbi, Sidney Strulovicci of Temple Brith Sholom, offered the closing benediction.

The third to offer a "eulogy" was Morris Noss, president of the CCDC. He spoke of Haskell's countless contributions to civic, business, and industrial affairs of the community. He noted that Haskell was a charter member of the local Rotary Club and lived up to the motto of Rotary, "Service Above Self." He listed all the industrial developments Haskell had been involved in and explained that in all of these developments, men felt inspired by Haskell because he developed a feeling of trust and friendship in the room of participants—"a feeling of men believing each other and liking each other." Noss claimed it was a personal victory for Haskell to witness the recent repayment of the stockholders of the CCDC.

After all the tributes, Haskell was handed a plaque, made exclusively in Cortland, and presented "for dedicated service to his community. . . ." In addition, Haskell received from Veterans of Foreign Wars Post 2354 their annual Citizenship Award. Indeed, the testimonial dinner was fit for a king.

The testimonial tribute was not just for a man who was a leader in the fields of law, religion, business, and industry but for a man who was also a husband, father, and grandfather. The largest table in the room was filled with the Haskell patriarch's children and grandchildren. Joe and Barbara Haskell had five children: Jim, Tom, Joe Jr., Connie, and Mary Ann. Bob and Jean Haskell Sweeney had eleven children: Shaun, Robert Jr, Gary, Colleen, Diane, Michael, Linda, Patrick, Margaret, Maureen, and William. The deceased Charles Haskell had two children present: Robert and Elizabeth. Haskell's wife Mildred was not overlooked. A tiny charm was presented for her charm bracelet. Noss said the bracelet now had seven charms representative of her husband's countless achievements.

The guest of honor was expected to offer commentary next, and Haskell did not disappoint. Like a well-prepared lawyer, with three sheets of handwritten comments on yellow legal pad to guide him, he gave what would be his last major public talk:

> It is with mixed emotions that I express our appreciation for this wonderful evening. . . . I would not be human without feeling some sense of pride and gratitude at these laudatory remarks—but somehow I also have a feeling of deep humility and doubt as to whether any individual is worthy of the tributes I have heard here tonight. . . . all this wonderful community and helpful spirit started with the War Bond drives around 1917 or 18. Then came the service clubs—breaking down barriers of race, religion, and indifference to our fellow man. [Many who shared in the common goal of] making our community and state and nation a better place [in which] to live have passed away—but tonight somehow it seems that their spirit at least is in this room—and they have returned again smiling in memory's mirror. I would be most contented to accept this grand affair as a symbol with others . . . none walk alone. . . .

Five years after his death, the city of Cortland's Common Council decided by a unanimous vote to name a downtown street in Haskell's honor. Haskell Place is parallel to Main Street and connects Orchard Street and West Court Street. Located behind a bank building and Main Street stores, today Haskell Place is little more than an alleyway and hardly seems a fitting memorial for the man who Mayor Morris Noss at the time made this assertion: "Few men have done as much for Cortland as Albert Haskell Jr. His whole life was devoted to Cortland . . . and the people of Cortland don't know a fraction of what he did for the city." Haskell Place is a mere fraction of the lasting kind of tribute merited by Albert Haskell's remarkable life of service. He has earned much more, and not just for his actions and words. According to a quote often attributed to the famous poet and civil rights activist, Maya Angelou, in the end "people will forget what you said, people will forget what you did, but people will never forget how you made them feel." Haskell accomplished much for others because he had a knack for "humanizing society," for making folks feel their input was sincerely valued and that they had a personal stake in seeing a project through to its fruition.

Will the city ever see a lawyer like Haskell again? Maybe. Stranger things have happened. Joe Haskell Jr.'s son Timothy resides in Cortland and is set to earn his law degree in the spring of 2023 from the Syracuse University Law School. A fourth generation Haskell would be welcomed to set up practice in Cortland. He has a superb role model in his great-grandfather.

Actually, Albert Haskell Jr. presents a fine example for everyone on how to relate to others. Theodore Fenstermacher once said about Haskell: "His office was a kingdom where the least sat side by side with the greatest." The large oak desk from Haskell's office is being used today at the Cortland County Historical Society. The artifact is a reminder of when "the Crown City" had a most remarkable and benevolent "King" who modeled how we all should be living in service of others.

Notes

CHAPTER 1

Haskell's birthdate and middle name: Interview of Joseph Haskell Jr., on Labor Day, 2015, on February 22, 2022, and email to author on March 1, 2022.

History of park and pavilion at Dwyer Memorial Park in Preble. "National Register of Historic Places Registration Form: Little York Pavilion" (PDF). Retrieved February 12, 2022.

The song "Sidewalks of New York": Smith, Chrysti M. (2006). "Trip the Light Fantastic," in *Verbivore's Feast: Second Course: More Word & Phrase Origins.* (Farcountry Press: Helena, Montana), 320.

Poem by David Starr Jordan: Biography of poet in "David Starr Jordan '72" (PDF), in *Cornell Alumni News,* I (6): 39, 43 (May 10, 1899). Accessed online on February 12, 2022.

CHAPTER 2

The 1912 split in the Republican Party: Coletta, Paolo Enrico (1973). *The Presidency of William Howard Taft* (Lawrence: University Press of Kansas).

CHAPTER 3

The Dillon Brothers' theatre in Cortland: Information provided by Mindy Leisenring of the Cortland County Historical Society (2018).

Al G. Field: Rice, Edward Le Roy (1911). "Al G. Field," in *Monarchs of Minstrelsy* (New York: Kenny Publishing Company), 214.

Political background on Charles Evans Hughes: Henretta, James A. (Spring 2006). "Charles Evans Hughes and the Strange Death of Liberal America" in *University of Illinois Law and History Review*, Vol. 24, No.1.

1917 Emergency Loan Act: Garbade, Kenneth D. (2012). Birth of a Market: The U.S. Treasury Securities Market from the Great War to the Great Depression (Cambridge, MA: MIT Press), ch. 5.

CHAPTER 4

Major General Ray Barker: See *World War II Graves*, online at https://ww2gravestone.com/people/barker-ray-wehnes/. Accessed February 14, 2022.

"Ted Fenstermacher, a prominent Cortland attorney who served as a chief prosecutor of Nazis field marshals in the Nuremberg war crimes trials following World War II": Persico, Joseph E. (1995). *Nuremberg: Infamy on Trial* (London: Penguin Books), 361, 383, 449. Also, death of Goering: Kershaw, Ian (2008). *Hitler: A Biography* (New York, NY: W. W. Norton & Company), 964.

CHAPTER 5

Izzy Einstein and Moe Smith: Miller, Nathan (2003). *New World Coming: The 1920s and the Making of Modern America.* (New York: Simon and Schuster), 103–4.

CHAPTER 6

The "Black Hand Society": Dash, Mike (2009). *The First Family: Terror, Extortion and the Birth of the American Mafia*. (London: Simon & Schuster).

CHAPTER 7

Early history of homicides in Cortland County: One file on "Hangings" and one on "Murders" in the Cortland County Historical Society's archives. Accessed in August of 2011.

Unsolved 1894 murder of Patrick Quinlan of Homer: Sweeney, Martin A. (2012). *Death in the Winter Solstice: A Narrative of a True Murder Mystery in Homer* (Cortland, NY: Cortland County Historical Society).

1924 murder of John Reale by Eugene Graham: "A Spectacular Murder Trial," in *The Seven-Valley Villager* of April 25, 1963.

CHAPTER 8

Connection of the Ku Klux Klan with Prohibition: Quarles, Chester L. (1999). *The Ku Klux Klan and Other Racialist and Anti-Semitic Organizations: A History and Analysis* (Jefferson, NC: McFarland & Company), 62.

Connection of the Ku Klux Klan with President Harding: Wade, Wyn Craig (1998). *The Fiery Cross: The Ku Klux Klan in America* (New York: Oxford University Press), 165.

Sources used to reconstruct the story of Haskell and the Klan:

Langley, Roger. "The Night the KKK Struck at Marathon," *Syracuse Herald-American*, Sunday, May 2, 1965, 3.

The KKK solicitation card cited is in Haskell's scrapbook along with these articles found in the *Cortland Standard:* 4/10/24, front page; 4/11/24, 2 & 6; 4/12/24, 2; 4/16/24, 2; 4/17/24, 2; 5/2/24, 7; and 5/15/24, 2.

Information in the 1924 *Directory* provided by Mindy Leisenring, Director of the Cortland County Historical Society.

CHAPTER 9

The case of the death of Alton Howe: Photocopies of clippings from Cortland and Syracuse newspapers of 1924 provided by Steve Malchak of Marietta, NY, who owns Alton Howe's Boy Scout uniform.

CHAPTER 10

Brief explanation of tuberculosis in dairy cattle: Grange, John M.; Yates, Malcolm D.; de Kantor, Isabel N. (1996). "Guidelines for speciation within the Mycobacterium tuberculosis complex. Second edition." (World Health Organization PDF). Accessed online February 16, 2022.

CHAPTER 11

Information on Lizzie Halliday: Telfer, Tori (2017). *Lady Killers: Deadly Women Throughout History* (New York: Harper Collins Publishers), 79.

Information on Reddy's sentence: "Reddy Committed to Hospital for Criminally Insane," in a news clipping (unnamed paper) dated November 19, 1926. Provided via email by Tabitha Scoville, Director of Cortland County Historical Society, on January 11, 2022.

CHAPTER 12

History of John S. Draper and the Allen Gang: "Judge T.L. Massie and Two Court Officers Murdered by Allen Gang at Hillsville," in *The Roanoke Times* (March 15, 1912).

The verdict and death of Fred Fadik: Two news clippings provided by Tabitha Scoville, Director of the Cortland County Historical Society on January 13, 2022, from its "Murders" file:

"Fadik Anticipates Verdict By Pleading Manslaughter," in *Cortland Democrat* (June 14, 1929).

Death of Fred Fadik announced in an unnamed newspaper (August 13, 1937).

CHAPTER 13

Death of Haskell's son Jimmie and ensuing dramatic changes in the Haskell household, including death of Regina, wedding of Haskell and Mildred Aungier, and Mildred's death: Interview with Joe Haskell Jr. on December 6, 2018, and on February 22, 2022. Emails from Joe Jr. to the author on February 25, 2022, and March 1, 2022.

Biographical sources for Senator Clifford P. Case of New Jersey and NYS Attorney General Louis Lefkowitz: Wikipedia online. Accessed on January 18, 2022.

Catherwood Library: Catherwood Library website. Accessed January 19, 2022.

It should be noted: Lusk Field House on SUNY College at Cortland campus is named after Clayton R. Lusk.

CHAPTER 14

Milk strikes outside New York State: *New York Times*, for St. Louis: 8 November 1931, 6 and 15 November, 25; for central Illinois: 31 October 1931, 5; for Houston: 15 February 1932, 3; for Sioux Falls, SD: 1 September 1932, 3; for Atlanta: 24 September 1932, 32; 25 September, 16; 27 September, 1; 28 September, 21; 29 September, 15; for Chicago: 17 July 1932, 15; and for Indiana: 20 September 1932, 15.

The Sioux City Milk War: *New York Times*, 14 August 1932, 8; 15 August, 14; 16 August, 2; 18 August, 42; 19 August, 19; 20 August, 28; 21 August, 7; 30 August, 36; and 1 September, 1.

Text of report of the New York State Milk Control Board: New York State, Milk Control Board, (March 1934). *Report of the Milk Control Board to the Governor and the State Legislature* (Albany: J.B. Lyons), 3.

Reporter concluded the 1933 strikes "possibly . . . brought New York State closer to martial law than at any time since the Revolutionary War." *New York Times*, 13 August 1933, Section 4, 1.

Success of the DFU by third day of strike in 1939: *The Union Farmer*, 25 September 1939, 1; Dyson, Lowell K. (1982). *Red Harvest* (Lincoln, NB: University of Nebraska Press), 172–73.

CHAPTER 15

Brief history of the Crusade for Freedom: Cummings, Richard H. (2010). *Radio Free Europe's "Crusade for Freedom"* (Jefferson, NC: McFarland & Company), 2–3.

Transformation of the American Heart Association in 1948: "History of the American Heart Association" (2022). Online at https://www.heart.org/en/about-us/history-of-the-american-heart-association. Accessed February 17, 2022.

Early history of Community Chest: "A Brief History of United Way" (2022). United Way of Tompkins County website at https://www.uwtc.org/brief-history-united-way. Accessed February 17, 2022.

Quote on civic engagement by Robert D. Putnam: Putnam, Robert D. (2001). *Bowling Alone: The Collapse and Revival of American Community* (New York: Simon and Schuster), 58.

CHAPTER 16

Gen. Lucius Clay's quote on need for interstate highway system: Smith, Jean Edward (2012). *Eisenhower in War and Peace* (New York: Random House), 652–53.

CHAPTER 17

Biographical material on Richard F. Torrey of Syracuse: Found on his September 30, 2012 online obituary at https://obits.syracuse.com/us/obituaries/syracuse/name/richard-torrey-obituary?pid=160546385. Accessed February 5, 2022.

CHAPTER 18

Early history of Le Moyne College and its oldest dormitory, Nelligan Hall: Le Moyne College website. Accessed February 12, 2022.

EPILOGUE

Notice of Albert Haskell Jr.'s death: *Cortland Standard,* September 21, 1964.

Albert Haskell Jr.'s funeral Mass and Joe Jr.'s recall of incidents at the Lake and interactions with his grandfather: Interview of Joe Jr. on December 6, 2018, and on February 22, 2022.

Albert Haskell's pets and Cadillacs: Joe Jr. email to the author on February 25, 2022.

Haskell family in attendance at the tribute banquet in 1964: Interview of Joe Jr. on February 22, 2022.

Birth order of Jean Haskell Sweeney's eleven children: Provided by the 11th, William "Bill" Sweeney.

Cortland Common Council's unanimous vote to create Haskell Place to honor Haskell and comments of Mayor Noss: *Cortland Standard,* October 22, 1969.

Maya Angelou's quote on making an impression on people: Chang, Rachel (2020, 2021). "19 Inspirational Maya Angelou Quotes," in *Biography.* Online at https://www.biography.com/news/maya-angelou-quotes. Accessed February 19, 2022.

Theodore Fenstermacher's description of Haskell's office: Conklin, Walt (undated). *Cortland Standard* article describing the testimonial dinner for Haskell on January 25, 1964. Accessed in Haskell scrapbook.

Haskell's oak desk: Was donated by Tom Meldrim to the Cortland County Historical Society.

References

"A Brief History of United Way" (2022). United Way of Tompkins County website at https://www.uwtc.org/brief-history-united-way. Accessed February 17, 2022.

Article on NYS milk strike of 1933. *New York Times*, August 13, 1933, Section 4, 1.

Article on third day of NYS milk strike in 1939. *The Union Farmer*, September 25, 1939, 1.

"A Spectacular Murder Trial," in *The Seven-Valley Villager,* April 25, 1963.

Cameron, W. Bruce (1994). *A Dog's Journey* (New York: Forge Books).

Case, Senator Clifford P. of New Jersey. Obituary online through *The New York Times*. Accessed on January 18, 2022.

Catherwood Library. Catherwood Library website, courtesy of School of Industrial and Labor Relations, Cornell University (Ithaca, NY). Accessed January 19, 2022.

Chang, Rachel (2020, 2021). "19 Inspirational Maya Angelou Quotes," in *Biography.* Online at https://www.biography.com/news/maya-angelou-quotes. Accessed February 19, 2022.

Coletta, Paolo Enrico (1973). *The Presidency of William Howard Taft* (Lawrence, KS: University Press of Kansas).

Cortland Common Council's unanimous vote to create Haskell Place to honor Haskell and comments of Mayor Noss. *Cortland Standard,* October 22, 1969.

Cummings, Richard H. (2010). *Radio Free Europe's "Crusade for Freedom"* (Jefferson, NC: McFarland & Company).

Dash, Mike (2009). *The First Family: Terror, Extortion and the Birth of the American Mafia.* (London: Simon & Schuster).

"David Starr Jordan '72" (PDF), in *Cornell Alumni News*, I (6): 39, 43 (May 10, 1899). Accessed online on February 12, 2022.

Death notice for Albert Haskell Jr. *Cortland Standard,* September 21, 1964.

Dyson, Lowell K. (1982). *Red Harvest* (Lincoln, NB: University of Nebraska Press).

Early history of Le Moyne College and its oldest dormitory, Nelligan Hall. Le Moyne College website. Accessed February 12, 2022.

Garbade, Kenneth D. (2012). *Birth of a Market: The U.S. Treasury Securities Market from the Great War to the Great Depression* (Cambridge, MA: MIT Press).

Grange, John M.; Yates, Malcolm D.; de Kantor, Isabel N. (1996). "Guidelines for speciation within the Mycobacterium tuberculosis complex. Second edition." (World Health Organization PDF). Accessed online February 16, 2022.

"Hangings," file in the Cortland County Historical Society's archives. Accessed in August of 2011.

Haskell, Jr., Albert. Scrapbooks of news clippings, letters, programs, and other ephemera dealing with activities of his life from 1911 to 1964.

Haskell, Jr., Joseph. Interviews and emails from 2018 through 2022.

Henretta, James A. (Spring 2006). "Charles Evans Hughes and the Strange Death of Liberal America." *University of Illinois Law and History Review*, Vol. 24, No. 1.

"History of the American Heart Association." Online at https://www.heart.org/en/about-us/history-of-the-american-heart-association. Accessed February 17, 2022.

"Judge T.L. Massie and Two Court Officers Murdered by Allen Gang at Hillsville," in *The Roanoke Times* (March 15, 1912).

Langley, Roger. "The Night the KKK Struck at Marathon," *Syracuse Herald-American*, Sunday, May 2, 1965.

Lefkowitz, Louis. NYS Attorney General. Obituary online through *The New York Times*. Accessed on January 18, 2022.

Leisenring, Mindy (Director of the Cortland County Historical Society in 2018). Information on the Dillon Brothers' Theatre on Groton Avenue, Cortland, in the early 1900s and information in the Cortland City *Directory of 1924.*

Malchak, Steve of Marietta, NY. Photocopies of news clippings from Cortland and Syracuse newspapers of 1924 on the strange death of Alton Howe.

"Major General Ray Barker," *World War II Graves*, online at https://ww2gravestone.com/people/barker-ray-wehnes/. Accessed February 14, 2022.

Milk strikes outside New York State in 1931 and 1932. *New York Times*, for St. Louis: 8 November 1931, 6 and 15 November, 25; for central Illinois: 31 October 1931, 5; for Houston: 15 February 1932, 3; for Sioux Falls, SD: 1 September 1932, 3; for Atlanta: 24 September 1932, 32; 25 September, 16; 27 September, 1; 28 September, 21; 29 September, 15; for Chicago: 17 July 1932, 15; and for Indiana: 20 September 1932, 15.

Miller, Nathan (2003). *New World Coming: The 1920s and the Making of Modern America* (New York: Simon and Schuster).

"Murders," file in the Cortland County Historical Society's archives. Accessed in August of 2011.

New York State Milk Control Board. *Report of the Milk Control Board to the Governor and the State Legislature* (Albany: J.B. Lyons, March 1934).

"National Register of Historic Places Registration Form: Little York Pavilion" (PDF). Retrieved February 12, 2022.

Persico, Joseph E. (1995). *Nuremberg: Infamy on Trial* (London: Penguin Books).

Putnam, Robert D. (2001). *Bowling Alone: The Collapse and Revival of American Community* (New York: Simon and Schuster).

Quarles, Chester L. (1999). *The Ku Klux Klan and Other Racialist and Anti-Semitic Organizations: A History and Analysis* (Jefferson, NC: McFarland & Company).

Ramsey, William (1906). *A Book of Toasts* (New York: Dodge Publishing Company).

Rice, Edward LeRoy (1911). "Al G. Field," in *Monarchs of Minstrelsy* (New York: Kenny Publishing Company).

Scoville, Tabitha (Director of Cortland County Historical Society in 2022). "Reddy Committed to Hospital for Criminally Insane," news clipping (unnamed paper) dated November 19, 1926, provided via email on January 11, 2022. Also, provided via email on January 13, 2022, two news clippings dated 1929 and 1937 from Society's "Murders" file on the verdict and death, respectively, of Fred Fadik.

Sioux City Milk War. *New York Times*, 14 August 1932, 8; 15 August, 14; 16 August, 2; 18 August, 42; 19 August, 19; 20 August, 28; 21 August, 7; 30 August, 36; and 1 September, 1.

Smith, Chrysti M. (2006). "Trip the Light Fantastic," in *Verbivore's Feast: Second Course: More Word & Phrase Origins*. (Farcountry Press: Helena, Montana).

Smith, Jean Edward (2012). *Eisenhower in War and Peace* (New York: Random House).

Sweeney, Martin A. (2012). *Death in the Winter Solstice: A Narrative of a True Murder Mystery in Homer* (Cortland, NY: Cortland County Historical Society).

Telfer, Tori (2017). *Lady Killers: Deadly Women Throughout History* (New York: Harper Collins Publishers).

Torrey, Richard F. Obituary of September 30, 2012. Online at https://obits.syracuse.com/us/obituaries/syracuse/name/richard-torrey-obituary?pid=160546385. Accessed February 5, 2022.

Wade, Wyn Craig (1998). *The Fiery Cross: The Ku Klux Klan in America* (New York: Oxford University Press).

Index

Page references for figures are italicized.

Adams, A. Carley (judge), 106, 111
Alexander, Glenn (supervisor of the town of Cortlandville), 201
Allen, Ross, 202
Allen Gang, 133–34
American Cancer Society, 174; Friendly Red Door project of Cortland chapter of, 174; Haskell as director of the Cortland chapter of, 174
"The American Flag: Forever Float That Standard Sheet" (poem, 1861), 13
American Heart Association, 174; Haskell as member of New York Heart Assembly of, 174; Haskell's letter to Walter Grunfeld regarding, 174–75
Ames, Morse E. (judge), 140
Angell, H. K. (attorney), 161
Angelou, Maya (American poet), 222
Anson, Fred, 78
Antonuck, Frank, 135–36; charge of murder reduced to manslaughter in death of, 134, 135–36; David Deverick hosts poker game where Fred Fadik stabbed, 135; Haskell represents Fred Fadik charged with murder of, 135, *136*; imprisonment and death of the killer of, 136; John Clinch discovers a severely wounded, 134–35; prisoner John Guy donates blood for, 135
Auburn Prison, 99, 136
Avery, Otis and Margaret, 89

"baby boom," 198, 199
Badger Northland, 181, 198; Massey Ferguson bought out, 198
Baldwin, Charles, 161
Barker, Ray (US major general), 66
Barry, Franklyn S. (superintendent of schools), 200
Bender, Denny, 70
Bennett Hotel in Cincinnatus, NY, 81
billiard parlors in city of Cortland, NY, 6
Birdlebough, M. S., 104
Black Hand Society and Dominick Militona, 82–83; Alexander Carbone and association with, 82–84; Charles Sardo extorted by, 81–82, 83, 84; Haskell's prosecution of, 83–84, 85
A Book of Toasts (1906), 9
Borden's milk, 166, 168

Boyden, U. H., 99
Brewer, Edward A. "Ted," 57
Briggs, John B. (mayor of Homer, NY), 150
Brockway Motor Truck Company, 82
Brown, Ralph Adams, 152
Buckley, Daniel and Mrs., 79–80, 81
Bush, Frank, 78
Butler, Arthur, and Haskell's first trial case, 74–75
Butler, Ralph, 148

Cameron, Fr. Joseph, 50
Cary & Company, 181, 183–84, 205
Cascadilla School in Ithaca, NY, 15
Case, Clifford P. (US senator from New Jersey), 152; Cortland Republican dinner addressed by, 152; political career and voting record of, 152–53; Sen. Joseph McCarthy openly criticized by, 152
Catherwood, Martin P., 154; Haskell and, 154; library in Cornell University's I. L. R. school named after, 154; as New York State Industrial Commissioner, 154; as second Dean of the New York State School of Industrial and Labor Relations at Cornell University, 154
Catholic Diocese of Syracuse, NY, 209, 213–14, 215; Bishop Walter A. Forey, D. D., of, 212, 213, 215; David F. Cunningham, Auxiliary Bishop of, 214; Haskell and, 211, 213, 215
Champlin, George M. (judge), 69, 75, 77, 81, 136, 161
Chase, Levi R. (US Air Force major general), 202
"Chat" (friend of Haskell in S.U. Law School), 30–31, 34, 37–38
Chocolate Shop of Cortland, NY, 49
Chris–Craft Corporation, 203–4, 205, 206, 207; gold ring presented to Haskell for efforts on Corsair plant of, 207; ground–breaking ceremony for, 204; Haskell and acquisition of William Diescher's farmland for, 203–4
Chrisman, Frank W., 78, 83, 104, 111, 122, 130
Christ the King Retreat House in Syracuse, 212, 213; Haskell and, 212, 213
Cincinnatus Chamber of Commerce, 195
Clark, Edward H., 66
Clements, Harold M., 104, 109–10
Coffey, Charles P. "Cabbey," 41
Cold War, 174; Crusade for Freedom Campaign and Haskell during, 174; Radio Free Europe and, 174
Congdon, Grove, 86–87; Clifford Congdon and, 86; Haskell prosecutes child neglect case against, 86–87; Mrs. Congdon testifies in court against, 87
Connors Hotel, 81
Coon, William, 131, 136
Cornell University Law School, 23, 43, 85; comment by Haskell about Ithaca weather while at, 25; correspondence received by Haskell while at, 23–38, 40–42
Cortland Airport, 198–99, 201–2, 204; C. B. Friday, Director of NYS Bureau of Aviation, and 198–99; City of Cortland and, 199; Cortland Aeronautical Association and, 198; Cortland Flying Club, 199; Haskell's opinion on, 204; local industries in need of, 201; problem of ownership of, 202
Cortland Auto Supply Company and Haskell, 137
Cortland Cart & Carriage Company of Sidney, NY, 33, 42, 43, 198
Cortland Central School, 5, *22*; banners placed by Haskell on, 12–13, 16, 58; Delta Epsilon at, 8, 11; education of

Haskell at, 5–20, 210; Haskell and commencement week in 1911 at, 18–20; Haskell and dances at, 10–12, 14, 17; Kappa Zeta and Haskell at, 8–9, 24; sports at, 5–8, 14–16, 27
Cortland Civil Service Board, 53; Haskell as secretary of, 53, 132
Cortland Common Council, 222
Cortland Country Club, 55, 57, 140, 152, 184, 199, 200
Cortland County Agricultural Society, 171; Haskell named a director of, 171
Cortland County Bar Association, 86, 140, 215, 219
Cortland County Bus Lines, Inc. and Haskell, 137
Cortland County Chamber of Commerce, 3, 47, 48, 177, 178, 179, 180, 189, 190, 194, 195–96, 199, 201, 204, 206, 220; brochure touting advantages of life in Cortland put out by, 200; Carl Cooper and, 177, 179; Cortland County Development Corporation (CCDC) created by, 180, 181; Haskell and Dan McNeil on recruiting new members to, 190; Haskell caters 1914 dinner for, 47; Haskell chairs committee of legislative affairs for, 179; *Herald American* credits Cortland's "bright future" to, 193–94; history of Haskell and hotel exploratory committee of, 194, 195–96; Richard M. Day and, 191
Cortland County Courthouse, 88; comments on skylight in, 90
Cortland County Development Corporation (CCDC), 155, 178, 179, 180, 183, 189, 191, 198, 199, 201, 206, 207, 221; goal of, 180; Haskell as first president of, 155, 157, 180, 183; Haskell re-elected as president of, 194; Haskell steps down as president of, 206; New York State Department of Commerce and, 182, 206; Noss succeeds Haskell as president of, 206; officers elected in 1958 to, 194; prominent business leaders in community support goals of, 180; Syracuse *Post-Standard* of 1962 gave history of the five enterprises brought into Cortland since 1957 by, 204–6
Cortland County Holstein Club, 172
Cortland County Hospital, 175; Haskell on the Board of Trustees of, 175
Cortland County Sesquicentennial, 177–78, 180; Haskell and "Brothers of the Brush" during, 177
Cortland Elks Club, 43, 50, 55, 58, 173, 209; Valentine's Day Dinner in 1918 of, 209
Cortland Junior Chamber of Commerce (Jaycees), 199
Cortland Knights of Columbus, 209, 211; Haskell as deputy grand knight of, 209
Cortland Moose Club, 55
Cortland, NY, as "Crown City," 1, 58
Cortland Normal School/SUNY College at Cortland, 6, 47, 48, 122, 182, 200, 201–2, 207, 215; Haskell and, 201–2, 215
Cortland Park and Shop, Inc., 207
Cortland Rotary Club, 57–67, 173, 220; early fund-raising projects of, 65, 67; first officers and directors of, 57–58; 45th year of, 66; Haskell as co-founder of, 55, 57; Haskell as 1922–1923 president of, 64; Haskell's longevity noted by, 66; Haskell teased about effects of his "Beezum" by, 187, 200–201; KKK prank/hoax played on, 59–64, 103; 90th Anniversary Gala Dinner of, 64–65; summation of Haskell's life at 1963 meeting of, 67, 220; "The Unveiling of the Mazuka" and prank played on James A. Farrell by, 58–59

Cortland Rural Cemetery, 51, 135
Cortland Traction Company, 16, 17, 47, 137; Haskell and, 137; streetcar of, 17, *52*
Cortland Trust Company, 132; Haskell as president of, 132, 143
Cortland Veterans of Foreign Wars, 177; Haskell and, 177
Cortland Wagon Company, 198
Cortland Y.M.C.A., 66, 178, 194; Haskell and Industrial Club Study Group of, 178
Costello, Frank J. (mayor of Syracuse), 211
Cowan, Helen DeEtta "Ettie," 88, 89; indicted by D. A. Haskell, 89. *See also* Graham, Eugene "Gene"
Craig, Hal, 177
Crampton, Fred, 167, 171
Crandall, William G., 99, 172, 214
Crowley, James Harold "Sleepy Jim," 211

Dairymen's League, 97, 162, 163, 164, 165, 166, 168; Fred H. Sexauer opposed milk strikes by members of, 164; milk strikes denounced by Cortland members of, 164
Dalton, Edward, 47
David Harum Hotel in Homer, NY, 70, 71
Davis, Rowland L. (judge), 85, 88, 89, 99
DeGraw, Bernard (Rev.), 108
DeGroat, Harry DeWitt, 48
DeVico, Dominick, 69
Dewey, Thomas E. (NYS governor), 153, 211
Dillon Brothers' Cortland Theatre, 49, 50; minstrel show attended by Haskell at, 49–50
DiOrio, Gasper, 77–78
A Dog's Journey (Bruce W. Cameron), 219
Donahue, Elizabeth, 146
Dorset, "Pete" (attorney), 177
Dowd, Louis R. (judge), 83, 127
Doyle, Harry J. (also "Deac" and "Judge Doyle"), 26, 31, 32, 34–35
Durkee Domestic Bakery, 184; Haskell assists with Beaudry Wallpaper plant purchase by, 184
Dwight, John Wilbur (congressman and House Minority Leader), 29–30
Dwyer, William J., 90, 187

Edlund Machinery Company and Haskell, 137
Eggleston, Joseph E. (judge), 86
Einstein, Isidore and Moe Smith, ("Izzy and Moe"), 70–74, *72*, 81; D. A. Haskell enforces 18th Amendment with help from, 70–74; Harry Cortright and, 70
Eisenhower, Dwight D. (general and president), 149, 152, 174, 179; General Lucius D. Clay charged with proposing an interstate highway system by, 179
Elm Tree Hotel in McLean, NY, 12
Emergency Loan Act of 1917, 55
Empire Hall of Cortland, NY, 50

Farm Bureau, 48
Feeley, George, 200
Fenstermacher, Theodore "Ted," 66–67, 142, 180, 220, 222; applies Oliver Wendell Holmes' quote to Haskell, 220; Goering and Nazi field marshals prosecuted by, 66–67; Haskell's "kingdom" described by, 222
519 East Buffalo Street, Ithaca, NY, 25
Folmer, Louis (assemblyman), 150, 156, 157, 192, 200, 201
Forcucci, Sam, 177
Forshee, Frank, MD, 93

Gordon, Janet Hill (NYS senator), 155; Grunfeld comments on Haskell's fitness for post vacated by, 156;

Haskell declines third chance to run for NYS Senate upon seat vacated by, 155–56, 157; politics behind four-county 46th Senatorial District post vacated by, 156
Graham, Eugene "Gene," 88–99; commendations received by Haskell for prosecution of, 99, 101; delivered to Auburn Prison by Sheriff Henry, *100*; Dominic Colasurdo as witness against, 88, 90, 96; Ernest Crane as witness supporting, 95; Fred Graham testifies at trial of, 96–97; Fred Stone testifies at trial of, 92; Fred Van Schaick testifies at trial of, 92, 97; Goldie Trim testifies at trial of, 93; letter from prison to Haskell by, 99; Lula Van Schaick testifies against, 88, 92; murder trial attorneys representing, 90; Patrick Kane as uncooperative witness in trial of, 96; release from prison of, 99; seven-day trial for murder of John Reale by, 89–99; two children testify in trial of, 91
Graziani, Enrico "Harry," 127–30; autopsy of, 128; funeral Mass for, 130; Haskell extracts a confession from murderer of, 127; Mike Yuradi, aka Mike Reddy, and murder of, 127–31; Mrs. Graziani and, 128; Mrs. James Commando witnessed murder of, 128; neighbors and Officer George Dafoe apprehend murderer of, 128; Rosie Reddy and murderer of, 130, 131–32
Greek Peak ski resort in Virgil, NY, 66, 182, 184–85, 200; architect Robert Tallman placed a plaque on ski lodge at, 184; Gov. Harriman in 1958 attends opening day of, 184–85; Gov. Harriman in 1957 inspects progress of, 182; Robert Thompson and, 184, 185–86, 187; Rotarians credit Haskell's "Beezum" with snowfall at, 187; Thompson and Haskell's amusing correspondence about snowmaking at, 185, *186*, 187
Grinnell, Edgar (chief of police), 128
Grunfeld, Walter W., 67, 174–75, 192–93; Haskell and, 174–75, 192–93; 1963 presentation to Rotarian Haskell by, 67

Hannum, David, 171; *David Harum: A Story of American Life* by Westcott and, 171; note to Haskell from the niece of, 171
Harriman, Averell (NYS governor), 150, 151, 182, *183*, 184, 190, 192, 200; close defeat of Ives for Governor by, 152; letter to Haskell regarding future of the economy from, 190
Haskell, Albert, Jr., 1, 5, 17; admitted to the Bar, 50; adoption case for Eva and Bob Baxter handled by, 140; amusing letter from Edward E. Blodgett to, 212; aphorisms kept in small black books by, 23–24, 28, 43; Briggs Cadillac of Homer and, 220; cartoons in 1927 depicting career path of, *132*; character of, 131–32, 140, 141, 220; collegial relationship of Cortland lawyers and, 137–38; death of, 147, 219; as director and attorney of the Second National Bank, 132; and election as District Attorney of Cortland County, 55–56, 64, 143; heart attack experienced in 1962 by, 141, 155, 174, 203; as humanitarian, 178; insurance companies represented by, 137; Irene F. Jennings honored as secretary to, 141; as "King of Crown City," 222; law practice first opened by, 53; letter from Raymond G. Castle to, 214–15; as member in diverse local organizations, 209; as "Mr. Chamber of Commerce," 4; as "Mr. Cortland," 3, 4; oak desk used at Cortland

County Historical Society was owned by, 222; personality of, 58, 220; pets of, 219–20; photographs of, book cover, *125*, *132*, *150*, *183*, *197*; physical appearance of, 3, 58, *125*, 143; plan of action to attract new industry outlined by, 192, 193, 195; poetry used in legal response by, 54–55; *pro bono* legal work for Cortland churches by, 212; as public speaker at dinners, 50, 51–52, 53, 140, 154, 172, 176, 177, 180, 183, 184, 192–93, 195; record as district attorney garnered by, 131–32, 143; referenced as "the 'elder statesman' of Cortland's industrial growth" by Herbert C. Howe, 187; religiosity of, 181, 183, 185–86, 209, 221; retirement as district attorney announced by, 131; role of women in relocation of industry explained by, 192, 193; school boards in Cortland County represented by, 138; seat on the NYS Codes, Public Service, Internal Affairs and Revision Committee assigned to, 148; seller of Twentyman Building in Cortland represented by, 141; starts reading law in Jas. Dougherty law office, 24–25; supports Hughes for President, 53; tale of the amazing "besum plant" and, 66, 187; tale of the lake bass and gold watch told by, 65; "What Rotary Means to Me" explained by, 67; William F. Fitzpatrick, President of the New York State Bar Association, pays ultimate compliment to, 141

Haskell, Albert, Sr., (Albert's father), 5, 17, *21*, 42, 43; death of, 51; wrote 1909 article on waning interest in the automobile, 198

Haskell, Charles Kelly (Albert's son), 43, 140, 219; death in head on car crash, 140; Haskell and claims filed by Estate of, 140

Haskell, James Albert "Jimmie" (Albert's son), 43; Haskell in Republican primary election one week after death of, 148; 1932–1933 St. Mary's basketball team captained by, 145, 146, *147*; 1925 letter to Santa Claus written by, 124–25; sudden death in high school of, 145–46; yearbook dedication and a memorial prize as tribute to, 146

Haskell, James "Jim" (Albert's brother), 5, 33, 36, *44*; production of a motorized commercial vehicle on hold due to death of, 43; sinking of the *Monroe* and death of, 42–43

Haskell, John (Albert's brother), 5, 51, 134

Haskell, Joseph Charles (Albert's son), 43, 146, 219

Haskell, Joseph, Jr., (Albert's grandson), 222; recollections of Albert Haskell Jr. by, 216, 219–20

Haskell, Mary Gibbons (Albert's mother), 5, *21*, 28, 33, 37, 51; death of, 134

Haskell, Mildred Cecilia Aungier (Albert's second wife), 137, 146–47, 216, 221; Altar and Rosary Society of St. Mary's Church presided by, 152; death of, 148; Haskell weds, 146; relationship of Joe Haskell Jr. and Jean Haskell with, 146–47; Republican Women's luncheon chaired by, 152

Haskell, Nellie (also Nellie Richardson; Albert's sister), 5, 28, 37

Haskell, Regina Mary "Jean" (Albert's daughter), 43; children of Robert and, 159; Robert "Bob" Sweeney weds, 159

Haskell, Regina Shaughnessy (Albert's first wife), 24, 35, 43, 49; death of, 146, 175; dramatic changes to

Haskell household with the death of, 146–47; emotional response of Jean Haskell Sweeney to "home movie" showing, 148
Haskell, Timothy (Albert's great-grandson), 222
Haskell, Tom (Albert's grandson), 65
Haskell cottage on Little York Lake, 17, 28–29, 48, 65, 216; annual hosting of Cortland Bar Association at, 137; Haskell able to relax at, 147; local Catholic priests find recreation at, 216; sale of, 147
Haskell Place in Cortland, NY, 222
Hatfield, Alfred Griffith (or Al G. Field), 49
Hatfield, Louis I., 33, 42
Hegeman Farms milk plant in East Homer, NY, 165, 169
Henry, Frank M., 69, 78, 79–80, 81, 82–83, 99. *See also* tubercular cattle scandal in Cortland County
Hill, James P. (judge), 90, 91, 99, 119, 122, 124
Hoag, Floyd W. (attorney), 109, 111
Hoagland (mayor of the city of Cortland, NY), 53
Hockenbury, Myron D., 195–96
Homer Chamber of Commerce, 3, 189, 220; Edmund Karam and, 189; Haskell attends first annual banquet of, 189
Hoover, Herbert (president), 148
Hope, Leighton, 157; credentials of, 157; Haskell and, 157; political career of, 157
Hotel Cortland, 66, 180, 183, 184, 190, 196, 210
Howe, Alton (14 years old), 115; Leon Witty discovers lifeless body of, 116; mysterious death in Homer of, 116–18; verdict of suicide supported by Haskell in death of, 117–18
Hughes, Charles E., 53
Hull, Bob, 26, 31, 32, 34, 35
Interfaith Center near the State University College at Cortland, 216; Haskell and, 216; James McDonald, a founder of J.C. Penny Company and, 216
Interstate 81 highway (or Penn-Can Highway), 150, 180, 191, 194, 195, 199, 201, 203; gravel pits in Homer viewed as detriment to a proposed, 180; Haskell addressed Marathon's opposition to, 192–93; Haskell supported a route through Cortland County by, 201; Irving Ives's position on siting of, 150–51
Ives, Irving M., 149–52; construction of St. Lawrence Seaway opposed by, 151; as founding Dean of the School of Industrial and Labor Relations at Cornell University, 149; Haskell arranged a 1954 campaign stop in Cortland for, 150; Haskell helped to oust Joseph A. McGinnies as Assembly Minority Leader and replace with, 149, *150*; Haskell's political ads supporting run for governor by, 151; letters of appreciation to Haskell from, 152; political career of, 149–52; rally in Watertown, NY, sees tomatoes tossed at, 150

Keating, Kenneth B. (US senator), 157; Cortland Republican Committee dinner of 1963 addressed by, 157
Kelley, Charles J., MD, 93, 175
Kelley, Daniel, MD, 57
Kellogg, O. U. (attorney), 127, 130
Kelly, Paul, 134
Kennedy, John Fitzgerald (president), 158; Haskell's response to assassination of, 158
Kenney, Robert C. (mayor of Cortland, NY), 155
Kerr, Robert, MD (mayor of Cortland, NY), 158

Kesler, Harry E. (judge), 135
Kinney Hotel in Truxton, NY, 81
Kolton, Harry and Mrs., 81
Korean War, 214
Ku Klux Klan (KKK), 64, 103–13; activity in 1924 Ebensburg, Pennsylvania of, 105; anti-Catholicism in Cortland County and, 108, 109; arrest and prosecution of Cortland "king kleagle" of, 106–7, 109–12; Claude McKinney's experience during raid by, 104, 110; Eighteenth Amendment and, 107–8; First Amendment of the Constitution and, 106; "hate list" by 1920 of, 105; invitation to Homer Town Hall to attend recruitment meeting of, 105–6; origins in Tennessee of, 105; President Warren G. Harding as member of, 105; raid on Central Hotel in Marathon, NY, by, 103–4; rally in Marathon, NY, of members and protestors of, 108–9; Robert L. Rice enters guilty plea for raid on Marathon by, 112; testimony of Lyman Cronk in trial of local, 111–12

Lefkowitz, Louis J. (NYS attorney general), 153; letter of appreciation to Haskell from, 153; long political career of, 153
Lehmann, Herbert Henry (NYS governor), 144, 163–64, 165
Le Moyne College in Syracuse, NY, 141, 210, 211, 214, 215, 221; Ed Sullivan and fundraising for, 211; Haskell receives honorary doctorate degree from, 214; Haskell's relationship with, 211, 214, 215; Haskell's support of Nelligan Hall fund of, 211, 214
Little York Park (also Dwyer Memorial Park), 16, 17, 149; Cortland County vote and purchase of, 149; Haskell's concession stand at, 30, 38, 47; pavilion at, 16, 37, *39*, 41, 47, 48, 51, 219
Lucy, Henry D. (attorney), 137
Lusk, Clayton R., 50, 53, 134, 137, 139, 141, 143, 156; career in law and politics of, 134, 154; death of, 153–54; Haskell clerked for, 50, 53, 134; Haskell seeking NYS Assembly seat held by Irving R. Rice is a challenge to, 145; letters to Haskell in 1953 and 1958 from, 137
Lynch, Francis J., 52

Mack, Joseph (mayor of Cortland), 158, 201
Maher, William C. (attorney), 134
Manning, Claude, 138–39; attorney Donald Mahwhinney represented, 138; Haskell and Robert Sloan represented county in case brought by, 138, 140; letters of congratulations received by Haskell for success in case brought by, 139–40; Lusk, Buck, Folmer, and Ryan also represented, 139; negligence suit against Cortland County by, 138–39; witnesses to accident causing injury to, 139
Marathon Chamber of Commerce, 192–93
Marine Midland Trust Company of Southern New York, 137, 196; Cortland touted in national advertising campaign spearheaded by, 196, *197*; Haskell presented plaque for thirty-three years of continuous service with, 199; Hugh H. Williams and, 196, *197*
Matteawan State Hospital for the Criminally Insane, 131; infamous serial killer Lizzie Halliday housed at, 131
Mayer, Leo, 146
Mayette, Edgar, 53

McAuliffe, Ed or Edmund or "Eddie," 6, 9, 25–26, 27, 29, 30, 31, 32, 33–34, 35
McEvoy, Daniel J. (judge), 141
McEvoy, Harold "Deke," 146
McEvoy, John, 128, 212
McEvoy & Hartnett Furniture Company of Cortland, NY, 54
McEwen, Robert W. (president of Hamilton College), 181
Mcgrady, Patrick or Pat, 195, 210
Meldrim, Leo, 202
Metcalf, George H. (attorney), 83, 88, 89, 90, 95; letter to Haskell about children bringing joy sent by, 124
milk crisis of the Great Depression, 160–71; Assemblyman Haskell offered his "Four Point Plan" for, 161–62; Assemblyman Haskell worked with Cortland dairy farmers during and after, 161, 171–72; Attorney Haskell successfully represented the Central New York Cooperative Association during, 170; Central New York Cooperative Association, Inc. formed in Cortland and joined Metropolitan Cooperative Milk Producers during, 169; Cortland dairy farmers charged with rioting during, 161; Dairy Farmers Union (DFU) organized strikes and a settlement during, 162–63, 166, 170–71; farmers meeting at Cincinnatus Central School urged by DFU to strike during, 164; Homer S. Rolfe, president of the Metropolitan Bargaining Agency, urged members not to strike during, 164; John J. Dillon criticized New York State's Rogers-Allen law during, 162; John L. Lewis and organized labor supported the 1939 milk strike during, 170; New Deal regulations over NYS dairy industry declared unconstitutional during, 170; New York City Mayor Fiorello LaGuardia brokered an end to the 1939 milk strike during, 170; New York State Milk Control Board created during, 160; New York State Senator Rhoda Fox Graves expressed confidence in a 19-county strike during, 166–67; non-strikers organized for their own protection at Heuvelton, NY, during, 167; violent milk strikes in mid-West during, 160; violent milk strikes in New York State during, 160–61, 163, 165, 166, 167, 168. *See also* Wright, Archie
Miller, Frank, 78
Molinari, Joseph (judge), 139
murder cases in Cortland County before 1924, 87–88

Nason, Philip S., 65
Natonio, Dominick, 83
Newman Foundation of Cortland College, 215–16; Haskell supports, 216. *See also* O'Heron, Fr. Edward J.
New York Holstein-Friesian Association, 172; Haskell recognized for fifteen years membership in, 172
New York State Association of Industrial Development Agencies, 190; State asks Haskell to help organize, 190–91
New York State Board of Estimate and Control, 122
New York State Bureau of Farms and Markets, 122, 123–24
New York State Conservation Department office building in Cortland, 205
New York State Department of Agriculture, 168
New York State Department of Commerce, 180, 182, 192, 200; Haskell invited to speak at Third Annual Statewide

Industrial Development Workshop sponsored by, 201
New York State Department of Public Works, 194, 204
New York State Joint Legislative Committee on Industrial and Labor Conditions (or "Ives Committee"), 149; Haskell retained as attorney of, 149
1923 Rotary District Conference in Montreal addressed by Haskell, 65
Nix, William, 50
Nixon, Richard (president), 149
Northway, Selah E., 6, 13, 23, 27–28
Noss, Morris (Cortland business and political leader), 3, 178, 180, 199, 202, 203, 204, 206, 221, 222; comments made in 1969 about Haskell by, 222; Haskell and, 155, 178, 206
Noyes, Holton V. (NYS Agriculture and Markets commissioner), 163, 165, 169; speech before the New York State Farm Bureau Federation critical of farmers given by, 168
Nuremberg war crimes trials, 66

O'Connor, Charles J., 190
O'Heron, Fr. Edward J., 216; Haskell and, 216
123 Prospect Street, Cortland, NY, 5, 42
Onondaga County Penitentiary, 77, 84
"Opportunity" (poem), vi
Ottinger, Albert (NYS attorney general), 122, 124
Otto, J. Austin (NYS assemblyman), *150*

Parker, Alton B., 86
Patriarco, Dan, 75, 77
Payne Aldrich Tariff of 1909, 29
Pellerin Detective Agency, 79
People's National Bank of Pulaski, Virginia, 133–34; in legal suit against Lewis H. Hewitt, Haskell and Maher represented, 134; legendary attorney John S. Draper assisted in representing, 133; three trials finally ended with verdict favoring, 134. *See also* Allen Gang
Pickert, Claude, 78
Port Watson-Tompkins Street Sewer, 155, 181; Cortland County District Superintendent of Schools Chester A. Lacy's letter to Haskell about, 155; Haskell's radio broadcast of 1961 regarding, 155
Preble Milk Cooperative Association, 171–72; Haskell as attorney for, 171–72
Preble Rod and Gun Club, 177; Haskell as member and toastmaster of, 177
Prohibition law (18th Amendment), 69, 73, 81, 103, 116; D. A. Haskell's enforcement of, 69–73, 77–81
The Purple Pennant, 6–17; businesses advertising in, 7; Haskell as editor-in-chief of, 7, 8, 18; physicians advertising in, 11
Putnam, Robert D., 178
Pyrke, Berne A., 124

racial stereotypes, 49, 50
Reale, John, 88, 91, 93, 95, 96, 97, 98, 99; widow of the murdered, 90, 93. *See also* Graham, Eugene "Gene"
Republican primary election of 1933, 148; amusing accounts in *The Homer Post* about getting out the votes for Haskell, 148
Richardson, George B. (Albert's brother-in-law), 36
Richardson, Leslie "Lester" (Albert's nephew), 28–29, 30, 32, 36, 37, *45*; KKK hoax played on Cortland Rotary Club with help of, 62–64
Robinson, A. N., 104, 110
Rockefeller, Nelson A. (NYS governor), 153, 154; Cortland school children interacted with wife of, 154;

Haskell's endorsement of, 153; 1958 Cortland County Republican Committee dinner meeting addressed by, 191
Rogers, Clifford, 79–80
Roosevelt, Franklin D. (NYS governor; president), 143, 145; Cortland County and New Dealism of, 148; Haskell's opposition to a federal welfare system proposed by, 148, 193
Roosevelt, Theodore (president), 53, 86
Ryan, Edward, 50–51

Second Vatican Council, 217
Shay, Richard J., 141; Haskell, Foley & Shay's right to have their stairway over another person's premises successfully litigated by, 142; Haskell & Foley law firm joined by, 141
Shea, James A., 50
Sheffield Producers, 162, 164, 165, 166, 167, 168
"Sidewalks of New York" (song, 1894), 17
Singer, Leland, 25, 33, 35–36; trip to D.C. described by, 36
Skateland, 152, 192
Slocum, Clarence, 81
Smith, Alfred E. (NYS governor), 119, 151
Smith, Donnal V. (president of Cortland State Teachers College), 182
Smith-Corona (later Smith-Corona Marchant or S-CM), 155, 181, 191, 196, 201, 205, 206–7; Cortland as "typewriter capital of the world" because of, 207; Elwyn Smith and, 191, 196, *197*; groundbreaking ceremony in 1958 for, 191; impact of labor shortage and personal computer on, 206–7; issue of water line to, 206; Rorapaugh Farm on Route 13 and, 183, 189; Wilbert L. Smith II and, 196, 198
Sobey, Albert, 79–80
Sputnik, 181–82; impact on U.S. educational system by, 182
Stafford, Colleen Sweeney, xvii
St. Anthony's Roman Catholic Church in Cortland, NY, 130, 213; Carmen Basilio speaks at Holy Name Society event at, 213; Haskell presented a life membership in Holy Name Society of, 213
Steger, Don, 177
Stevenson, Adlai (presidential candidate), 152
Stiles, Rena, 167
St. Mary's Cemetery in Cortland, NY, 130, 134, 219; Haskell buried in, 219
St. Mary's parochial school in Cortland, NY, 3, 141, 213, 220; Bob Martin honored for 20 years coaching football at, 211; Haskell as general chairman of Parish Development Fund for construction of annex to, 212–13
St. Mary's Roman Catholic Church in Cortland, NY, 51, 134, 141, 152, 209, 210, 214, 217–18, 219; Haskell as manager of a crisis between the laity and Fr. George May at, 217–18; Haskell as president of Holy Name Society of, 209, 210; Haskell's funeral at, 219; Holy Name Society of, 209, 210–11; letter to Haskell from Father O'Brien of, 215; Monsignor Martin J. Watley and, 213; St. Patrick's Day Banquet of 1955 of, 210
Sutton, James, 89
Sweeney, Robert "Bob," 159; Sweeneys related to, 159
Swor, Bert ("Dean of Minstrel Comedians"), 49

Taber, John, 149, 189–90

Taft, William H. (president), 36, 53
Tammany Hall, 150, 151–52
Taylor, Leland "Lee" (attorney), 155, 192; letter to Haskell from, 215
Temple movie theater on Groton Avenue, Cortland, NY, 35
Testimonial dinner of 1964 for Haskell, 3–4, 220–22; bracelet charm presented to Mildred Haskell at, 221; Cortland V.F.W. annual Citizenship Award presented to Haskell at, 221; ecumenism at, 221; Haskell responds to tributes offered at, 221–22; Haskell's children and grandchildren at, 221; Morris Noss' assessment of Haskell at, 221; plaque for "dedicated service" presented to Haskell at, 221; Ted Fenstermacher's assessment of Haskell at, 220–21; Very Reverend Nicholas J. Sullivan's assessment of Haskell at, 221
30 Charles Street, Cortland, NY, 105, 137
Thompson, Elmer, 78
Thompson, Hunter S., 218
Thompson Boat Company, 203
Tioughnioga Club, 86
Tioughnioga River, 58
Titchner, Walter, 12, 26–27, 34
Tobin, James F., 86
Torrey, Richard F., 207; letter to Haskell from, 207
Trinity Equipment Corporation, 180, 181, 182, 183, 194–95, 200, 202, 205; Haskell introduces to Rotary George Feeley, president of, 194; Haskell welcomes Gov. Harriman to cornerstone laying for, 182, *183*; history of, 194–95; Pall merged with, 202; Rotary recognizes Haskell's role in bringing to Cortland, 194
tubercular cattle scandal in Cortland County, 119–24, *123*, 143, 171; eleven indicted, convicted and sentenced for roles in, 120–22; Haskell commended for successful legal handling of, 122–24, 131; Mycobacterium bovis and, 119; New York State regulations and, 119
Tully Chamber of Commerce, 192
Tyler, Chris, 59, 61, 63, 64

United Way (or United Fund), 148, 175–77, 193; Community Chest and Haskell before there was, 212; Community Chest as forerunner of, 175; Haskell's role in fund-raising for, 175; Randolph V. Miller's letter to Haskell about campaign work for, 175–76

Wagner, Robert (NYC mayor), 151
Wagner, Robert F. (senator), 211
Wales, B. Roger (NYS senator), 143, 144; Bert Lord of Chenango County takes the seat of, 145; contested "gentlemen's agreement" on filling vacant seat of, 144; Haskell makes bid for senatorial office upon death of, 143; Haskell withdraws name from contest over vacant seat of, 144–45
Walsh, James, MD, 128
Walsh, Thomas or Tommy, 103, 108
"white slavers" in Truxton, NY, 85–86; George Shaw and case of, 85–86; Lark Thorington and case of, 85
Wickwire Bros. wire mills, 48, 130, 135
Willcox, Spiegle, 66, 152, 158
Wilson, Joseph H., 122–23
Wilson, Malcolm (NYS lieutenant governor), 201; business climate of Cortland in 1959 touted by, 201
Wilson, Woodrow (president), 36, 53
Wolner, Louis or "Lou"(supervising principal of Homer schools), 3, 66, 189, 198; efforts to bring summer theater to Homer Town Hall addressed by, 189

World War I (or the Great War), 43, 48, 50, 52, 53, 55, 57, 78, 105, 210; peace conference at Versailles after, 173
World War II, 66, 173, 199, 214; Cortland War Finance Committee during, 173; Dumbarton Oaks Conference during, 173; Haskell encouraged the purchase of war bonds during, 173; Haskell's disdain for Ireland's neutrality during, 154; 1944 Armistice Day speech by Haskell during, 173–74
Wright, Archie, 162–63, 164–65, 166–67, 168, 170; DFU lost political power in 1939 with the red-baiting of, 171. *See also* milk crisis of the Great Depression, and Dairy Farmers Union
Wright, Earle W., 212

Yaman, James, 201
"Your Day and Mine" (poem by David Starr Jordan), 17–18